2

Seraffyn's
Mediterranean
Adventure

Seraffyn's
Mediterranean
Adventure

by

Lin and Larry Pardey

Pardey books

By the same authors

Cruising in *Seraffyn*
Seraffyn's European Adventure
Seraffyn's Oriental Adventure
The Self-Sufficient Sailor
The Care and Feeding of Sailing Crew
Capable Cruiser
The Cost-Conscious Cruiser
Storm Tactics Handbook
Details of Classic Boat Construction
Bull Canyon: A Boatbuilder, a Writer and Other Wildlife

DVDs

Storm Tactics: Companion to Storm Tactics Handbook
Get Ready to Cruise: Offshore Sailing, Part One
Get Ready to Cross Oceans: Offshore Sailing, Part Two
Cruising Has No Limits

Lin and Larry's Newsletter and Cruising Tips:
www.landlpardey.com

Copyright ©1981, 2011 Mary Lin and Lawerence F. Pardey
First published 1982 by W.W. Norton and Company, subsequently by Cruising World books,
McGraw Hill Ltd, Sheridan House Inc.

Library of Congress Cataloging in Publication Data

Pardey, Lin.
Seraffyn's Mediterranean Adventure

1. Western Mediterranean—Description and travel.
2. Mediterranean Sea—Description and travel.
3. Sailing—Mediterranean Sea. 4. Pardey, Lin.
5. Pardey, Larry. 6. Seraffyn (Cutter)
I. Pardey, Larry. II. Title
D974.P3   910'.0916381   81-3983

ISBN – 978-1-929214-16-7
Printed in the United States of America

To Steve Doherty
with appreciation for everything he taught us

Contents

~~~~~

Acknowledgments

~~~~~

People are the bonus in cruising, and the yachtsmen, fishermen, and natives we met throughout our Mediterranean voyaging proved this again and again. It would have been impossible to tell the story of every special afternoon or evening we had during those two and a half years. I would like to thank Rosemary and Francoise Greaser, Sarah Westwood, Robin Morgan, Alex Carozzo, and all the members of the wonderful Club Adriaco who were not mentioned in this book but are well remembered.

Several people either provided photos for this project or helped us take pictures of *Seraffyn*. They include Peter Phillips, Carlo Sciarrelli, Sasha Von Wetter, and Richard Blagbourne.

Mary Eisenlohr, who typed much of this manuscript, deserves special credit for working through the heat of a California summer.

The encouragement offered by Mary Baldwin and Ellie Moyer kept me going on slow days.

Portions of this book have appeared in *SAIL* magazine. Patience Wales the editor lived up to her name. Many thanks for your suggestions.

And finally, we would both like to thank the customs officials in various Mediterranean countries who in their innermost hearts believe in free trade.

Foreword to the 30th Anniversary Edition

"It won't be the same. I just know it. That's why I'm afraid to go cruising again," Kim laments. Kim Bushnell grew up on her family's thirty-foot sailboat as they meandered from Canada, down the Mississippi River, then out into the oceans of the world. She met a sailor in the Indian Ocean, married, helped him build a boat, then took her six-month-old daughter to sea. Though that marriage didn't last, she never gave up her love of sailing. Now she and her two children have cruised throughout the waters of the Pacific Northwest on a boat she built. Her children are grown, she is single, and it is easy to sense her restlessness, her desire to once again sail out onto the open ocean.

I nod as I tell Kim, "I worried about the same thing forty-five years ago when we were just getting ready to go cruising. I'd read so many books about voyaging adventures that happened ten or twenty years before we were ready to go, I thought we'd missed the magic. I worried about it again when we came back from cruising and started to build *Seraffyn's* big sister *Taleisin*. In fact we purposely didn't sail *Taleisin* to the same places at first, just because we were worried we'd be disappointed by the changes we'd encounter. But you know what? As different as things were -- physically, socially, politically -- when we eventually did revisit old haunts, the people we met, the adventures we had, never disappointed us."

I think I am primed to give her that answer because both Larry and I have just been re-reading *Seraffyn's Mediterranean Adventure* in preparation for this special edition. The political situations in many of the countries we visited have changed dramatically since this book was originally written. Yugoslavia, a place where we not only got arrested by the military but also were included in the life of tiny island communities, no longer exists. It was, just as the people we met three decades ago warned us, torn apart by civil war soon after Tito died. But in the ensuing years, the islands we loved along the Dalmatian coast have become even more welcoming to sailing visitors, and you can now sail into Albania without fear of being arrested. Gibraltar is no longer a smugglers' haven or the scene of fence-side weddings at a closed, armed border since Spain joined the European Union. The list of physical changes in ports we visited could fill a book. Yet friends, who are currently cruising in the Mediterranean Sea, send us letters filled with stories of pleasures they are finding there right now.

The wonderful historical sites still cause cruisers to wear out their sandals as they roam through the ruins of history. Intriguing anchorages still lure more adventurous sailors away from the enticements of towns and cities. The often-fickle winds and currents still challenge sailors, and just as they did back then, people tell us it is impossible to sail in the Med. Yet we still hear of sailors who wait for the night breezes and sail across velvety smooth seas without turning to their engines except to maneuver into port. Today, more cruisers take the time to visit the far eastern reaches of this inland sea than was the case back then. Some venture north into the Black Sea, waters that were off-limits to us back when we cruised on *Seraffyn*. More Israeli ports are open to voyagers.

The red tape of officialdom, though, may be different but it is still there. Only now, there are websites and electronic translators to help you through it all. (Though we are told many potential difficulties can still be avoided by adhering to the old adage: just act dumb and smile a lot.)

It is what hasn't changed that we feel makes this book not only relevant for today's sailors but also one of our favorites. The sheer variety of sights, sounds, flavors, and pleasures available inside this relatively small inland sea is unbeatable. The seamanship required to navigate its waters safely, to anchor securely, still tests those who voyage here. The leisurely pace of life you will experience once you slide comfortably into European rhythms will lead to many experiences similar to those we write about in this book.

The original introduction to this book, written almost thirty years ago, still holds true today. And that is why I urge Kim to get back out to sea. I remind her that voyaging onboard a small, well-found vessel is a unique way to move gently into other people's lives, then move onward again with time to savor what you have seen and learned. In a world more rushed than ever, life afloat moves at a pace that is humane and natural. So in spite of its occasional inconveniencies and sacrifices, the life described in this book is one we still find to be elegant beyond most others.

Lin and Larry Pardey
Kawau Island, New Zealand

June 2011

Introduction

〰️

"You've been cruising for how many years? Don't you get tired of just sailing around all the time?"

People ask us these questions everywhere we go. At first glance it must seem like this is all there is to a cruising sailor's life: prepare to make a passage, sail, arrive, celebrate, swim, party, go sight-seeing—and then prepare to make another voyage. For people who have been cruising less than two years, that assessment is probably right.

But as the years pass and cruising becomes more than just a vacation from the realities of your shore-based life, subtle changes begin to take place. One day you turn to your partner and say, "This is our way of life, the other world is the myth."

That is when you look back over the past year's voyaging and become aware of those things you did besides sail, sun, and swim. If you are an average cruising couple like ourselves, you spent about a third of your time working to earn your cruising funds. You met some extra special people and moved into their lifestyle long enough to taste their joys but only sense their pains. You probably worked twice as hard as a person living on a normal income because you had to invent economical improvements for your boat or a neighbor's boat, and maybe you scraped and saved for a rewarding trip inland to ski or explore, climb a mountain or hear an opera. That trip was sort of like a well-earned, much-needed holiday from a way of living that other people think of as the ultimate vacation. And laced through all of your adventures was the connecting thread of successful voyages fraught with moments of fear, hours of discomfort, and days of unbelievable beauty.

INTRODUCTION

This book is the story of the sixth, seventh, and eighth years of our cruising life. We spent them in and around the Mediterranean—an especially interesting area because of the variety of cultures represented along the Mediterranean shores. More than any other period in our cruising life, these years demonstrate why we don't get tired of "just sailing around all the time."

CHAPTER 1

~~~~~~

Gibraltar

There are two mooring areas for visiting yachts in Gibraltar. The first is called the "destroyer pens"; the second, the "marina." During the four winter months we spent at Gibraltar, the first area earned its name over and over again; the second one didn't quite make it.

We had been advised to sail *Seraffyn* alongside the rock airport runway that forms one side of the marina area. Two hundred boats of all types lay stern-to against rickety wooden floats that extended out from shore to a huge dilapidated barge, which lay sunk in eight feet of water. There was just enough room to set our anchor about one hundred feet from the docks. As soon as it grabbed hold and we lowered our sails, the two of us launched *Rinky Dink* over the side. Larry took our passports, *Seraffyn*'s registration documents, and his wallet and rowed ashore to arrange our port clearance. I set about furling our sails properly and packing our shower kits along with fresh clothes.

We had been at sea for five days. The voyage south from Seisembra, which is on the west coast of Portugal, had been eventful, but now my only thoughts were on the huge rock fortress that towered over us. The Rock of Gibraltar! Its name brought back school-lesson memories of Homer, Nelson, the Great Wars, Britain's vanishing empire, and insurance companies.

As I watched Larry row back toward *Seraffyn,* the wonderful reality of our life as cruising sailors flooded over me. We were able to be right in the middle of this history-packed part of the world—complete with our own comfortable beds and cooking facilities. We could explore till our feet were weary and then come home to be surrounded by familiarity. If we got tired of exotic foods or restaurant cooking, we could search out our favorite ingredients and cook our own. We could travel with no bags to pack, no hotel reservations to make, and no train or plane schedules to worry about.

Larry brought to mind some of the less pleasant realities of our life when he rowed up and said, "Got to lift our anchor and tie stern to that dock. The customs officials won't come on board until we are alongside. Besides, the fellow who owns that big trawler warned that the holding ground out here isn't too good."

I cranked in the anchor chain while Larry set our sculling oar in place. Then we moved to an empty spot between a handsome, English, forty-foot sloop and a thirty-foot French cutter. We dropped our anchor, warped *Seraffyn* into place, and sat back to wait for the officials.

Gibraltar, lying as it does, in the entrance to the Mediterranean is a voyaging yachtsman's crossroad. Charter yachts bound outward across the Atlantic for the Caribbean winter charter season stop here for final duty-free stores, engine parts, repairs, and provisions. European yachtsmen and cruisers like ourselves coming south to avoid the harsh northern winters stop here to take stock after the often rough passage from England, across the Bay of Biscay, and down Portugal's exposed coastline. Some scatter into the Med, others continue along the classic, sunny, trade-wind route to the Canaries, Barbados, and Panama. All have one thing in common. They know this is the last major, English-speaking enclave they will visit for a long time. There are no yacht chandlers within fifteen thousand miles east of Gibraltar and three thousand miles to the west, where those specialized items such as rigging parts, motor spares, bottom paints, bronze and stainless fastenings, charts, or maritime navigation publications can be bought at reasonable prices. Because of this, Gibraltar's yachting community is always in search of craftsmen. Since all the skilled Gibraltarians are kept busy by the British Navy shipyards, visiting craftsmen can work on foreign yachts with no questions asked and no fuss about work permits. If a Gibraltarian yachtsman asks you to work on his yacht, he can help you get a proper six-month working visa in one day. You are then eligible for income taxes, which are only about 1½ percent and not worth evading. We had heard reports of this laissez-faire attitude toward foreign workers from sailors in northern Spain, and it was the reason we planned to spend some time in Gibraltar. We were, in November of 1974, quite broke.

Technically we had lots of assets, we just did not have any cash. We had made a classic mistake. As we visited the small villages and towns on the north coast of Spain, we saw wonderful small bronze and brass antiques. My mother, who lives in California, had always said, "If you see anything interesting send it along, I'd enjoy helping you sell it." So Larry and I carefully purchased some beautiful bronze candlesticks from a seventeenth-century Spanish church that was being torn down, old bronze andirons, and church keys. Our scrounging days in the flea markets always turned up a treasure or two. We shipped them off and waited for the cash to roll in. But like most small investors, we could not stop buying once we had started; by the time we reached Gibraltar we had invested six months cruising funds in antiques and had only two hundred dollars cash left plus five or six weeks worth of food stores on board (fortunately, because of our wandering life, no bills were due). A few days before we reached Gibraltar an inherent flaw in our scheme dawned on us. It would take time for those antiques to reach their destination, time for them to be sold and the money forwarded to us, and time for us to arrange to cash the foreign checks. Even with good luck we could not hope to see any cash for two or three months. I was a bit worried.

But as we sat waiting for our port clearance, several local yachtsmen came around to introduce themselves. After the usual "Where you coming from, where you going?" one of our first visitors said, "Hope you're not here to get any repair work done, it's almost impossible to find anyone who is at all skilled and not too busy."

The customs men arrived and had us fill out a health clearance, a crews list, and a local visa permit; then they welcomed us to Gibraltar. After that, both of us eagerly headed for a long-anticipated hot shower. The water was hot, but the so-called marina had the dirtiest shower facilities we have ever used. Within a day of arriving we sounded like all the rest of the old-time residents, "They charge all of us twenty-five dollars a month, give us each ten feet of dock space for our sterns, then only have one washroom for two hundred people and that's impossible to keep clean." Yet for all of the griping, our stay in Gibraltar's marina introduced us to some fascinating people and boats plus a winter full of variety and adventure.

A day or two after we arrived, we moved *Seraffyn* into the spot we had rented by the month. Her storm anchor was hooked snuggly under the huge links of chain laid on the bottom between each dock, and her stern was secured to dock cleats. Larry suggested we take a walk over to the destroyer pens, where visiting yachts that drew more than six feet were forced to lie. These pens, built by the British Navy during World War I as an area for mooring and servicing their destroyers and supply ships, are in the old commercial part of the main harbor near the fuel dock and warehouses.

I am glad we chose to moor *Seraffyn* in the marina. Not only were the destroyer pens almost a miles walk from town, they were also an unsafe place to keep any but the largest steel yacht. Rough wood and concrete pilings supported fifteen-foot-high piers that could only be reached by rickety ladders. Cleats were few and far between. Fender boards rubbing against oil-coated piers, plus a slick of crude and fuel oil on the water, meant every boat in the pens had a bathtub ring of black around its topsides. We learned the worst about the pens a month or two later when winter storms blowing through the Straits from the Atlantic set up a three-foot surge inside the mooring area. Then hulls laying against the pier lost paint, stanchions, and rail caps. During one storm in early spring when over one hundred boats filled the pens three deep all the way around, we saw a forty-foot steel cutter with three-sixteenth-inch plating sustain a one-foot-deep, three-foot-long dent from surging against a wooden barge at the northeast end of the pens. Several boats lost bowsprits, pulpits, and pushpits (stern pulpits) during the same three-day blow. Our advice to anyone entering Gibraltar with a deep-draft vessel is: Do not stay in the pens for more than one day to load stores. Anchor outside near the north side of the runway. During westerly blows or southwesterly storms move around to the Mediterranean side of the rock and anchor off the other end of the runway. If you do decide to moor in the pens for more than a day, choose a spot on the western side as far to the south as possible. Tie alongside a vessel that has higher topsides than you do and tend your lines and fenders constantly during a blow.

In spite of the problems in the destroyer pens, eight or ten new yachts came in to moor and stock up each week during the winter. When we were there *Shamrock V,* an old J class America's cup challenger, came through sailed by a delivery team who was taking her north to England for a complete re-fit. We later heard they had had an excellent nine-day passage, beating all the way in fifteen- to twenty-knot head winds. They had to shorten sail because the masthead band slipped one foot due to some rot in the fifty-year-old spar.

Voyager, a fifty-foot schooner owned by Peter Phillips and bound for New York, stayed in the pens after a year of exploring the Med without an engine. This beautiful black-hulled Nova Scotian flush-decked schooner caught our eye immediately. As we looked her over one fact stood out. She was obviously new, but her spars were old, her fittings were old, and so were her sails. When we called hello to her owner, Peter explained the riddle. "I had a beautiful old schooner that sailed wonderfully but leaked like a sieve. Every day-sail was an adventure. When I got estimates on rebuilding her properly, the costs were

Voyager. Designed by John Alden.

so high they staggered me. Then I got an idea. I contacted a Nova Scotian yard near Lunenburg and asked what it would cost to build a new deck and hull and use all of the fittings from my old boat—ballast keel, spars, deck hardware. Well, in 1973 it cost me fifty thousand dollars for a new hull and deck, and I had a boat with all the charm of my old one and none of the problems, except for the hunk of iron that's called a motor and that hasn't worked in a year." As we walked away from *Voyager* Larry and I named several interesting old boats that would have cost their owners less money and trouble if they had been rebuilt Peter's way instead of piece by miserable piece.

An Ocean 71 fiberglass ketch also lay in the pens that first day. We admired the wonderful maintenance job her crew was doing. Since they were obviously busy, we did not stop and chat. But we came to know her skipper, Brian Hoare, and the cook, Cathy, well over the winter, especially after an event that occurred three days later, on Sunday.

As we walked hand and hand along the rock causeway back toward the marina, discussing our general plan of action, Larry reassured me, "Don't worry just because no one has rushed up to offer us work. Several people have come down to look at *Seraffyn* and ask who built her. I've talked to the guy in the repair shop at the marina, and he said he'd turn any woodwork our way. So don't appear too impatient or people will try to get us to work for less than we are worth. Besides, maybe some money will come in from the articles we've written."

When we reached *Seraffyn*, the man on the next boat had a note for us. It seemed that the Gibraltarian owner of a small shipyard had repossessed an older plywood cabin cruiser because of unpaid shipyard bills. It was basically sound but looked badly neglected and old-fashioned. Would we be interested in fixing it up for him? We were delighted with the prospect of a job that would help us start rebuilding our cruising kitty.

When a man walked up and said, "Do you ever race your boat?" we were eager to learn more about the Gibraltar Inter-Services Invitational race series. It seemed the British Army and Navy personnel stationed in Gibraltar had several sailboats they raced all year round, but to perk up the winter racing fleet they enjoyed inviting all of the cruising boats that sailed in to join the bi-monthly races. We agreed to participate, and when our visitor offered to provide crew for us, we asked for a husband and wife team and said that experience was not really necessary.

The next morning we walked over and looked at the down-at-the-heels thirty-foot powerboat *Susy*. Then we spoke to her owner about the changes he wanted, and at lunch time we drew up a proposal and contract for her renovation. By late afternoon we had not only a Gibraltarian working visa but also a check for £100 (U.S. $250) as a deposit on our next three-and-a-half weeks labor. At cocktail time Chris and Sandy Bunney and their friend Dick came down to introduce themselves as our new racing crew.

Within a week of arriving in Gibraltar our life had fallen into a pleasant schedule. We had a job during the week, yacht racing every other weekend, and new friends to share it all. So, as is tradition in the L and L household when everything is going our way, we splurged and went for a good dinner at a well-recommended local restaurant. Then we took a late-night stroll through the old town of Gibraltar.

CHAPTER 2

~~~~~

Of Work and Play

There is an invisible barrier in the sailing world. On one side stands the cruising sailor, who describes those who race as masochists standing in a shower in leaking foul-weather gear while they reach over and flush ten-dollar bills down the toilet. On the other side stands the racing man, who looks at cruisers as overloaded, slow moving boats with beer-drinking helmsmen who spend all day comparing anchors and anchor rodes. Fortunately events like the Gibraltar Combined Services Winter Invitational Regatta, with its arbitrary Portsmouth Yardstick rating, help break down this barrier—because there is a wealth of information to be learned by racing your boat, even if it was never designed for that purpose.

When we sailed *Seraffyn* over to the starting area for the race on Sunday we were delighted to see nineteen boats sporting eleven different national flags. The boats ranged in length from twenty-two feet on deck through several forty-five- to sixty-footers. The largest, *Happy Captain VI*, an Ocean 71, seemed to swarm with crew. Good-natured challenges flew from skipper to skipper in the milling fleet while the race committee tender came alongside each entrant, collected the 50 pence ($1.25) fee, concocted a rating on the spot, handed us a mimeographed diagram of the course, and then sped off to the next boat.

To avoid the confusion and to help familiarize our new crew with *Seraffyn*'s sailing gear, we took a spin out to the first buoy and back. We arrived just in time for the ten-minute warning gun. I must say that some of the antics on the line during that first race would have sent protest flags flying from the spreader of every boat in a more serious fleet. One forty-eight-foot ketch accidently got caught in irons right on the starting line. Another sixty-footer barged through the fleet with the skipper yelling, "Watch out, we've lost the winch handle!" But all nineteen vessels got across the short line safely and headed off on the thirteen-mile race. We were delighted with our start, and *Seraffyn*—sporting her huge 135 percent genoa, staysail, and main on a beam reach—loved the eight-knot breeze. We passed most of the smaller boats at the first mark. But before we had reached the south tip of Gibraltar, where the race course turned due east for four miles into the Mediterranean, the Ocean 71 reached majestically past to windward sporting a beautiful mizzen staysail.

Larry was sitting to leeward, tiller in hand while he percolated orders, "Chris, ease the genoa; Dick, move a bit forward; Lin, run below and see how close we can cut the tip of the Rock. I want everyone to be thinking of getting the spinnaker up as soon as we can!" A careful check of the chart showed deep water right up to the shore line. So Larry started describing what each of the crew should do to get our nine hundred-square-foot spinnaker set properly. All went right to plan as Larry headed *Seraffyn* to clear Europa Point at Gibraltar's tip by only two hundred feet. We slowly gained on the Ocean 71 as our increased sail area went to work. Her skipper for this race was one of the more successful local sailors, and when he kept *Happy Captain* on a reach heading much farther off the tip of the Rock, we began to wonder. Then Chris Bunney, who had arrived in Gibraltar only two weeks before, said, "I heard there's supposed to be a back eddy right near the Rock. All of the locals give it a one-quarter-mile berth." We did not have time to change our plans, but for some reason the back eddy was in a different place that day. All of a sudden *Happy Captain* and all of the boats near her began to go backwards toward the west while *Seraffyn* trickled ever eastward. Three hours later, after we finished drifting around the seemingly deserted course, we tied *Seraffyn* back in her berth and headed toward the tiny sailing club bar. The rest of the cruising-racing crews drifted slowly in to have a beer and meet each other. Listening to the talk, it finally became clear to us that we were the only crew who had not been warned to avoid the back eddy that is usually running two knots off the tip of the Rock. But more important, because of that, we were the only boat to finish the race!

Our trophy was presented the same evening, and we humbly accepted the prize we had won by a lucky mistake. Then we promised to give Brian, the skipper of the Goliath-like Ocean 71, *Happy Captain VI*, a rematch.

During the rest of the winter there were five more races with winds ranging from eight knots to one stormy race which was held in the lee of the Rock while the anemometer on the breakwater registered steady forty-five-knot winds with gusts to sixty. Because we went out and tried to push *Seraffyn* to her limits while other boats were near enough so that we could see improvements in our performance, we learned that in light winds with a choppy sea, *Seraffyn* goes better if she is heeled five or ten degrees by shifting all of her crew to leeward. In heavy winds we learned to make full use of her new reefing number two genoa.

The owner of *Mabel Amelia*, a handsome forty-two-foot wooden sloop designed by Buchanan and built by Moody's yard on the south coast of England around 1960, claimed the six-race series taught him to trust his boat. Don and Heather Hynd had bought *Mabel Amelia* in England and were sailing south toward the Caribbean with Maine as their eventual goal. When they stopped in Gibraltar to restock for the Atlantic crossing, they discovered Heather was pregnant. So rather than risk delivering a baby at sea, they were spending the winter in Gibraltar, where doctors were known to be well-qualified and where the local hospital had an excellent, though slightly old-fashioned, maternity ward. During the heavy-weather race which was held three months after we arrived, *Mabel Amelia* took first place with two English sailors and a vastly pregnant Heather as crew. Two weeks later their son was born. This racing experience helped Don decide that *Mabel Amelia* was too much boat to handle himself on a long ocean passage where Heather would have had to devote almost all of her time to taking care of a two-month-old baby. So he took on two crew, and Heather flew to the Caribbean to meet him. The two of them cruised the rest of the way along the east coast of the United States alone and sold *Mabel Amelia* in Maine so they could buy a smaller, more easily managed boat.

Barry Hollis, Gordon Butler, and Willy Keech were three English sailors in their early twenties who had pooled their resources and bought a wooden twenty-five-foot folkboat on the Solent. They had cruised together quite happily, enjoying life until one dark night when a Portuguese fishboat ran into them twenty miles offshore. Their engineless boat, *Piratical Pippet*, began taking on water immediately; they had to force the captain of the fishboat to tow them into port. The port captain of the small fishing village on one of the rivers on Portugal's south coast coerced the fishboat skipper into paying for the basic repairs on *P-Pippet*. But this incident left quite a dent in the boys' cruising funds. Within a few weeks of their arrival in Gibraltar, all three had a contract to lay tile in the new apartment buildings under construction just a quarter mile from the marina. With their dinghy racing experience to draw on, Barry, Will, and Gordon were our fiercest competitors that winter. The local joke was that the handicapper used to walk over to our mooring spots after we had started each race. He would weigh the junk the crews of *P-Pippet* and *Seraffyn* left behind on the dock. Then he would decide on our handicaps. All three of *P-Pippet*'s crew agreed that the race series confirmed what they had suspected during their previous five months of cruising; they needed more sail area. Because reports from some voyagers told only of trade-wind sailing and heavy winds, the boys had shortened their rig for cruising. Even though they carried a masthead genoa, they missed the four feet of mast they had removed. They also decided jiffy reefing would have been much better than the roller reefing the boat came with. As winter drew to a close, Barry, Will, and Gordon said that without the races, they would not have gotten out sailing during the winter and would not have discovered some of the problems on *Piratical Pippet* which needed attention before they could attempt further ocean crossings.

But most important, the Gibraltar race series introduced us to people who came from outside the cruising and marina society. Sandy Bunney had never sailed before and even though we tried to make her feel welcome on that first race, she refused to come along. "I might slow you down," she explained. But when we arrived back at the marina she came to tell us, "Dinner's waiting." After spending one evening with Chris, Sandy, and their four-year-old son, Phillip, in their British Air Force issue apartment, we felt like we had gained a family. We talked Sandy into racing with us for the rest of the series. I arranged to take her out for an afternoon sail with just another girl along, and she turned out to be fine crew. In fact she raced during the Boxing-Day regatta with her leg in a plaster cast from the knee down; we took first place with Sandy in charge of the mainsheet. Sandy and Chris gave us a key to their apartment, urged us to use their laundry facilities and bathtub, and shared their days off, showing us their

Gibraltar—from local sights to formal evenings at the officers' club.

Gibraltar is a whole country set on two and a half square miles of steeply inclined solid rock. The only flat land in the country is the one-thousand-foot-wide sand isthmus which connects it to Spain. About one half mile of this isthmus belongs to Gibraltar, and the border is marked by two electrified wire fences two hundred feet apart. One fence has a solidly locked and heavily guarded gate with a Spanish flag flying over the guard post. Two hundred feet away is an open gate with two seated British soldiers under both a Gibraltarian and a British flag. In between the two fences a white stallion grazes. We never learned who owned the horse, but we often watched it grazing placidly on Sunday afternoons while Gibraltarian families yelled across the grassy patch to their Spanish relatives who were locked out by the embargo of the tiny but strategically placed British dominated country. From the Bunney's back window we watched a wedding ceremony performed next to the northern fence by Spanish priests while Gibraltarian relatives shared the event through binoculars.

There were almost 29,000 people living in Gibraltar while we were there, with four thousand cars and an estimated five thousand dogs, all of which made the town area terribly congested. Yet one thousand feet up the Rock, the famous Gibraltar apes still roamed freely. Sandy and Chris drove us up to see the three dozen Barbary apes which are so carefully protected by the British Navy. According to legend, these fifty-pound animals swam across the eight-mile-wide Straits from Africa to seek refuge; when they desert the Rock, the British will lose the last of their empire. So not only are the apes given free run of Gibraltar, they are made ranking members of the Navy and receive monthly pay checks which must be used to make their lives more pleasant. They also can do no wrong. The apes, who in my opinion are vulgar, disappointingly small animals, taunted every visitor who stopped by their favorite playgrounds. The malicious animals ripped off car antennae, windshield wipers, and side-view mirrors. Although there are signs posted saying "Do Not Hand-Feed The Apes," while we were in Gibraltar one female tourist got too close to one of the larger apes. He grabbed the woman's long pearl necklace, which was not only strung on nylon thread that refused to break, but was also the kind that wrapped two or three times around the neck. So when the ape tried running off, clutching the pearls, the poor lady was almost strangled. Fortunately, one of her companions had a knife and cut the necklace. Unfortunately, several of the apes scrambled for the scattered pearls and popped them in their mouths.

Once we started working on the renovation of *Susy,* all sorts of interesting work offers came our way. As Larry struggled to get a nice finish on the poor-quality plywood of her interior, and while I tried to cover up and revitalize poor-quality hinges and hardware, we often discussed the error of postponing the search for ways to earn more cruising funds until we were almost broke. "Next time we start when we are down to three-months money. Then we can wait and be choosy instead of taking the first offers that come along," Larry commented as we planned the next job we had scheduled.

Our life fell into an interesting pattern when we finished *Susy.* Larry contracted to build a complete new interior for a twenty-five-foot miniature Colin Archer cutter built by a skilled, competent Danish sailor who had cruised on *Teddy* for two years and then sold her to Tony Barton in Gibraltar. I contracted to do the finish work—four coats of varnish on everything. Larry worked every morning on the woodwork in *Teddy* while I stayed on *Seraffyn* and wrote some articles. In the afternoon I would come over and varnish what he had built or add extra coats to build up a nice finish. Some afternoons Larry spliced wire for people who were changing their rigging or had broken steering cables. On rainy days he stayed on *Seraffyn* and wrote about things like oil lamps, sailing into tight situations without an engine, and boat maintenance.

About half-way through our winter in Gibraltar, as our cruising funds neared the two-thirds mark, politics wormed their way into our lives and directly caused two events which made our winter in this tiny colony especially memorable. First—because of bad crops in many parts of the world—sugar prices in all English colonies climbed overnight from 17 cents a pound to 90 cents. Second, the local bakers went on strike; and third, the ship bringing the monthly supply of propane to Gibraltar was locked in a Spanish port due to the embargo.

When we ran low on propane it seemed only natural to declare a long weekend and sail sixteen miles across the Straits to Ceuta, the Spanish-owned equivalant of Gibraltar, an enclave that clings to a rocky promontory on Morocco's north coast. We had heard this was a duty-free port where good wines could be had at one-fifth the price of those we drank in Gibraltar. A ship's captain had told us there was a propane depot there. So our weekend as smugglers started when we mentioned to one of our neighbors in the marina, "We're headed across the Straits to buy some propane, do you need any?"

By Friday over fifteen people who were living on boats in the marina had asked us for everything from refills for their tanks to fresh meat, sugar, and most of all yeast and flour to make the bread Gibraltarian bakers refused to bake. As our requisition list grew ever larger I began to worry. I recalled incidents where yachts were confiscated in Columbia and Venezuela when the owners innocently (or maybe not so innocently) supplied residents of the country with radios and watches from duty-free Panama. Larry made a simple suggestion to calm my fears. "Before we leave, talk to the customs man at the post outside the marina. You seem to be good friends with him."

So after I finished getting *Seraffyn* ready to go on Friday, I strolled past the customs post. My friend was at his desk filling out his endless forms. During our months stay I had met his wife and his two sons and admired his new motorcycle. So I decided the open approach was best. He listened to our plans for the weekend and then suggested we step outside the customs office. "You know people from Gibraltar can't visit Ceuta because of the embargo," he told me and then quickly continued, "so when the Spanish harbor official comes to clear your papers and says, 'Did you have a nice voyage from Algeciras?' just say 'yes.'" This bit of conspiracy between the officials of two tiny port enclaves perched on the sides of hostile countries was a delightful change from normal politics. But the customs official grew more serious as he told me, "Don't worry about the propane. That's a government-run business here. They have no propane so they don't care if you import it. But fruit, vegetables, flour—you'll be stepping on the toes of local shopkeepers if they find out. So if you bring me ten pounds of flour and five pounds of sugar and come back after dark, they won't hear about your little venture. And remember, don't bring back more than a few bottles of sealed wine. But if you find me some sweet Málaga wine, put it in a fruit jar and bring it along."

Larry chuckled when I repeated our smuggling instructions. The next morning when we woke there were nineteen empty propane tanks lined up on the dock astern of *Seraffyn*. We set *Rinky Dink* right side up on top of the cabin and loaded the six forty-pound tanks into the dinghy. Then we lined the thirteen smaller tanks along the cabinsides and lashed them firmly in place with canvas to protect the decks and varnish.

A voyage across the Straits is almost always a beam reach because winds funnel into the Straits guided by two five thousand-foot-high chains of mountains. A two- or three-knot east-going current always rushes through the Straits as cold Atlantic waters rush in to replace water lost by evaporation on the land-locked sea. To lay Ceuta on one tack we had to keep *Seraffyn* on a close reach headed twenty degrees above our course in a lovely ten-knot westerly on a sunlit shirtsleeve day. Four hours later, when we eased sails for the final reach into the gold-colored stone city which lay behind the long protecting arms of a man-made breakwater, I lounged on our absolutely dry decks and asked Larry, "Why didn't anyone else from the marina sail over when they ran short of propane? Some of them have been doing without for a month now."

"Most of the boats are torn apart," was his explanation. "They came to Gibraltar to winter and once they tied their dock lines they tore apart the gear that had been hassling them all year long. Then they sent out for parts or contracted for repairs. Which boat can you name that doesn't have its engine apart or rigging off or electronic gear at the repair shop? Besides, the reports of winter gales is a real psychological barrier."

The customs man had been right. As soon as we tied our dock lines in the surging but safe inner harbor reserved for small fishing boats and occasional visiting yachts in Ceuta, a broadly smiling Spanish immigration official called to us, "Did you have a nice trip from Algeciras?"

Because of this mutual deception we had no papers to fill out, and as soon as *Seraffyn* was properly secured we went for a walk into town. We found food prices excellent, wine ridiculously low priced, and a pastry shop to rival any we had ever visited. Thus far reassured, Larry suggested we follow the plan that had formed during our short passage —inspired no doubt by visions of our smuggling profits. We put extra chain down with our twenty-five-pound CQR anchor, added two more stern lines with chaffing gear, locked *Seraffyn,* and asked the military dock guard to watch her. Then we found the bus depot and headed for Tangiers.

After a one-hour wait at the border guard post, we began an interesting sixty-mile ride across Morocco's barren countryside through oasis and white-washed villages into Tangiers—the port made famous by tales of Barbary pirates, smugglers, and refugees.

We checked into the well-recommended Grand Hôtel de France and settled into a red-carpeted room complete with mammoth bathtub, unlimited hot water, double bed, and delightful wrought-iron balcony overlooking the luxurious gardens. A leisurely bath; a siesta; an afternoon stroll through the hotel grounds to look at the eighteenth-century décor and art objects from all of North Africa; then a seven-course, Moroccan-style dinner served impeccably by turbaned waiters; a night in the old, slightly decadent but nonetheless elegant hotel; breakfast in bed on a linen-covered tray—what a wonderful contrast to our normal life, and we enjoyed every minute of it. Moreover, the cost of a day's tour through one of the oldest, largest, and most intricate casbahs (shopping cities) in North Africa and the bus trip from Ceuta to Tangiers and back was less than sixty dollars. These are the interludes of extravagant, but reasonable, luxury that keep me from feeling that I gave up something better when I chose to join Larry in his life of wandering.

We arrived back in Ceuta Sunday evening, and early Monday

On a corner in the Casbah.

morning Larry located a taxi-type pickup truck, loaded all twenty propane tanks—including *Seraffyn*'s—then headed west into the hills. I walked into the market section of town with my shopping lists. On the ground floor of the three-story granite building that houses the farmers market with its three hundred stalls, I found one stand with wonderful, reasonably priced vegetables and dried fruits. Because every bit of food that comes to Gibraltar must be imported from England by way of Tangiers, I had not seen produce of this quality and variety for over a month. After I made my selection I asked the lady who ran the stand if she would watch my purchases while I did the rest of my shopping. By 1000 I had a mound of fresh food three feet tall stacked with the standkeeper. I left it there while I went to rendezvous with Larry at the Three Barrels (Tres Barriles)—a small wine shop we had discovered the afternoon before.

Larry and the portly owner of the keg-crowded room were deep in a comparison of the various red wines stored in fifty-gallon casks which lined the walls two deep. With his spirit really into the smuggling mood, Larry reminded me, "The customs man told us—no wine in sealed bottles. So I've brought our five-gallon water jugs. We'll buy it bulk and the worse we'll have to do is pour it overboard. Come on Lin, taste this red one, it's only thirty-two cents a litre." The proprietor also entered into the smuggling spirit and searched his back room until he found over a dozen empty, four-litre plastic containers left from the olives he served as hors d'oeuvres. Before we finished he had introduced us to that wonderful drink served in southern Spain, medio-medio: a mixture of half Málaga sweet wine and half dry white wine, served very cold. We took three gallons back with us. His neighbor just down the narrow stone street was a ships chandler, and after only a short consultation we were told that 100 two-kilo bags of sugar, 100 one-kilo bags of flour, and at least ten kilos of yeast would be at our boat in one hour. (Now that we are thousands of miles from Gibraltar I must admit we also ordered 18 bottles of Fundador brandy and sparkling wines at less than one dollar each.) So we hired a taxi and carted 105 litres of wine, 100 pounds of fruit and vegetables, 40 pounds of fresh meat, and 50 pounds of ice back to *Seraffyn*.

Sure enough, an hour later the chandler came down to *Seraffyn*. "But there is a big problem," he called to us in Spanish. "The guard at the gate asks if you have an export permit."

The soldier in charge of customs patiently explained, "You can't be buying all of this butane, food, and sugar for yourselves. It won't even fit inside your boat! Therefore it must be a commercial venture and for that you need an export license and to get that license you must go to the big office building across the street." I do not know how I held my temper, but when I looked across the harbor to where Larry was transferring the mound of propane bottles, liquor, and food from the dock to *Seraffyn*'s deck, I had to agree. I was not even sure she could carry it all. So I patiently filled out twelve different forms in eight different offices—guessing at some of the items I could not translate easily—while visions of our first smuggling voyage being a complete financial disaster flashed through my mind. One hour later I arrived at the last step in the monopolylike game: the accounting office. I am not sure if the uniformed accounting officer really had a twinkle in his eye as he looked over each form, his fingers beating a constant tattoo on his beat-up old adding machine. But when he finally pulled the two-foot-long tape from his machine and wrote his signature across my formal two-month export license with the flourish of a matador, he presented me with a bill for seventeen pesetas, or, thirty-one cents.

This fearsome objective out of the way, I returned to help Larry lash down the last bottle. Then we carefully loaded two hundred bags

The last bits of semi-contraband supplies being loaded on board.

of flour and sugar plus all of the fruit into the forepeak, on the cabin sole, behind the lee clothes of the quarter berths and into the lazarette lockers. The brandy went into semi-secret storage areas under the floor boards.

With the decks clear, we sat back to enjoy a lunch of crusty Spanish bread, farmers cheese, and red grapes with some chilled medio-medio before the smallest ocean-going, sailing cargo ship began her voyage across the Straits.

Seraffyn sat almost three inches low in the water when we untied our stern lines and winched away from the dock to where our anchor lay in ten feet of water. We set her full main and staysail to work clear of the harbor, then lifted the anchor and hooked it in its spot on the bobstay. "We'll set more sail when we see what it's like outside," Larry told me as he steered for the harbor entrance. Overhead, fat white clouds scurried along toward the east, and a community of seagulls cackled at us from the stones of the breakwater. Less than a quarter-mile offshore we could see tumbling whitecaps galloping into the Mediterranean. Even though we only had twelve or fifteen knots of wind right where we were, Larry glanced at the top-heavy load of butane bottles in the upright dinghy and said, "We must have two thousand pounds of extra weight on her, and most of it's high. I'll put two reefs in the mainsail now: we can always shake them out later. You check everything below once more before we get out into the open."

Minutes after *Seraffyn* was snugged down to double reefed main and staysail, we cleared the outermost point of Ceuta, where high mountains blanket the Atlantic winds. Larry's expression was a de-lightful mixture of concern and pride as our overladen little vessel heeled sluggishly to the first gust, then stubbornly and proudly chal-lenged the eight-foot seas and thirty-knot winds. She seemed to defy each roller as it attacked her from a seventy-five-degree angle. Her bowsprit would threaten to pierce each whitetop then lift and surge ahead as if to say, "Try and catch me!" Within minutes she was close reaching at five and a half knots, oblivious of her load. Light showers of spray crossed the foredeck but the cockpit stayed dry. *Seraffyn's* work-boat heritage showed itself that day. Her ample beam and heavy displacement helped her carry the load yet sail smartly and comforta-bly. I went below to make hot coffee and tea while Larry readjusted Helmer (our self-steering gear) to make up for the current.

The December day drew to an early close, and it was dark by the time we came into the lee of Gibraltar Bay. The wind drew aft until we were running wing and wing as we passed Europa Point, Gibraltar's southernmost tip. The ten-second light flashed its welcome, and in the parking lot on a hill behind the lighthouse we noticed the headlights of two cars. Larry took our big flashlight and shone it on our mainsail. The car headlights began flashing. "Must be the Bunneys checking to see if we made it across all right," Larry said.

And sure enough, as soon as we maneuvered into the marina dock Chris and Sandy were right behind the customs agent. "Did you have a nice voyage?" my customs friend asked. With *Seraffyn*'s stern to the dock and the cabin oil lamps glowing brightly it was impossible to miss the pile of stores we had aboard. "Did you purchase any liquor in sealed bottles?" the customs man asked. "Only some bottles of sparkling wine and brandy for our own use," Larry honestly answered. "And did you find me any sweet wine?" the customs man asked. Larry reached into the lazarette locker and handed over the gallon jar that had once contained olives and now held medio-medio. "Well then, you must be tired from your rough sail. I think tomorrow morning would be soon enough for your customs clearance. Have a good night."

Our dock was soon buzzing with people from the marina who came to get their butane bottles, and each seemed eager to buy as much flour, yeast, and sugar as they could. Within an hour *Seraffyn* was almost empty, and we went off with Chris and Sandy to taste a bottle of Carta Blanca sparkling wine, introduce them to medio-medio, and toast our first and last voyage as professional smugglers.

The next morning Cathy, the cook on *Happy Captain*, came by. "Several of the people with boats in the pens would like copies of the instructions you gave me for making bread. Do you have any left?" she asked. The day after the bread strike started I had written a three-page outline of instructions and given copies to friends—along with some of my original three-pound supply of dried yeast. I found more copies and poured Cathy some tea. "You really should write a book about cooking at sea," Cathy said. Every time I saw Cathy during the next two weeks she repeated, "When are you going to write a proper seagoing cooking guide?" Finally, with Larry and Cathy urging me on, I wrote a book proposal and sent it to a small nautical publisher in New York. Three weeks later a five-page letter came back from Steve Doherty at Seven Seas Press: "I already have a nautical type cook book, but I know people would like to read a book about your voyages on

Seraffyn. " So Cathy's kind suggestion plus the bakers strike had started a chain of events that was to have a profound and interesting effect on our cruising life.

Our Gibraltarian winter seemed to glide by quickly. Our cruising fund came ever closer to the four-thousand-dollar goal we had set ourselves. The vicious winter storms sweeping in from the Atlantic or surging out of the Mediterranean came twice a month to confirm some of the sea stories locals told us. Because of the sheer 1700-foot-high cliff on Gibraltar's east side, thirty-five-knot easterly winds would pile their force against the Rock, build up pressure, and finally tumble down the western slope of the city at sixty knots. We watched one of these williwaws lay the fifty-four-foot British Navy training yacht *Adventure* flat on her beam ends as the crew cast off from the mooring with the main and small jib set. Another day, after Larry had to chase after his large handsaw when a sixty-knot gust of wind blew it away, I watched a heavy-set woman get blown ten feet from her boat's stern

That is Larry working away at his temporary bench next to Teddy.

onto the dock without ever once touching the boarding ladder. While the winds blew, the days turned so cold that we got out our propane heater and connected it to one of the burners on our stove. But between the three-day-long storms, days were sunny and often warm enough for us to dress in shorts and tee shirts.

Larry had offers of more work than he could handle. Some checks trickled in from sales of our antiques and articles. Occasional voyages to Ceuta, races, and local events on shore kept our weekends full. As March drew to a close we finished *Seraffyn*'s varnish work and gave her bulwarks some extra paint. Around us other boats were starting to sparkle as their owners reinstalled fittings, motors, and electronic gear. By April 1, when we stored the last of Larry's tools in their locker, bought traveler's checks, and paid the nineteen dollars we owed the Gibraltar government for income taxes, the first charter boats—including *Happy Captain*—were under way and bound for Greek, Spanish, and Italian ports.

Mabel Amelia was already on her way to the Canary Islands with Willy and Barry from *Piratical Pippet* as crew. That voyage was one more step toward an interesting life for Barry Hollis. During the next years we heard through the grapevine how Barry crewed back from the United States on board Ed Greeff's forty-seven-foot yacht, *Puffin*, raced the Fastnet, then went on to help deliver a fifty-foot ketch to South Africa. Now, five years later, Barry—who had started off as the rigger for a small shipyard in Portsmouth, England—is skipper on the highly rated race boat *Arles* while his wife works on board as cook.

Sandy and Chris Bunney came down to wish us good-bye when we cast off our lines. "Keep our house key, you'll need it. You'll be back, there's no other way out," Chris called as we cleared the marina.

On Wednesday, the second of April 1975, we steered well clear of Europa Point and that back eddy we had come to know so well. After six years of voyaging, *Seraffyn* finally poked her bowsprit into Ulysses' sea: the wine-colored Mediterranean.

CHAPTER 3

~~~~~

An Introduction to the Med

Estepona, the first Spanish port east of Gibraltar, is shared half by
a fishermen's co-op and half by a modest, seldom-used yacht club.
The morning after we arrived, we set fore and aft anchors in the small
mooring area near the club then sat on deck watching the heavily
loaded fishboats mumbling past us to tie at the far end of the harbor.
After the last boat came by, I climbed into *Rinky Dink* and rowed over
to buy some ice and see what the fishermen were catching.

When I secured *Rinky* below the stone steps that lead to the co-op's
auction building, the last commercial buyers from towns as far away
as Grenada and Málaga were loading their vans with crates of fresh
fish and Crustaceans. In the middle of the auction-house floor there
was a pile made up of ten different kinds of fish five to twelve inches
long, prawns of all sizes, clams, oysters, mussels, and miniature lob-
sterlike creatures that were four and a half inches long. A fisherman
patiently explained that since commercial buyers are only interested
in complete twenty-five-kilo boxes of sea food, the fishermen throw all
of the odd bits from their catch into the pile. The auctioneer then
shuffles the pile with his shovel and sells it by the kilo to local housewives. I joined the handful of women who had walked a mile from
town, and we watched while shovels, full of *mariscos* (the Spanish word
for any food that comes from the sea), were emptied onto a piece of
newspaper—the contents then weighed and sold for less than fifty
cents a pound.

As soon as I had my mariscos, I found the iceman in back of the
auction building and paid for a fifty-pound block of ice. The iceman
called to one of the fishermen who were now lounging around the

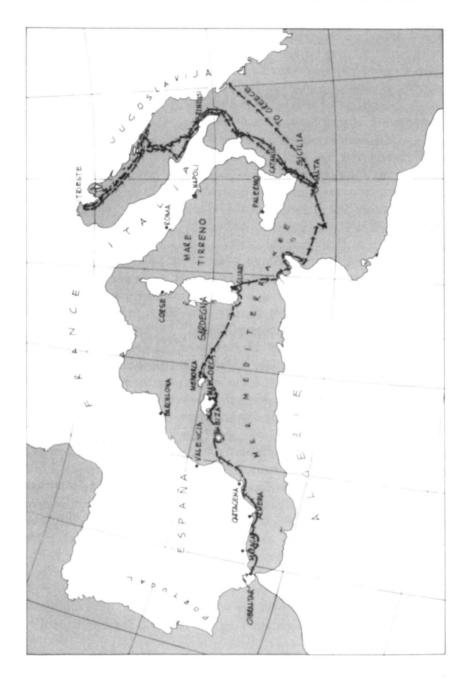

dock, "Come help this little lady carry her ice." There were several volunteers, and the unfortunate fellow who came forward first hefted the block onto his shoulder and followed me to where six-foot-eight-inch-long, fifty-five-pound *Rinky Dink* lay bobbing happily among heavy wooden fishing dories and rough rowboats. Before I could let out a shout, he jumped three feet from the quay into the dinghy. *Rinky* tilted dangerously, threw the startled fisherman in the water, ice and all, then bounced upright without a drop of water inside. The dockside loungers were roaring when the poor fisherman came to the surface and sputtered, "Why didn't you tell me your dinghy had no substance!" The Spanish flew fast and furious between the loungers and the soaking fisherman, and I could not translate much of it. But somehow my would-be assistant's temper was cooled to laughter by his fishing friends. The ice was replaced in *Rinky*, and three laughing fishermen held the dinghy solidly in place so I could get in.

As I rowed home with my ice and the equivalent of a shovel-full of mariscos, I planned a paella (pie-ā-ya), which is the Spanish national dish—a combination of rice, assorted sea food, green vegetables, and pimento, seasoned with cumin and saffron. After seeing the way odd-lot fish were sold, I appreciated how the women in Spanish seaports came to invent this special meal.

Smuggling has been a major part of the economy in almost every port within a fifty-mile radius of Gibraltar for over two centuries. English cigarettes and whiskey are frantically sought by Spaniards who have to pay very high prices for low-quality local substitutes. It is rumored that one of the reasons Gibraltarians chose to remain under British rule instead of joining Spain when there was a vote supervised by the United Nations in 1967 is that several of the most influential and wealthy people in Gibraltar are wanted by the Spanish guardia for smuggling. Because Estepona is so close to Gibraltar, the local customs officials are known to be more ardent than other Spanish port officials in their entry inspections of visiting yachts. We were lucky and had no trouble at all when we sailed in; the officer just asked to see our passports and ships papers. But when friends from Gibraltar sailed in a few days later, with a British flag flying, and tied to the sea wall, they were delayed for two hours by bureaucratic hassles.

We rowed over for drinks on their boat and, at dark, decided to go to town together for dinner. Shirley, Grant, and I walked along the quay toward the yacht club while Larry rowed out to *Seraffyn* to get his wallet. It was a particularly dark evening. The harbor was quiet and still. The three of us waited under a street lamp in front of the club, wondering what was taking Larry so long.

When he finally arrived Larry was white as a ghost. "I was almost shot!" he stammered. It seems a local policeman was sneaking a nap under the yacht club veranda when Larry rowed up to the concrete launching ramp. The sound of Larry tugging the dinghy onto the ramp woke the policeman, who came running at Larry. He drew his revolver and stopped just a few feet away with it cocked and aimed at Larry's forehead.

Larry later explained, "I was terrified. I couldn't think of any Spanish words to slow him down." Fortunately the policeman shone his light at Larry and the tiny dinghy, then cooled down enough to listen to Larry's halting explanation. Sputtering and angry, he launched into a lecture on how people shouldn't be rowing around the harbor at night without a light. "The guy was still waving his gun around all this time," Larry told us. "I felt much better when he finally put it back in his holster and told me to get going."

During all of our cruising in Spain this was the only time we had anything but courteous treatment from either officials or the Guardia Civil. In fact these men are almost ruthless about protecting foreign tourists from problems of any kind. The incident near the yacht club simply involved an over-zealous and startled local policeman who had heard one too many smuggling stories.

The next morning a portly Spanish man was yelling from the patio of the yacht club. "Hello, Hello Canadian!" he called, waving his arms. Since we were the only boat flying a Canadian flag, Larry rowed ashore in *Rinky Dink*. When he came back twenty minutes later he told me, "I've invited Luis and his wife by at 1430 for drinks." Margot Isnor was a thirty-five-year-old Canadian who had met Luis during a holiday in Spain. They were married only a few weeks later and together opened a small marine store at the far end of town. These two warm and friendly people decided it was their job to show us why they loved southern Spain so much. The day after we met, we piled into their van and drove through small villages and along country roads until we were on the side of a mountain two thousand feet above the Straits of Gibraltar. A fresh easterly wind chilled us as we stood on the sunny, green-covered slope. Below us the confused blue water of the Atlantic rushed in to mix with the warm green water of the Mediterranean.

The wind whipped the already churning sea and laced it with white. Cargo ships, ore carriers, and tankers passed below like glowing toys visibly tossed by the overfalls and swell. Between us and the cold-looking sea, fish hawks glided, swooping and darting, their cocked heads watching the sea below. Every few minutes one of the gold-colored hawks would dive straight for the sea. Other hawks near him would break their gliding pattern, fold their wings, and tumble downward, then struggle back into the windy sky with fish in their beaks.

A spell was cast over all of us by the glowing blue, white, and green of the windy scene. We climbed into the van in silence and not until we parked at a small café where Luis said we would taste mussels prepared by a chef who loved sea food, did any of us feel like talking. Our new friendship deepened while we savored a tray-full of sweet-tasting mussels that had been steamed open in a sauce made from fresh tomatoes, onions, and lemon juice lightly seasoned with oregano and red wine.

I hate haulout time. It is one of the evilest necessities of a cruising sailor's life. Unfortunately even the best anti-fouling paint only keeps marine growth off the bottom of boats for seven to ten months. *Seraffyn*'s underbody looked like a garden after almost a year in the water. Barnacles clung like little white volcanoes all along the rudder fittings, orange bushes an inch high grew in patches under the turn of the bilge, and green grass everywhere else. All of it made *Seraffyn* sail sluggishly in light winds. To get optimum sailing performance and for generally good maintenance it is prudent to check all of the underwater fittings once a year for signs of wear or electrolysis and to scrape any barnacles out of through hull fittings, such as cockpit drains, so they do not plug up when you need them most.

Since we are always on the move, every place we haul is new to us; each hauling setup is different, and usually we have to contend with a language barrier. Larry becomes like a nervous mother hen when someone else is handling *Seraffyn,* putting rough wood and metal cradles around her and dragging her out of her natural element. Since *Seraffyn* was damaged by careless shipyard handlers in Jamaica several years ago, I don't blame him for his concern. This time we decided to haul in Estepona because the foreman at the yacht club seemed vitally interested in doing a careful job for us so that we would tell other cruising people about his yard and about his brand new ways of doing things. So when *Seraffyn* had been settled into a cradle and hauled clear of the water with little more than the usual fuss and bother, and when Larry was satisfied with the way she was supported, I thought the worst was over and that only some hard work lay ahead.

Even scrubbing the smelly green scum and barnacles off the bottom was not as bad this time as usual. The club had some long-handled brushes and pails of sand. Larry wet the brush, dipped it in the sand, and scrubbed while I hosed down behind him. The next day the two of us sanded the white topsides by hand in less than three hours. The weather cooperated by staying warm and still so the glossy white enamel lay on easily under Larry's three-inch-wide Grumbacker brush. I should have known things were going too well.

The next morning dawned gray, windy, and cold. We were scheduled to re-launch on the high tide in five hours, which gave us three hours to paint *Seraffyn*'s bottom and two hours for the paint to set up. We climbed into grungy work clothes—ones we save just for painting the bottom. I pulled out two large paint brushes, a bag of rags, a gallon of kerosene, and the four quarts of so-called "unbeatable" bottom paint the sailors at Gibraltar's naval yard had sold us for half the price of normal anti-fouling paint.

Larry climbed down the ladder from *Seraffyn*'s deck and opened the first can. It was so thick he had trouble stirring it. "Lin, the navy fellows said not to thin this with anything but to heat it up if it was too thick to go on," Larry called up to me. "How about putting it in the oven for a few minutes?" He put the lid of the brown gooey paint lightly in place and handed it up to me; I set it in the oven, which was still warm from heating the cabin that morning.

Anti-fouling paint contains tremendous amounts of copper and other metals. It is at least two and a half times heavier than regular paints. Larry was waiting impatiently below. I reached into the oven, grabbed the can with one hand, and turned to climb out of the cabin —then that goddamned can slipped through my fingers. When it hit the cabin sole the top flew off, and paint sprayed across the cabinets and floor boards and half way up my leg. It spattered the white cabin top and left splotches like runny manure on the blue settee cushions. I stood in the middle of the slowly creeping, gooey brown puddle that covered almost a third of *Seraffyn*'s pristine scrubbed teak floor boards. My mind was a complete blank for just a minute, then I ran shrieking on deck, "Larry, bring rags, kerosene, help! Quick!"

When Larry climbed into *Seraffyn*'s paint be-spattered cabin he set to work in complete silence, mopping and soaking rags in half a quart of mudlike paint. I tried to help, but in *Seraffyn*'s confined floor space there is only room for one person. Larry exploded, "Get out of my sight!" I stood there staring horrified at the mess I had made just because I had rushed a bit too much. "Quick," Larry growled from his kneeling position. "If I see you here one minute longer I'll kill you."

I climbed down the ladder feeling absolutely terrible. Everywhere I stepped brown toe prints marred the clean teak decks. Tears were streaming down my face as I tried to clean the paint from between my toes.

Larry was still furious when he emerged with two shopping bags full of paint-soaked rags. "Get out of my sight," he yelled again as soon as he saw me. I certainly did not blame him. The tide was on its way in. The bottom was not painted, and we needed that full tide to re-launch the boat. I had wasted most of a quart of paint that cost sixty dollars a gallon and I felt sure our bare teak floor boards would be stained forever. So I went and sat behind the clubhouse building for twenty minutes until Larry's mumbles became more subdued.

When I peeked out and saw Larry furiously painting away on the far side of *Seraffyn*'s long keel, I sneaked over, got the other brush, and began painting the near side. Quiet as I was, Larry noticed my feet moving along under the ways car. He threw down his brush and, without warning, came around the end of the keel, grabbed me, and threw me—brush and all—off the side of the launching ramp into the cold gray water. How could I get angry? I would have done the same thing if he had made a mess like that! (Of course I would have had a much harder time throwing Larry off the dock than he had throwing me.) I guess the sight of me bobbing to the surface be-draggled and sputtering, but still clutching the bottom-painting brush, was just enough to break Larry's evil spell. With all of his aggressions gone, Larry helped me from the water, got me a towel and dry clothes, then said, "The hell with catching todays tide!" He set to work getting the last traces of bottom paint off me.

Nature was on my side that day. By high tide, storm winds in the Mediterranean had set up such a surge in the harbor that it would have been impossible to re-launch *Seraffyn* even if she had been ready. The wind had been blowing for twelve hours; it continued for only twelve hours more but created a surge three feet high that ran across the harbor. Water pushed up the ramp ten feet to where a freshly painted *Seraffyn* sat proudly, then tumbled under the cradle and ran across and down the ramp to form miniature breaking waves two feet high behind us. For three days this continued, so we could not be re-launched and had plenty of time to search out the last traces of bottom paint from between strakes of varnished tongue and groove mahogany or bare teak in *Seraffyn*'s galley. The club did not charge us the usual daily fee for the extra time on the ways, and Luis and Margot introduced us to more of the highlights of Estepona while we waited.

This surge is a real problem throughout the Med. Even the best planned harbors with mazes of breakwaters end up with surges that wear on dock lines and tempers. At sea this energy translates to chop and sloppy seas, which are one more reason people say, "You can't sail in the Med, there's either too much wind or too little and the waves are the worst in the world." We had heard this comment so often during our winter in Gibraltar that we had almost come to believe it —until we remembered the thousands of sailors who had moved cargo ships and warships throughout the Med for thousands of years.

A fresh westerly wind blew the day after we finally re-launched *Seraffyn*. We beat out of Estepona early on the gray, wintry day. When we cleared the harbor we reached off across the lumpy sea carrying reefed main and staysail. Just a few hours later, when we came through the breakwater entrance of Spain's newest, fanciest man-made harbor —José Banus—the westerly wind was up to a gale. We could see a whole area of empty docks at the far end of the harbor so we did not think to stop at the harbormaster's office. Besides, we could not have rounded up into the wind in the narrow area at the harbor's entrance. In fact, there was no room to maneuver until we reached the area where the empty docks lay. Booming voices came over the office loud speakers, but the strong wind carried their words away. I took down all sail and *Seraffyn*'s speed dropped from six knots to about two. Larry got out a long mooring line, ran it through a stern hawse pipe, and cleated it. "Let's slow the boat down and head right next to that end pier," he suggested. "You steer and as we pass that big mooring ring I'll try and slip the line through it, snug the line, and stop *Seraffyn*. If I miss, round up into the wind. I'll drop the anchor, and we can warp back to the dock and pick up the anchor later." Larry's stunt worked wonderfully. I steered a wide series of zig-zags to slow *Seraffyn* down as much as I could then headed as close to the ring as I dared. Larry had just enough time to shove the line through the ring and wrap it back around the stanchion of the boom gallows as our wind-filled rigging kept us moving relentlessly down the harbor. All five and a half tons of boat squeaked to a halt and we were just gloating over our bit of grand-standing when two angry uniformed dock attendants came rushing down the broad concrete docks on bicycles, yelling, "Why didn't you stop at the office!" They climbed off their bicycles and came to our dock end, where the strong wind kept *Seraffyn* clear and comfortable—still dangling from one stern line. The bigger official began to say, "You can't stay here!" Just then a particularly strong gust of wind rushed through the harbor. I tried to think of the right Spanish words but all I could do was point. Those two bicycles flew off the dock. The two attendants ran toward them and stood watching in stunned silence as their bikes sank into the murky storm-tossed waters and disappeared in twelve feet of water. The two men walked away without saying a word to us. We never saw them again though a maintenance man came down after we had properly secured *Seraffyn*'s bow to a mooring buoy, stern to the quay. He threw a grappling hook on a long line until he snagged and lifted each mud-covered bike.

CHAPTER 4

~~~~~~

Along the South Coast
of Spain

A few minutes after *Seraffyn* was secured in José Banus, the two
of us hurried over to the port captain's office. We had not received any mail for over a month. As usual, we had had our bank hold
everything until we knew which port we would most likely visit. Then
we had sent a letter asking for everything to be packed up together and
sent care of the port captain's office. The friendly marina manager had
our mail pack ready for us. He told us we were welcome to leave
Seraffyn where she was and charged us the fees for his harbor, which
were twenty times higher than the normal Spanish port fee of fifteen
cents per night.

José Banus is a privately owned development. From the manager's
office on the third floor we could see over the tops of the fancy restaurants, shops, and apartments that surrounded the half-empty marina.
Just ten feet behind the stucco and tile simulated Spanish town, there
was nothing—just desert shrubs and a narrow road leading off into the
distance where the old village of Marbella lay. José Banus is just an
expensive façade designed to lure northern Europeans who supposedly would buy or rent an apartment with a mooring in front of
it for their yachts, then spend the long dark winters and their money
in sunny Spain. José Banus is a safe harbor, but in spite of the elaborate
planning, no one had thought to provide a warm-water shower for
visiting yachtsmen.

Our mail pack contained delightful letters from thirty friends, but
not the one letter we needed. Just after New Years, Larry's folks had
written that they were planning a springtime visit to Spain—probably
around the first of May. It was now the nineteenth of April. We did

not know when or where they would be arriving and we were concerned. It may seem strange, but only when it came down to the wire did we think of a simple solution: we went to the telephone office and called the Pardeys. When I say simple, I mean relatively simple. Telephone systems in most parts of the world are far different from those in the United States. To place a long distance call you must find the telephone exchange, give them a deposit, sit and wait while they place your call, then line up at a cashier window to pay your fees. This sometimes takes up to three hours of sitting in a waiting room full of restless people. Because of time differences around the world, we have had to find telephone offices at 11:30 at night to reach friends at a reasonable hour, their time. But in spite of the hassle, it is still better than the foul-ups that can occur if you have guests meet you and depend on arrangements confirmed only in letters, which are sometimes lost or delayed. (Larry's parents had written. Their letters arrived three weeks after they did.) The telephone call cost us fourteen dollars, but we knew which airport to go to and which flight number to check on. If we had called only two weeks earlier, the Pardeys would have known to fly into Málaga, which is only sixty miles from where we were with *Seraffyn*. Instead they confirmed their charter flight for Valencia because it was close to the Balearic Islands, which we had mentioned as our goal for the summer. When we eventually met Larry's folks after a day on a bus and two on a train, we decided that we would tell any future visitors not to make final plans until we telephoned them. We also resolved to be more conservative in estimating our times of arrival so we could be waiting at a harbor near the airport a few days before our guests arrived.

Meanwhile, we had eight days left to find a nice place to leave *Seraffyn* while we rendezvoused with the Pardeys. Not only is José Banus too commercial, it just isn't the kind of port visitors from Canada hope to find when they cruise in the Mediterranean.

We headed east on a light, warm west wind. The sea was restless, with a two-foot chop from some wind which must have blown from the east the night before. We were making little headway with our genoa set on the spinnaker pole and the mainsail slatting and banging as we lifted to each wavelet. So just after lunch, when we were both trying to sunbath in the nude and enjoy the green hills that slipped slowly by three miles to port, Larry suggested putting up our huge blue and white spinnaker. As soon as it was set we dropped the mainsail and genoa. The power of the 960-square-foot, 1.2-ounce nylon spinnaker added a knot to our speed. Twenty-four-foot *Seraffyn* still bounced up and down, sometimes quite quickly in spite of her 11,000-pound displacement. But without the sound of slatting Dacron sails, life was most delightful.

Larry was on deck reading, Helmer was steering, and I was below looking for a pen and paper to answer some letters when I felt a slightly larger jolt. Then Larry shouted, "Lin, come quick!" He was pointing at our masthead. We have two spikes in the masthead fitting to discourage seagulls and cormorants from perching there while *Seraffyn* is at anchor. Somehow the spinnaker had gone up when *Seraffyn* leaped off a sloppy swell. The spikes grabbed the soft nylon cloth, and we now had a mass of blue nylon billowing like a cape over our whole boat—thirty-five feet above our heads. I cannot explain my reaction, but for some reason I took one look and dashed back below for my underpants. By the time I had climbed on deck again, pants half on, the spinnaker had taken charge of matters. There was a small ripping sound, a twang, and the sail came free, shook itself gently, and filled into a beautiful bell shape again. Then Larry started to laugh. I fell in love with Larry originally when I heard that laugh. And now I fell in love again. When he asked, "How were your underpants going to help get that sail free?" I replied, "All I could think of was, What if I had to go up the mast without any pants on?"

Later when we took the spinnaker down, a close inspection showed only a small snag in the cloth, which a bit of stretching and pulling remedied. But Larry did have to remove the two seagull stoppers and straighten them the next time we varnished the mast.

There was a sloppy sea just outside the breakwater when we sailed into Málaga. Inside, the maze of piers and stone breakwaters seemed to magnify this into a two-foot surge that kept every boat in the harbor restlessly lunging and rolling. We set *Seraffyn*'s bow anchor in fifteen feet of water near the big farmers market. Then, on the suggestion of two local yachtsmen, we took a long stern line to the mast of a 150-foot ship that had sunk the year before and positioned *Seraffyn* head to the worst of the surge. Our beamy little ship with a 27 percent ballast ratio moved with the surge a bit but was not too uncomfortable to live on. *Piratical Pippet,* the folkboat we had met in Gibraltar, lay behind us and she was not moving too violently. But abeam of her a thirty-two-foot English Rival Class sloop was rolling through thirty-degree arcs and whipping so badly that the owners had to crawl when they were on deck and could not cook below. We learned that the Rival had a 50 percent ballast ratio but only eight and one half feet of beam and very rounded underwater sections with a fin-type keel. So her ballast acted like the pendulum on a clock, accenting the surge in the harbor and prolonging each roll.

Next to the Rival, tied stern-to the stone steps of Málaga, was the sad remains of a once-handsome English yacht. We learned the story of the dismasted, neglected thirty-five-footer from the local officials. It seems two young men were sailing along the coast near Torremolinos on a breezy winter day when their mast came down. The offshore winds were not very strong; reports vary from force 3 to force 5. Due to some technical difficulty, the engine did not start. But the two sailors were able to attract the attention of a Spanish fishboat that was working nearby. The fishermen pulled up their nets and came alongside, then agreed to tow the yachtsmen thirty miles into Málaga.

When the two boats reached port, the fishermen asked for $75.00 to compensate for their lost fishing time and fuel. The two sailors refused to pay, saying that the price was too high and that, besides, they had never offered to pay anything. The Spanish fishermen went to the port officials, who instituted an investigation which kept the fishermen tied up in port for five days. They had a formal hearing at which the English sailors were represented by an English and Spanish speaking consul official; the court awarded the fishermen $1100 for the tow, lost time, and inconvenience. The two yachtsmen did not have the funds, so their boat was chained up while they returned to the United Kingdom to earn enough to pay the judgment and buy a new mast. Five months of being neglected in a fishermen's port where dories and work boats surged up against the untended yacht had turned it into a near derelict. Although there is probably another side to this story, if the facts we heard are true, our sympathies lie with the fishermen. They have to be out at sea; that is the way they earn their living. We yachtsmen go to sea for pleasure, so we should be prepared to take care of ourselves or to pay if we request assistance. If the British sailors had arranged a price before they accepted a tow, there would have been no problem.

Thirty miles east of Málaga we found a fine port. Motril is a pleasant and safe harbor with no city nearby. Its long breakwater just out from a fertile alluvial plane which is covered with a green carpet of

The sad remains of the dismasted English yacht.

sugar cane. There is a small pension near the harbor, along with two or three homes and a customs guard post that has a small dinghy dock. One other yacht plus eight or ten fishboats lay in the sandy-bottomed harbor. *Seraffyn* had plenty of room to swing to two anchors. The customs guard agreed to watch our dinghy, and a bus only two hundred yards away took us three miles to a modern village—where we began our treck to Valencia.

Larry's mother had always dreamed of castles in Spain. So we used her visit as an added reason to stop in the most beautiful city I have ever seen: Grenada. The elaborate gardens and fountains, rose bushes in full bloom, snow capped mountains in the background, and cheerful Spanish youngsters in full flamenco dress made our two-day visit to this ancient inland Moorish capital a highlight of our Mediterranean cruise. We did have a bit of special luck since we arrived on a local holiday when everyone was celebrating in traditional costumes.

It is easy to visit Grenada from almost any southern Spanish port from Málaga to Almería since buses leave every two hours for the beautiful mountain drive to the cool highlands. The express bus cost us less than five dollars round trip, and almost one hundred small, clean pensions offered rooms for less than ten dollars per night per couple.

The four of us sailed to Almería, one of the larger commercial ports on the south coast of Spain, where we decided to get butane since our tank gauge read only 5 percent—which would have given us only enough fuel for five more days. In our eleven years of cruising in thirty-one countries, we have always been able to refill our butane tank without much trouble. Our tank is rated at 225 psi, so it can hold either propane or butane. It has a reverse-threaded female fill fitting and a pressure release valve so we can fill it from another tank of the same size or larger by connecting the two tanks, hoisting the full one above the level of ours, and opening the valves on both tanks plus the pressure release valve on ours. Since fill fittings do vary in foreign countries, Larry has made a two-foot-long transfer tube. One end has a fitting for our tank; the other is ready to take a local fitting, which we secure in place with hose clamps. We usually take our tank ashore, find the local butane depot, and have it refilled. Whenever we have had to buy a local fitting, they have rarely cost over a dollar at the hardware store. We have needed only five different fittings to work worldwide. Butane is easy to find and exceptionally reasonable, plus it is consistent in quality. The same is not true of kerosene, which sometimes clogs burners or makes your eyes smart if it is dirty or if the local refinery is not up to standard. Alcohol is even worse because in smaller island countries it just is not available.

We unfastened our tank and, while the Pardeys went off to explore the beautiful castle that overlooks Almería, Larry and I headed toward the customs gate to hail a taxi. Then we ran into a snag that is unique in our cruising annals. The customs man would not allow Larry to import an empty butane tank into Spain without paying fifty-five dollars duty. It took us over three hours to find another customs agent, who led us to the head of customs—who, in turn, wrote a special release that finally convinced the guard to let us take our battered tank to the main fuel supplier for a refill. But the guard demanded that we prove we had brought back the same tank within four hours. Fortunately the agent saw the humor of the whole situation and refused to accept a fee; in fact, he bought us a drink of local wine when we finally cleared up the mess.

Seraffyn is too small for long-term guests, so the Pardeys spent a few days on board and then moved ashore to explore and learn about Spain on their own. A full gale started to blow the next day and vented its fury for two days. Our anchor slowly started dragging through the soft mud on the bottom no matter how much chain we let out. So Larry put on his wet-weather gear, set up our folding thirty-five-pound Jornfardling fisherman anchor with thirty feet of chain and three hundred feet of five-eighths-inch nylon, then rowed it well to windward in bucking spray that was tossing *Rinky Dink*. It held perfectly. That is the rare occasion when our twenty-five-pound CQR on three hundred feet of five-sixteenths-inch BBB chain could not hold us.

Later that afternoon I rowed ashore (or rather was blown ashore) wearing wet-weather gear to tell Larry's parents we did not think it was safe to leave *Seraffyn* untended while we joined them for dinner. As I was walking along the length of the harbor toward their hotel I watched a three hundred-foot freighter drag its anchor and crash up against the rock sea wall. It seems Almería is well-known for its hard, dredged bottom with soft mud on top. The winds were at least gale force, and the only way I got out to *Seraffyn* again was to hitch a ride on the local pilot boat—the pilots had seen me struggling to row against the strong wind on a choppy sea.

As soon as the storm winds lay down to force 6 from the south, we set sail bound for Javea on the east coast of Spain, just opposite the Balearic Islands. Larry's parents planned to explore by bus for a while and meet us later for a voyage to the islands.

We cleared Almería Harbor carrying double-reefed mainsail and staysail. Occasional stronger gusts buried *Seraffyn*'s lee rail as the surprisingly cold wind blew off North Africa's desert. The barometer was rising, and gray clouds were starting to break up—so occasional blue patches winked at us for the first time in three days. As we approached Cabo Gato the wind increased and so did the sea. We cleared the cape by two miles and headed down wind, running wing and wing in almost thirty-five knots of wind. The seas grew terrifying. Even Larry, who is far less easily concerned than I am, felt their fury. "Close the companionway completely," he told me as the steep crumbling, following seas threatened to climb right over our transom. *Seraffyn* steered beautifully, Larry at the helm to help the wind vane. But on Larry's suggestion I pulled the mainsail down to slow our rush over the forty-five-degree angle that each wave face made. Thank God our mainsail has no battons, because we could not have rounded up to pull that sail down. Even without battons to worry about I had a hard time clawing down the reefed sail and putting a gasket around its billowing folds.

With her speed down to five knots, *Seraffyn*'s stern lifted to each wave. Only a bit of spray now wet the side decks. Under short canvas with the cabin secured and everything battoned down, my fears soon abated and I joined Larry in the security of the cockpit, one hand firmly on the lifelines, seaboots and foul-weather gear keeping me warm and dry.

A large freighter slowly passed us, headed dead into the sea as we rode the roller coaster twenty-foot waves. The ship's bow would plunge straight off one sea and bury completely in the next, and spray would fly its whole length; the ship would roll first to starboard, then to port and lift roughly over the next steep wave. We were far more steady on board our little sailing ship.

There must be a counter-current right at the cape which causes these short, steep breaking seas and earns Cabo Gato its reputation as Spain's Cape Horn because only five miles later the seas calmed and we set the mainsail again. Two hours later we were sailing over smooth seas with a warm, full moon and full sail set—Cabo Gato only a memory.

By the time we reached Javea after hopping from port to port for ten days, we noticed our bottom paint—which was only six weeks old —now had over three inches of weed on it. This added drag slowed us so much that *Seraffyn* could barely be maneuvered in winds under three knots. So we had to haul once again at the Javea yacht club and scrape and repaint *Seraffyn*'s bottom. It took us two years to learn that we had been caught in a bit of a swindle. An unscrupulous bosun's mate in Gibraltar had been selling yachtsmen metal primer, claiming it was the same anti-fouling paint used on navy patrol boats. The money we had tried to save was wasted and we had to pay the cost of a second haulout. This time we bought sealed, labeled cans of the copper bottom paint that local fishermen used. It lasted nine months and carried us through the islands that are a part of some of our fondest cruising memories.

CHAPTER 5

~~~~~

Ibiza

By the time we set sail from the Spanish mainland toward the Balearic Islands, the weather patterns of the Mediterranean were no longer such a mystery. Our barometer, weather reports from the English Channel and the Atlantic, plus an incredible little book called *Instant Weather Forecasting*—along with a bit of practice—gave a better weather forecast than we got from any local radio station. It is no wonder that weather predictions for any one area of the Med are completely wrong fifty miles farther on. This long narrow sea has a labyrinth of mountains and plains on its north side. Weather from the Atlantic rushes through a corridor across France and is diverted by the hot air flowing north off Africa's deserts. Cold blasts from the Russian steppes fall thousands of feet and roar down the Adriatic and Aegean. Winter low pressure buildups over mountainous Czechoslovakia and Romania suck gusty sirocco winds from Libya's heated sandy flatlands. The peaks of Sardinia, Corsica, and Sicily block each of these winds and divert them into the gusty storms that drove the wreck of the Apostle Paul's ship onto the shores of Malta almost two thousand years ago.

We had learned to look at a topographical chart of the half of the Med we were sailing on and to mark large pressure systems in the Atlantic and Europe along the edge of the chart. Then we would trace any obvious canyons in the mountain chains that might turn into a wind tunnel between the weather system and us. If the systems were very stable, there would be little wind that day except for local thermals right near the land. But if a European pressure area was moving and our barometer was going up or down by at least three millibars

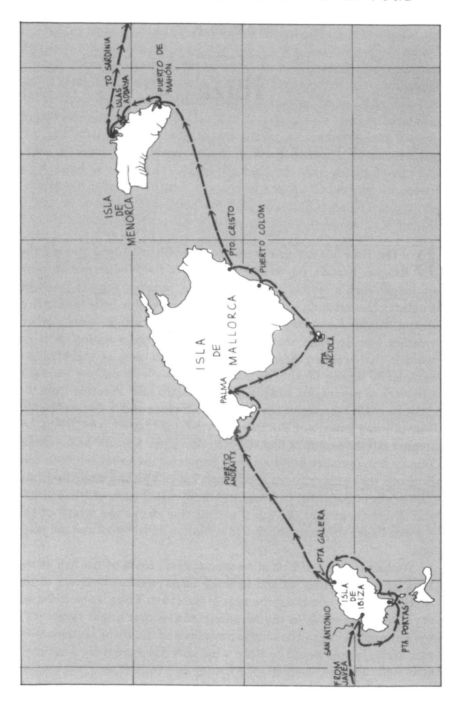

every two hours we would almost always have a fresh wind for longer passages.

Alan Watts's *Instant Weather Forecasting* has twenty-two photos of cloudy skies. Alongside each photo is a graph showing the most likely weather changes that follow such clouds and how long the changes are likely to take. We can think of no major wind increase during our two years of voyaging in the Med that was not preceded by one or another of the cloud patterns Alan Watts labeled "expect deterioration."

The day we chose to sail between Javea and Ibiza, the barometer was dancing up and down each time we tapped it. A lovely fresh breeze blew from the south sending *Seraffyn* skimming along at six knots over a shimmering, beam reaching sea. Larry's folks lounged back enjoying a day of sailing we have rarely equaled. A beautiful sunset cast orange and pink fingers across the hills of Ibiza. No one wanted to go below and climb into their bunks until the lovely south wind died almost at midnight, and we lay becalmed three miles from San Antonio's breakwater. I took the first watch, reading a yachting magazine that had arrived in our Javea mail pack. The glow of our stern lamp was enough to light the page and reflect off *Seraffyn*'s big genoa, which lay limp and quiet as we waited on the calm water. The red light of the breakwater end winked a welcome and beckoned us onward.

At 0230 a light breeze whispered across the water from shore carrying the warm fragrance of sage and rosemary. I should have woken Larry so he could take his watch, but I was entranced by the gliding pattern of a long tack to starboard and a short tack to port—using our hand bearing compass to determine the safe limits of my beat up the gulf into San Antonio. When the tip of the breakwater lay only a few hundred yards away, I called softly to Larry and he soon climbed on deck. Together we reached into the long harbor and chose a clear spot among a fleet of yachts and work boats and tried to let out *Seraffyn*'s anchor and chain quietly so the Pardeys would not be disturbed. After we had bagged and furled our sails, Larry poured two glasses of wine. Then we lounged against the cabinside, my head on Larry's shoulder. The town lights glowed across the black water, and the full moon slowly rose from behind the rounded hills.

Making port in a strange land at night is a magical part of cruising. All sorts of surprises greet you when you wake and survey your surroundings in the light of day. Unfortunately, San Antonio was a disappointment with its flat, unimaginative new tourist hotels crowding the main streets. But that was the only disappointment we had in all of the varied anchorages and harbors of the Balearic Islands.

We gunkholed around Ibiza bound for the main city, where the Pardeys would take a ferry back to the mainland for their flight home. When we approached the passage between Ibiza and Formentera it looked like a sailboat was anchored on the other side of the low sand-and-rock peninsula which forms Ibiza's southernmost tip. "They sure picked a poor spot to anchor," Larry commented. "It's a lee shore with this wind." Once clear of the point we were shocked to find a twenty-five-foot sailboat lying almost upright—high and dry on a sandy patch of beach, its landward side resting on large boulders with bunk cushions between the hull and rocks.

Larry worked *Seraffyn* in as close as he felt safe and said he would row ashore and offer to use some of our spare anchoring equipment to pull the hapless sailor off at high tide. But the owner saw us approaching and yelled, "Help is on its way!" The day after we sailed into Ibiza Harbor his miraculously whole but badly scratched boat was towed in with only a broken rudder. The single-handed sailor had dozed off while his boat lay becalmed several miles offshore at night. A breeze sprang up while he slept; the wind vane, which was still set, steered the boat off until the mainsail started pulling. He did not wake up until his boat hit the beach. By good fortune the boat had chosen the only sandy spot in over two miles of rocky coastline for its grounding. The light surf had gently moved it up the beach until the boat rested against several large round boulders.

Ibiza Harbor with its well-publicized town was a delightful place to stop. Its long sea wall was busy with local fishboats. Yachtsmen were welcome to tie stern to the wall then land and thread their way three blocks to town, stepping over fishnets, weights, and poles while fishermen sat in the sun mending nets or rigging new ones. A clean, reasonably priced marina lay on the far side of the harbor protected by stone breakwaters. It had a well-run hoist and nice café but was a two-mile walk away from town. Right in the center of the city was one of the oldest working shipyards in the Med. An ancient capstan that had been used on a sailing ship was mounted in the middle of the dirt shipyard. An equally ancient huge chain ran through a system of blocks and tackles so that the horse the shipyard owner rented by the hour from the farmer across the road could haul and re-launch vessels

The sixty-foot power yacht in the background is being hauled out of the water with this one-horsepower winch.

The sweet-hulled Ibizan fishboats.

weighing up to one hundred tons on a concrete slipway. Several handsome old Ibizan cargo schooners still sporting their spars and sails lay tied to the shipyard quay. All of them had been converted to working vessels by the addition of old-fashioned slow-speed diesel engines. This anchorage had room for visiting yachts, but there was one distinct disadvantage: it was right next to the main sewer outlet of the town. At low tide the stench was extremely noticable. So after a complete tour of the harbor, we found a quiet and safe anchorage right in the center and set our hook.

During the early 1970s the town of Ibiza was a favorite hangout for hippies and dropouts from all of northern Europe. The old-fashioned town with its tree-clad plaza and sidewalk cafés became a trading center for foreign youths who sold their handicrafts and drugs from blankets spread along the wide sidewalks. By the time we arrived in June of 1975 the wave of hippies had crested and strict police control had stopped drug sales, so the young foreigners who remained were some of the finer craftsmen. We threaded our way among their blankets and looked at intricate jewelry fashioned from silver and copper wire decorated with sea shells. Unique clothes, hand-embroidered blouses, lovely leather work, plus handsome macramé items were hard to resist. Tourists in colorful costumes ranging from short shorts to full-length caftans mingled with local fishermen and Catholic, Ibizan ladies dressed from head to toe in black. Just three blocks from the main street of town, life went on as it had for centuries. In the cool of evening, Spanish families sat in front of their white-washed, tile-roofed little homes chatting with neighbors and watching vendors sell fish, wine, and fruit.

We were looking for a special place to have a farewell lunch with the Pardeys before they boarded their ferry for Valencia. So Larry and I spent a quiet hour threading our way through tables, tourists, shoppers, and motorscooters on the various sidestreets leading off the main promenade. We found at least a dozen tiny cafés that looked delightful. The fare ranged from ice-cream and Coke to mussels in red wine sauce. Then Larry noticed a tiny balcony with two people eating at a cloth-covered table. I climbed the steps next to the balcony and found a miniscule, clean restaurant run by a young Ibizan couple. I reserved the balcony table at La Rosa and after we enjoyed a superb lunch of salad, fried sword fish steaks, and flan (baked cream caramel pudding), that restaurant became a second home for us.

A week after Larry's folks left for Canada, a mail pack arrived that had several unexpected checks for articles and antiques. When we decided to celebrate we asked Andrea at La Rosa what the difference was between their 80 peseta per person paella and the 100 peseta paella. She told us that they added extra shrimp and clams. "Well, what if we give you 150 pesetas ($2.55) per person?" Andrea went into a serious conference with her husband, who did all of the cooking, then said, "Here, sit on the balcony with this wine and bread. In one hour you will see a 150-peseta paella."

Our mail, our schemes, and the kaledioscope of people on the street fifteen feet below made the hour fly. We saw Andrea rush off with her market basket and return twenty minutes later with it full of tiny packages. Right at the end of an hour Andrea and her husband proudly presented us with a masterpiece of saffron-cooked rice crowned with prawns, lobster pieces, squid, mussels, clams, chicken breasts, spicy garlic sausage, fresh green peas, and three kinds of fish decorated with bright red pimentos.

Ibiza Harbor became our base for sailing forays to the calas and harbors of the neighboring islands. We now had a book to write and scheduled ourselves so that we could work together four mornings a week to discuss each chapter, write outlines, type up the results, then edit each other's work. Since I had to do all of the typing for both of us, Larry would work on *Seraffyn* for two hours in the afternoon or do any necessary shopping. Three days a week were time off for sailing and exploring ashore. Once the book writing project got beyond its embryo stage we found it added a new, sorely needed dimension to our cruising life; it gave us a reason to set to work each morning, and our alarm clock became redundant. We were awake before it rang. While our morning coffee and tea brewed, ideas came spurting out, "Don't forget to tell about that crazy cat in Cartagena," Larry would say. "Have you mentioned the trouble we had with *Seraffyn*'s sheer clamp?" I would ask.

Larry and I are not the only long-term cruisers who have found that this life needs some additional purpose besides the challenge and sheer pleasure it offers. Maybe that explains why so many voyagers write. Not only does writing offer a way to share the joys, pains, and triumphs of living with the sea, it also offers a reason for being there. Other cruising people fill their lives by collecting and classifying shells; some study to become naval architects or marine biologists. One we know of turned to studying philosophy; another, the intricacies of the Spanish language. Those who find no occupation to add to their voyaging usually return home or settle in foreign lands after two or three years and set to work at their old occupations for a while before they voyage off again. Not one of us can say exactly when the exciting life of a cruising sailor needs an added dimension. Maybe it is just as simple as a statement Larry made when we were first together, "Everyone needs to add something new and different to his life every three or four years to keep alert and growing."

A few weeks later we set sail for the beautiful sand lined bay at the north end of Formentera. Only two other yachts lay behind Isla Espalmadora—the island that offered some protection to the moon-shaped bay. One flew a Canadian flag; the other, an English one. We anchored well away from them so we could swim overboard nude in the crystal clear, pale blue water. Late in the evening the four people from the other two yachts rowed ashore and lit a fire on the white sand beach. We put on bathing suits and light sweatshirts, lit *Seraffyn*'s oil-burning anchor light, then took a flashlight and rowed toward the warm glow of their fire.

"Come and join us," four friendly voices called over the quiet water. Eager hands helped haul *Rinky Dink* up the beach. "Didn't want to disturb you when you anchored way off at the far side of the bay," Mike said as he pulled an edge of blanket over to make us a seat by the welcome warmth of the fire. Mike and Frankie Rodgers had set sail a year earlier on their very small twenty-four-foot bilge-keeled plywood sloop. They had had some wild adventures in the canals of France as they wound their way from Paris to Marseilles. Their stuart-turner inboard engine sometimes worked, sometimes did not. But soft-spoken Mike was willing to work hard and well at any job that came along to supplement his $50-a-month pension from his ten years in the British Army. Sitting next to his gregarious, eager wife, Frankie, was sometimes like sitting next to a volcano. Her exuberance would explode just when you least expected it. Her warm laughter and adventuresome spirit combined with an excellent knowledge of the French language had won them many friends. Her ability to live comfortably on a budget that averaged less than $150 a month won my admiration, especially since she eagerly entertained her friends with budget-minded delicious meals and ever-ready cups of strong English tea. We met them at various ports during the next years cruising, and each time we saw the bright varnished and green hull of *Scarab* Mike and Frankie had more adventures to share with us.

Eric and Chris Rhodes, a Canadian couple in their late forties, bought their thirty-foot English built sloop *La Russe* in Poole, England, and brought her to the Mediterranean through the Canal Midi. Now they were spending a year learning about her and planning the changes that would make *La Russe* capable of crossing the Atlantic to eventually reach their home in British Columbia. A delightful evening with this conservatively adventuresome couple was to be only a prelude to an interesting working relationship.

Unfortunately, the bay behind Isla Espalmadora suffers from the poor holding ground that is common in many shallow anchorages in the western Mediterranean. Heavy seaweed covers most of the bottom. It looks just like unmowed rye grass and waves gently in the flux of moving currents. We dropped our anchor in a large patch of sand, but when Larry put his mask and fins on to scavange for clams on the bottom eight feet below, he dug only four or five inches into the sand and found it covered a thick carpet of dead seaweed. When a brisk breeze blew up out of the northwest, the tiny island did not quite protect us; a low chop set up, and our anchor slowly started to rake a path through the sand and weed. Wispy clouds high overhead and a bouncing barometer made us leery of setting another type of anchor so late in the day. So we set sail and beat clear of Isla Espalmadora, then reached off for the tiny port of Sabina, twelve miles away. We did not want to spend the night worrying about dragging—*Scarab* and *La Russe* were not far behind us.

Sabina is well protected by two breakwaters. The village onshore consists of three small tourist hotels and two tiny stores. But the harbor is full of small fishing boats plus a landing for the ferry that arrives once a day from Ibiza. Most of the harbor is less than four feet deep, so we set our anchor on very short scope: three to one in the steeply shelving water just inside the breakwater. *Seraffyn* swung just clear of a beautiful forty-five-foot French yacht with oiled mahogany decks which lay on a permanent mooring.

It was calm that evening, so we rowed into the quay for wine and hors d'oeuvres with Mike, Frank, Eric, and Chris. "Do you believe in worms?" Chris asked when she learned that Larry builds and repairs wooden boats. Larry assured her that toredo and gribble worms love unprotected wooden hulls that sail in salt water. "We probably don't have to worry then," Chris said. "We've spent over half of the last year in fresh water canals." About an hour later in the middle of a discussion of new harbors and ports, Eric asked, "Where would you check for worms if you owned our boat?" Larry mentioned the bottom of the deadwood aft of the ballast keel, "Especially if you've ever run aground hard enough to scrape the anti-fouling paint off. I'd also worry about the area in back of the rudder post if it's hard to inspect between your rudder and stern post. People rarely get enough paint in there."

The next morning Eric and Chris rowed out to ask us, "What would you do if you thought you had missed painting a few spots between the rudder and stern post on your last haulout?" they asked. Without hesitating Larry said, "I'd find the nearest shipyard and haul to inspect the bottom right now. Once worms get into a hull they can bore three-sixteenth-inch holes at an inch a week."

Within two hours Eric and Chris steamed out of Sabina bound for Ibiza's marina to haul and inspect *La Russe*. "Chris couldn't sleep for worrying about worms," Eric called as they turned and smoked out the harbor entrance. *Scarab* followed shortly since Mike had been offered the job of scrubbing and painting *La Russe*.

At 0200 that night a summer squall drove thunder, rain, and howling wind across the harbor. We both rushed on deck to see the green light of the breakwater end fly past through the driving rain. Our anchor had slipped off the shelve into deep water, and *Seraffyn* was lying in the classic beam to the wind attitude that is a sure sign of dragging. Larry's first instinct was to let out more chain. That five-sixteenth-inch chain rattled over the winch cat head so fast we could hear its clank and crash above the howling wind and thunder. Larry set the clutch on the windless and within seconds *Seraffyn*'s bow came right into the wind. The shore lights stopped moving past. While Larry stood watching on deck, I went below and threw out a wet-weather jacket to cover his unclad body. Then I checked the charts for the depths outside Sabina Harbor. There was thirty-five feet of water over a sandy bottom almost to the far end of the mile-wide bay. A glance in the chain locker showed we had over two hundred feet of chain out now. Inside *Seraffyn*'s main cabin the underwater roar of a powerful outboard engine sounded clearly in spite of tempestuous weather on deck. As I climbed out to tell Larry about this a flashlight glared out of the rainy dark night; seconds later a powerfully built short man called to us in heavily accented English, "Are you all right? Can I be of assistance?" Pierre Bagnis, the Frenchman who owned the forty-five-foot yawl which lay on the mooring in Sabina, had come on deck to check *Baladin*'s mooring lines. He had seen us drag anchor, and, in spite of the dark, the driving rain, and the heavy winds, he had started his 45-horsepower outboard and come on his rubber dinghy to offer assistance. Only minutes after he arrived, the squall spent the last of its fury. The three of us crowded into *Seraffyn*'s warm, dry cabin and shared hot buttered rum on the absolutely calm sea as stars winked out from behind retreating storm clouds. Pierre earned our complete appreciation that night—even though we took some cross bearings and decided our storm chosen spot would be perfectly safe for the night.

We beat back into Sabina the next morning and tied to the stone sea wall. All during the next week mornings were filled with our growing book project and afternoons with our growing friendship with Pierre and his crew, Christine.

CHAPTER 6

~~~~~

Vespas, Covers, and a Crash

Our curiosity finally got the better of us. During the previous week in Sabina we had stuck to our writing schedule; scrubbed every inch of *Seraffyn*'s interior with fresh water, soap, and bleach; and gotten rid of a two hundred-pound stack of cans that were three-quarters empty, useless bits of line, and junk that really never would come in handy "some day." Now with *Seraffyn* smelling sweet, her varnish glowing, waterline showing, and five days of work behind us, we decided to sail to Ibiza and see if *La Russe* had been hauled and inspected. Another evening at La Rosa restaurant also seemed in order, since neither of the local cafés had looked the least bit interesting.

The day after we arrived, *La Russe* was lifted clear of the water on the marine hoist in the far side of Ibiza Harbor. The large mobile hoist carried her to the corner of a large gravel-covered area where she was carefully chocked up so her keel was two feet above the ground. Eric and Chris were glad they had hauled her for inspection. Worms riddled a six-inch-by-twelve-inch square of wood almost three inches deep just behind their lead ballast keel. When Larry and Eric removed the rudder, half a dozen quarter-inch holes tunneled into the stern post. Fortunately a probe with an ice pick revealed that the worm holes ended after only three-quarters of an inch. Eric asked Larry if he would help repair the damage, which was relatively minor, and find some way to prevent worms from being a nuisance again.

During the next week Larry spent his afternoons carving away an area that was an inch and a quarter thick all along the bottom of *La Russe*'s deadwood from rudder to the lead keel. Then he creosoted the wood, put a layer of roofing tar paper on, and added an inch-and-a-quarter piece of creosote-soaked mahogany to refill the gap. This sacrificial worm shoe was fastened in place with screws so it could easily be replaced. That way if *La Russe* grounded hard enough to scrape through her bottom paint, only the worm shoe would be exposed to gribbles and toredos who eat wood but almost never cross barriers such as tar paper or creosote.

The worm holes in the stern post were easy to fix. Larry drilled them out with a half-inch bit and put in wood plugs. Then he scraped all of the after end of the cupped trailing edge of the stern post down to bare wood and applied a liberal coating of creosote. Then he covered the whole area with eighteen-gauge copper bedded in Dolfinite fungicidal compound and secured it with large-headed copper tacks. He did the same to the leading edge of the rudder so that there would be no concern if the Rhodes missed getting paint on some spot because of the narrow gap between the stern post and rudder.

Eric and Chris wrote us letters for the next two years. As they explored more of the Mediterranean and headed for the Caribbean they often commented, "We're one of the few wood-boat owners that never worry about worms anymore."

Almost all of the major islands in the Mediterranean depend on tourism for their extra income. We found the islanders to be warm hosts. One Ibizan told us, "Of course we've learned to be good hosts. Invaders of some sort or another have been running over these islands for three thousand years!" One thing about the newest invasion of tourists is that few seem to stray more than a mile from their hotel. We, however, wanted to get some idea of what the islands are really like, so we took advantage of the Vespa motorscooters for rent at about five dollars a day from almost every hotel. These machines comfortably carry two people, a lunch, and a bottle of wine.

Although first-time riders of these somewhat clumsy little cycles will find the traffic in tourist cities a frightening obstacle and the rush hours well worth avoiding, once you get into the countryside, they open up whole new vistas. We would often pack a lunch, rent a Vespa, then toss a coin to decide whether to head east or west, north or south, and find a special place to spread our blanket, eat, and sunbath.

One day we invited Sasha and Anne-Christine Von Wetter, who were cruising on their torty-year-old English cutter, *Charmain,* to join us on rented Vespas. Our wandering took us to the far end of the island, where we parked the scooters against a rock, took off our shirts, and strolled along the beach looking for a good place to swim. About a mile along, the white sand dissolved into a jumble of rocks—a light surf broke against the base, and blue water turned to green as it filled with foam. We chattered like school kids; Larry and Sasha tried skipping flat stones along the ocean surges. Then we reached the rocks, climbed over, and met a sight that startled and delighted us. A tiny white sand cove, no more than four hundred yards wide, lay protected by a steep cliff. At each end huge rocks cut the cove off from outside viewers. Over a hundred Scandinavian people of all ages were swimming, sunbathing, and playing volleyball completely without clothes. There were no cars at the top of the cliffs. We had seen no buses on the road. The nearest hotel or town was seven miles away. I still don't know where these people came from or how they got to this lovely out-of-the-way spot where the only sign of outside civilization was the one little stand where a vendor sold cold soft drinks that lay in washtubs full of ice. We felt somewhat like intruders and without any discussion all four of us took off our bathing suits while we had a refreshing swim in the warm Mediterranean surrounded by friendly, laughing people. Then we climbed over the jumble of rocks at the far end of the cove, put on our swimsuits, and continued our circuitous walk back to the Vespas.

It is hard to decide where exactly to explore on each island you visit. To take your advice only from other cruising people means you may never leave the harbors most frequented by sailors who speak your language. To choose by the general navigation charts means you will miss any tiny coves which have little commercial value. The British Admiralty and American charts often do not put soundings in where vessels which draw less than six feet might enter. We have found it pays to locate every cruising guide there is for the area where you are cruising. Read it and compare it to others, then gunkhole into every spot you can where there is room to swing with water under your keel.

There are several cruising guides for the Mediterranean: some accurate; some useless. One of the worst is written and published by an Englishman named Bristow. It seems like he wrote the guide from tourist office information. I am sure he has never sailed into many of these ports. His book gives a detailed description of one harbor that did not even exist two years after the book was published. It seems developers ran out of funds after their elaborate planning and mail advertising campaign so the breakwater was never built. On the other hand, three of the guides we found were exceptionally helpful. The Royal Cruising Club of England puts out a pamphlet of favorite harbors and coves visited by their members through the years. These are hand-sketched and filled with usefull information such as, "Lady in white house on hilltop sells excellent farm fresh cheese." "Clams under large grey boulders on west side of cove."

H. M. Denham, who has roamed the Mediterranean for over thirty years in both naval vessels and his own yacht, has published a wonderful set of guides that include interesting historical notes. His seamanship and anchoring advice is first rate. But often his tastes differs from ours. In several ports which according to him "hold little of interest to visiting yachtsmen," we had wonderful mini-adventures. Unfortunately his guide to the Balearic Islands had not yet been completed when we were there.

The German Cruising Club Guide is one of the best we found. We cannot read German, but the hundreds of chartlets are clear and easy to understand, and a quick browse through a German-English dictionary gives you the words that are most important to know: rock, shoal, buoy. Different volumes cover each part of the Mediterranean. Ask German cruising sailors for a glance at theirs so you can find the publisher's address and order your own.

When we sailed out of Ibiza we were headed for the north side of the island where there was a 125-foot-wide, 700-foot-long cove called Portinatx. The English cruising guide had a chart of this "cala," the Spanish word for small coves along the coast of the islands. Our admiralty charts showed it as a one-quarter-inch-long indentation of the coast with less than one fathom of water. Pierre from the French yacht *Baladin* had raved about the tiny port, which is rarely visited by foreign cruising yachts. "Sail in bravely," Pierre told us. "There is deep water within ten feet of the cliffs on either side. When you see a tiny sand cove on your port side and a cave to starboard, put your boat into the north wind and look down. Just below the surface of the water you'll see a little piece of wood floating with a fishing weight on it. Pull that up and you'll find my own private mooring."

We glided along the coast of Ibiza on one of those special days we seemed to find five times a week in the Balearics. Warm sun glowed off the multicolored rocky edges of the island. Green fields lined the

shore and led back to white-washed farm buildings. The few hotels
that we saw seemed to gnaw on the upper edges of the sandy beaches
that nestled in coves cut by the restless sea. Five-to-eight-knot breezes
kept *Seraffyn* drifting along with her number two genoa set. With a bit
of extra work, changing sails, trimming to catch each shift of the wind,
we could average close to four knots on this kind of day. But usually
we settled in lazily, let Helmer steer, and trimmed sails only for major
course changes. We would then plan on a three-knot average. If we
limited each days voyage to fifteen or sixteen miles we could sleep in
as late as we wanted, get underway at a leisurely pace, eat lunch as the
changing vista passed before us, and arrive to set our anchor in time
for cocktails.

We were glad Pierre had told us about sailing in "bravely." Portinatx looked narrow when we first spied it from seaward. It looked
narrower still as we short tacked toward the sandy beach and small
hotel at its head. If we had been planning to anchor we would have
set two anchors to position ourselves in the confined space. With the
weeds that we could see waving on the white sand bottom twenty feet
below, I think we could not have slept soundly even with two anchors.
But Pierre's bit of floating wood was exactly where he had told us to
look. We pulled it up and found a carefully spliced three-quarter-inch
nylon line. As soon as we secured *Seraffyn*, Larry was overboard with
mask and fins. He followed the mooring cable down to a length of
five-eights inch chain that lead to a huge iron eye on a five-hundred-
pound block of concrete. This was *Baladin*'s winter mooring, and
within a day we understood why Pierre chose this enchanted spot.

For many reasons the Mediterranean is generally a difficult place
to make a living as a fisherman. After almost thirty centuries during
which the sea has provided food for the tables of most of southern
Europe and part of the Middle East, the fish close to shore have inher-
ited quite a wariness. More recent influxes of sport fishing boats and
scuba divers have decimated the fish populations close to resort towns.
During the 1950s and '60s pollution took its toll. To make matters
worse, the naturally narrow mouth of the Mediterranean cuts down
the chance of a quick regeneration of depleted sea life. But the skin
diving we found right at Portinatx added to the bits of encouraging
evidence that we saw throughout our two years in the Mediterranean.
Pollution control is working. Conservation attempts are working.
Jacques Cousteau even includes the waters near Sardinia among the

finest in the world for skin diving. But to find the good spots you have to get away from towns and large resorts.

We took *Rinky Dink* and rowed about a mile to get outside of Portinatx—away from where we figured local divers had been. Then we set the flukes of her ten-pound anchor between two rocks in twenty feet of water just outside the surf, which broke lazily against a rock cliff. Larry meandered along the surface in ever-widening circles; the orange tip of his snorkle and occasional splashes from his flippers made it easy to keep track of him. I am not such an energetic swimmer, so I stayed within fifty or a hundred feet of the dinghy, enjoying the view through my mask and surfacing from time to time to check on Larry. Every ten minutes or so I would climb up over *Rinky Dink*'s stern and warm myself in the sun. It took an hour for Larry to tire of chasing the elusive fish. "They're just too leery. Too many rocks for them to dive under. Don't want to ruin my spear by hitting a boulder instead of a fish."

So we rowed back into Portinatx. When we were only two hundred feet from *Seraffyn* Larry suggested, "You row the rest of the way, I'll snork along just for fun." Before I had reached the boat, Larry surfaced and called, "Tie up the dink and come on in. There are lots of fish here. If you scare them toward me I'm sure we'll have a few for dinner." Since the bottom was sandy Larry was less worried about damaging his double rubber-band spear. We snorkled along about twenty feet apart. Whenever we spotted a worthwhile fish, we would swim slowly toward it from opposite directions. With no rocks to hide under, the fish had to choose which way to escape. The three that chose to head toward Larry ended up in our oven an hour later sprinkled with oregano then covered with lemon, onion, and tomatoe slices.

We had finished our mornings writing. Lunch was a pleasant memory, and the two of us were lounging comfortably in the cockpit trying to think of ways to secure the sun cover more easily. Throughout our cruising years we have tried dozens of modifications to this basic necessity. People who cruise below thirty-five degrees latitude know they need one. Ideally a sun cover should protect 50 to 60 percent of the deck area. It should set high enough so that there is walking headroom under it; it needs side curtains to protect you from the glare of early morning and late afternoon sun; and it should be secured strongly enough to withstand twenty-five-knot winds and not flap too wildly or noisily yet be easy to get down if a forty-knot squall comes through the anchorage. Finally, the sun awning has to be stored away, so it should be compact and easy to fold. As you can imagine, we have been unable to figure out any one sun cover that meets all of these criteria.

Our first sun cover was made of four-ounce sail cloth for strength and light weight and had nine-foot spruce battons. That was a complete failure. It was noisy in the lightest wind. It work hardened and disintegrated in a squall after two years. The battons broke, and—even though the whole thing rolled up to be less than five inches in diameter —storing that nine-foot-long tube in a twenty-four-foot boat tried our patience. Then in Bermuda a friendly local sailor saw us painting *Seraffyn*'s bulwarks in the glaring midday sun. "Where's your cover?" he asked. "It blew away. We're headed for England now, probably won't need one for a few years," we replied. An hour later he returned and handed us a brand new complete-boat sun cover built for a thirty-five-foot sloop. "Sailmakers in England cut this one wrong. When they sent me a new one they told me to keep this one too," Laurie told us.

We had the white synthetic canvas (Acrilan) cover unrolled within minutes. It reached from bowsprit to boomkin, and the side curtains made *Seraffyn*'s deck seem like the inside of an Arab's tent. It shaded us completely, cut off our view plus any stray breezes, and took an hour and a half to put in place. But the two-part socketed aluminum tubes did work and store well. In the Azores, careful surgery removed the side curtains and all of the cover forward of the mast. That was far better. Finally, in England we borrowed a sewing machine and tailored it into the cover that we have used for six years now. The lightweight canvaslike material does have mildew on it but has never rotted. It is strong and quiet. The only change I would make is to sew three-quarter-ounce blue nylon to the underside of the cover to cut down glare. Our final cover reached only from the boom gallows to one foot aft of the shrouds. At its mid-point it is as wide as the boat, tapering slightly to the stern. An aluminum pole aft and one halfway along stretch the cover, and its forward corners are tied to the shroud. There is a nylon line stitched along the center of the cloth, its forward end is a spliced loop which hooks over a cleat on the mast. The after end ties to the back stay. There is a ring at the top center and for long stays in port we can move *Seraffyn*'s lazy jacks and hoist the cover on the main halyard over the boom for six-foot headroom. For short stays we rig it under the boom. Extra grommets along the sides let us secure a single four-foot-wide side curtain for times when the declining sun makes life uncomfortable. Three light lines per side secured to our lifelines hold the cover in place. For passage making the carefully folded cover with its collapsible poles makes a bundle seven inches by four and a half feet and stows against the sheer clamp above the forward bunk. In emergency situations or when forty-to-fifty-knot squalls whip through an anchorage we have found we can roll the cover from the stern and toss the whole thing down below "as is" in less then four minutes. We know because we had to get out of an untenable anchorage once in a squall and timed the whole departure. The ends of the aluminum poles have tennis balls over them to protect the decks or varnish work when it is being taken up or down. Our cover is now so easy to use that it goes up even if we just stop for lunch. That is important, because constantly glaring sun not only causes skin problems, it also tires you out and keeps potentially interesting friends from stopping by for an afternoon chat.

A small French sailing dinghy put off from the beach in front of the hotel and reached toward us. The muscular blond helmsman called, "May I come alongside?" Leroy Guy (Guy for short), the sailing instructor for the French-managed hotel, was soon on board with a glass of iced lemonade in his hand. Since most French people do not take their vacations until August, there were only a dozen guests. Guy had the afternoon off, and we had the cove to ourselves.

"In that round house lives a man who is the captain of one of Spain's largest crude carriers," Guy told us after a while. "He has seen your boat and fallen in love, but is too shy to come and introduce himself."

At 1800 Guy returned with four members of the Lopez family. During the rollicking cocktail hour that followed, we mentioned two things which later led to an interesting evening: I spoke of my fondness for champagne; Larry told how we were working to try and improve our Spanish.

After a sunny, laughter-filled three-hour sail with six eager Lopez relatives on board *Seraffyn* the next afternoon, Larry and I were sure José had invited us for dinner that evening at 2100. We showered on the foredeck, dressed in our summer finery, and only ate a light snack at tea time so we would not ruin our appetites.

Six bottles of three different brands of Spanish sparkling wines sat

Guy and Vera, a Norwegian ballet dancer, joined us for an afternoon sail.

on ice on the patio of the stucco and tile summer home built by José Lopez's father. Three cousins were in residence that week, all from Valencia. Carlos Graf was a well-known architect, Vivian ran an English school for Spanish businessmen. We never did find out what the third did.

All of our new friends spoke English quite well, but from the moment we were poured our first glass of delicious Spanish champagne, Vivian decreed, "You want to practice Spanish. We will help you. No more English tonight!" The mix-ups that occurred were hilarious, but Vivian's patience and the ever-flowing champagne got us over each language hurdle. Unfortunately by eleven o'clock when only one bottle of bubbly wine still lay in the bucket, both Larry and I were more than a little intoxicated on our empty stomachs. "Didn't they say dinner?" Larry whispered in an aside to me. "I'm sure they did," I whispered back.

At 1130 the telephone rang and José came back to announce, "Our dinner is now being served." We all walked to a small restaurant where our table was set on a tree-rimmed patio. The cool night rang with the calls of cicadas as we ate a succulent meal of lobster in garlic and tomatoe sauce. Our hosts relented on our Spanish lessons and Vivian later explained, "In Valencia we rise at seven AM then work until noon. We have our biggest meal of the day then and sleep until four PM. After that we work until eight or nine PM, so don't eat our last meal of the day, a light dinner, until midnight."

For the next four afternoons we were included in the Lopez family outings. On Saturday we slept in to recover from one more late "light Spanish dinner." About 1030 two thirty-five-foot sportfishing yachts came into the cala and anchored just off the beach—maybe three hundred feet away from us. We noticed them only because they were the only boats to enter the cove since we had picked up *Baladin*'s mooring. Both were registered in Ibiza, and almost a dozen people buzzed ashore in rubber dinghies then disappeared into the hotel.

By lunch time we had decided to set our alarm clock for early the next morning and leave this lovely bay bound for the island of Mallorca. So when the midafternoon sun beat hot on our deck, we spread a sheet on our forward bunk and lay down for a siesta under the cool breeze directed into our forward cabin by the galley sail (wind scoop).

The roar of large gasoline engines echoing across the still cove woke both of us from a sound sleep. I had just enough time to see it was still sunny then turn toward Larry. The jarring, crashing sound of metal hitting metal, then wood against wood did not drown out the rushing sound of waves breaking against *Seraffyn*'s side as she tried to pull away from the force of a thirty-five-foot powerboat moving at full throttle. *Seraffyn* heeled sharply then righted when the powerboat's engines stalled and gurgled into silence. I scrambled to get out the main companionway. Larry climbed out the forehatch. Two Spanish voices argued, "Let's get out of here quick!" "I can't start the motors!" "Shove off!" Three women shrieked and yelled, *"¿Qué pasa, por Dios?"*

Larry did not hesitate. He grabbed the end of *Seraffyn*'s mainsheet, tossed it over the bow cleat of the powerboat and secured it tightly. "Stay calm, Lin. Get some fenders and grab their stern line. Make it fast to the anchor winch."

Five Spanish people demanded an explanation of our actions in three languages, Spanish, French, and stilted English. "Slow down." Larry suggested, "I want to inspect the damages."

"We are in a hurry, write down the name of our insurance company and let us go," the driver of the powerboat said. Larry determinedly proceeded to extract *Rinky Dink* from under the bow of the powerboat, where she lay half swamped. In spite of the yelling, Larry baled out the dinghy, then climbed in and looked at Helmer, our self-steering vane, which lay bent over and twisted to a forty-five-degree angle. The end of our spruce and oak boomkin was split apart at the joint, and the boomkin stay chainplates were bent and had bitten into *Seraffyn*'s hull a quarter of an inch. Fortunately the curved bow of the powerboat had been so high it only hit the vane and not our transom. So the only damage to our planking was a few scratches caused after their engines quit.

Just as Larry was climbing back on board, the second powerboat came alongside the first and was secured. Then ten or twelve Spanish people started talking and yelling at us all at once. I could not count how many there were as things started moving too quickly. The skipper of the first powerboat, a younger man who worked for the repair yard in Ibiza during the week, climbed on *Seraffyn* and asked, "How much money do you want to fix it? Do you want to come back to our yard in Ibiza and have it repaired?" Before Larry could think of the Spanish to explain that we had planned to sail on to Mallorca in the morning, before he could even think of what was involved in repairing the damage so we could use the windvane and trust the boomkin to support our mast, we both heard the owner of the boat say to one of his friends, "Let's offer him one hundred pesetas [$8] and get going."

Larry saw red! Without a word he climbed out of *Seraffyn*'s cockpit and into the powerboat. I started after him. "Stay there and catch," Larry whispered. He grabbed the ignition keys and tossed them quickly to me before any of the Spanish people knew what was happening. For once in my life I actually caught something. I dropped the keys down the forehatch, and they obligingly slipped into *Seraffyn*'s bilge. Then all hell broke loose.

All ten or twelve Spaniards scrambled onto *Seraffyn*'s deck. Two men grabbed Larry and threatened to throw him overboard. I grabbed at a winch handle and started screaming at the men, who had scratched Larry's shoulder so that blood was now trickling down his chest. Larry was a tower of calm in the raging scene. "Cool down, Lin," he said in spite of the fact that both men were at him like mad terriers, pushing and shoving, trying to force him toward the stern of our boat while a babble of voices roared around us. Thank God Guy, the sailing instructor, came swimming along just then. His services as a translator soon got everyone somewhat quiet and all but the skipper and owner of the powerboat off *Seraffyn*. "Remember," he told the Spaniards, "I have almost twenty witnesses who saw you speeding inside the harbor and driving carelessly. One of the witnesses even took a photo of your collision."

Larry did some thinking and suggested a price of 8000 pesetas ($140) to repair what looked like two days work plus some glue and a bit of new wood. The owner got furious. He turned to his skipper, "You must have another set of keys. Get them and let's get going. They can call our insurance company." No one had any spare keys.

"Lin, go get the Guardia," Larry insisted. I started to climb into our dinghy. "I'll take you to the police," the owner of the powerboat insisted. So we climbed over his boat and into his rubber dinghy. Halfway to shore he stopped his outboard motor and said, "Tell your husband to accept four thousand pesetas. The police will take your cruising permit away otherwise." I said I felt Larry's price was too low and that their carelessness could have sunk our boat (and our home). "I'll have the immigration officials deport you," the owner threatened. "Let's get the police," I countered. This went on for ten minutes, but he never headed closer to shore. Finally he said, "If I give you eight thousand pesetas will you dive in the water and find my boat keys?"

He had not seen me toss them inside *Seraffyn* and seemed worried about missing some date. When I suggested we talk to Larry about it, he started the outboard and we returned to *Seraffyn*.

After twenty minutes of deliberation, heads hanging over the taffrail, and accusations from the Spanish women who kept calling us pirates because we had stolen their keys, the owner finally pulled out a huge handful of pesetas and counted off eight thousand. He offered them to Larry in exchange for a written release stating that we were satisfied and had no further claims. I retrieved the keys, and both boats roared away leaving Guy, Larry, and I stunned by the sudden silence.

"You can't have someone fix the damages for that little," Guy said as we had a drink of wine to calm our nerves. "I'll fix it myself," Larry answered, "but I'll need a work bench. Might be able to do it all in a day and a half. I know I shouldn't have stolen their boat keys. But all I could see was the rest of the summer wasted while we fought with lawyers and insurance companies and sat in Ibiza Harbor. I wanted some kind of immediate settlement or I would have gone for the police. Especially after they were so arrogant about the whole matter. Eight dollars, that's ridiculous.'"

It turned out that Larry had been wrong in his estimate of the work involved repairing our boomkin and wind vane. It actually took four and a half days.

José Lopez arrived just then in his family's small launch. He had seen most of the commotion through binoculars and wanted to hear about it. "You should have gone for the police," he said. "If a Spanish boat is involved in a collision with a foreign vessel in a Spanish port, the owner must deposit fifty thousand pesetas [$925] immediately or have his boat impounded while the local authorities meet and decide on a proper settlement. If he is at fault he looses his boat operator's license for a year. That's a way of making sure both boats can go on their way in a reasonable amount of time." José's words explained the owner's reluctance to take me ashore for the police.

The next morning Guy arranged for Larry to use the hotel work shop. By evening Helmer stood straight and proud again. The fractured boomkin was temporarily repaired and reinforced. The bad taste left by the only unreasonable Spaniards we ever met slowly faded as we set our alarm to wake us at 0530 so we could sail clear of Portinatx at first light.

CHAPTER 7

Puerto Andraitx

The alarm went off at 0530. I got up, tapped the barometer, and felt rewarded when its needle jumped up two millibars. The sun was just lighting the eastern sky. Our flag and telltales lay limp. So we took our time eating a light breakfast in the cockpit as the rising sun played color technician on the smooth water of the bay and the normally white rocks along its edges. By 0730 when Larry climbed on top of *Rinky Dink,* nestled on her cabin top chocks, he could see wind ripples on the water outside the rock and sand spit which protected Portinatx from the surge of the Mediterranean.

Larry unlashed our fourteen-foot oar and set it in place in the single-oar lock on the port side of the boat. As soon as I untied the mooring line, he began to row. With *Seraffyn*'s tiller tied slightly to starboard to counteract the thrust of the long oar, we steered a straight, slow but steady course one-quarter mile to where the rippled water promised a lovely breeze.

I had the main and genoa set before we cleared the point. When the sails lifted to the first puff, Larry pulled the oar right across the cockpit; its handle weight held it clear of the water while we trimmed sheets. About ten minutes later when we were moving along on a three-knot beam reach, Larry set Helmer to work, then stored away the oar. I climbed below and found the book he had been reading, handed it out, checked our course to Andraitx Harbor on the island of Mallorca, then set to work shortening a skirt Larry had bought me in Ibiza.

We have often been asked, "What do you do all day when you're sailing offshore?" For people who come down to the harbor to use their boat on weekends or two-week holidays, it is hard to imagine how much like home our boat is. But if you were to move on board and set off cruising for three or six months you would learn. On calmer days at sea, life goes on just as it would at anchor—with the boat's needs as far as trimming sails or changing course only a minor interruption. Since we love to be free to explore or skin dive in port, I use my at-sea time for household chores. I cook, clean, mend, or rearrange lockers while Larry stays clear of the carnage in the cockpit. Other days Larry goes on a riggers binge, checking the boat over for loose shackle pulls, frayed seizings, chaffed sail hanks. He will mend sails or figure out

Calm weather is time for reading, mending, and enjoying life.

some new gadget for the rigging while I act as go-for, finding that "two-inch piece of one-half-inch bronze I last saw in the corner of the tool locker." When the work list is short or nonexistent or when the weather is too boisterous for other work, we enjoy one of the great pleasures of cruising: time to read with few interruptions. I have seen Larry read all five volumes of Winston Churchill's *History of the English Speaking People* during one fifteen-day voyage. Sometimes we make love in the cockpit while we listen to Cat Stevens or Andres Segovia on the stereo. Sometimes we just talk or scheme.

As we sailed toward Ibiza, Larry said, "Lin, we've wanted to see the Swiss Alps, we couldn't afford to do it in the winter and go skiing. How about seeing them in the summer on a motorcycle?"

"Our cruising fund only has enough in it to last six months," I countered. "Buying a motorbike would really cut into that."

"We owe it to ourselves," Larry said. "I think we should look at it as an incentive. When we finish writing this book, we buy a second-hand motorbike and go exploring. If we don't take a chance and spend the money, we'll never see anything but ports around the Med. If we select the motorcycle carefully, we should be able to sell it again when we're finished. If our time schedule on the book goes true to form we'll be able to tour in August and September and be back to the boat when everyone is looking for people to do winter repair work. I hear Palma is full of charter boats all winter. Should be some work available there."

And so our day slipped away. Just after noon, we set our oversized spinnaker and *Seraffyn*'s speed skipped to five and a half knots over a smooth sea. A light haze cut visibility to less than four miles so we did not see the small outboard-powered ski boat until it was quite close. They zipped toward us, the nine-knot-wind muffling their motors roar. "Which way to Ibiza?" three Spanish voices called when they cut their motor forty feet from our side. We checked the chart and called the compass course. A man yelled back, "We have no compass! Point the right direction." Shrugging his shoulders, Larry held out his arm. The driver of the ski boat carefully lined up with Larry's outstretched arm, gave his motor full throttle, and roared off, happily pointed (we hope) in the right direction. Less than five minutes later they had faded from view, and we were left chuckling to ourselves as *Seraffyn*'s nylon spinnaker danced and pulled us toward a Spanish fishing village that became one of our favorite Mediterranean stopovers.

We had sailed less than eleven hours to cover forty-eight miles to Puerto Andraitx (An-dratch). Once we dropped the spinnaker and started beating between the one-thousand-foot-high cliffs that form the entrance to the fiordlike bay, we became aware of how hot it had gotten. After we set our anchor in twenty feet of water and began to furl our sails, both of us were sweating in the late afternoon sun.

"Come on, let's dive in and cool off. Then we'll put the boat away," Larry called as his head disappeared over the side and his feet made a resounding splash. I did not want to spend the night with a head full of wet hair. So I climbed off the bowsprit and slid down the anchor chain, took a few strokes to cool off, then clung to the chain surveying the dozen yachts anchored around us. People were going about their late-afternoon business. Several had waved when we first sailed in. The water felt wonderful, Larry was no where to be seen—but my field of vision was constricted by *Seraffyn*'s hull. All of a sudden something grabbed the back of my bikini bottoms. A squirmy, slimmy lump slid along my rear end. I screamed and squealed at the top of my lungs as I tried to get those bottoms off. Mud filled the water around me. Larry treaded water a safe thirty feet away, grinning from ear to ear. People on every boat stared in our direction. "It was only mud," Larry called. A well-directed spray of water sent him stroking away. And once I had maneuvered back into my un-muddied bikini I, too, began to laugh. Even today I can recall that slimmy, fishy feeling. I got mine back eight months later. But that is another story.

Puerto Andraitx is a mile-and-a-half-deep thumb print on the mountainous west side of Mallorca. It has no sand beaches, and this has been the saving grace of the tiny fishing port and the fertile valley behind it. German and Scandinavian tourists want beaches for sunbathing when they pay for Spanish holidays. All along the flat beaches of Palma, thirty miles to the southeast are huge hotels, shoulder to shoulder with condominiums, restaurants, and tourist shops. But in sleepy, beachless Puerto Andraitx there are only two small old hotels frequented by Spanish tourists and businessmen. Four restaurants on the quayside set their tables out for locals and the few tourists that ride in on a bus for two hours each day. Other than that, their business comes from the twenty or so foreign yachts that tie along the sea wall next to the local fishermen. There is a new marina across the bay from town. But three years after it opened, only fifteen or twenty small yachts tied there plus occasional transient racing yachts. The main commerce of the valley comes from farming and small vineyards.

When we went ashore to see if our monthly mail pack had arrived, an English yachtsman directed us to the post office. "It's the house with white lace curtains at the end of this street. See if the postmistress has any eggs for sale while you're there."

The only post office sign we found was a tiny brass plaque on the blue window sill. But as soon as we walked inside the open door, a three-year-old ran away calling, "¡*Mama!* ¡*Mama!* ¡*Turistas!*" The postmistress bustled in wiping flour from her hands. "What is your yacht's name?" she asked in Spanish. When we told her, she reached into a drawer in the desk that took up most of the front hallway and pulled out a two-pound registered package for us. "How long do you plan to stay here in Puerto Andraitx?" she asked. Larry told her three weeks or so. Then she carefully copied our name and *Seraffyn*'s off the package before handing it to us. "Now I will know you are part of our port," she commented. Just as we were leaving I asked, "Do you have any eggs today?"

"Not today," the postmistress said. "Come back tomorrow morning."

Larry remembered we needed postage stamps. When he asked for them, the postmistress looked slightly annoyed and said, "You can't buy them here, go to the tobacco shop."

Within a week we had fallen into the comfortably relaxed schedule of Puerto Andraitx. We bought our eggs at the post office on Tuesdays or Thursdays and our stamps at the tobacco shop, along with liters of light delightful red wine for twenty-one cents—when we remembered to bring our own bottles. On Wednesdays we took the eight AM bus four miles to the town of Andraitx at the head of the valley for farmers market day. Within three weeks we knew almost everyone of the housewives in the crowded morning bus. We would hold a lasso full of live chickens bound to be slaughtered or help store shopping carts in the overhead rack. At the market place in the open central square of the clean old town of about four thousand people I would fill my expandable nylon bags with farm fresh produce, local cheeses, fruit, and meat. Larry would carry each full bag to the corner of a nearby café, where the friendly owner kept an eye on our growing pile and the dozen or so other piles stacked in various spots around his shop by housewives from farms in the lower valley. When I was satisfied with my purchases, we would buy a cup of tea or coffee with a local sweet cake. We would then cash our weeks supply of travelers checks at the bank, mail any packages that required weighing or registering, and hail a taxi. On the way back down the valley we would stop at the ice plant and buy a fifty-pound block for seventy-five cents. The taxi ride usually cost us three dollars, but our shopping was finished for the week—and from a far better and less expensive selection of fresh food than was available in the three small grocers at the port.

Five mornings a week we would write until noon. Larry would take care of any errands while I prepared lunch. He has often said he learned more Spanish during our months in Puerto Andraitx than anywhere else since he had to describe our needs to the shopkeepers. I know he must have made a delightful impression because whenever I happened to go into one of the shops instead, the ladies would all ask, "Where's Lorenzo? Isn't he well today?"

Afternoons were filled with an ever-changing group of cruisers, summer visitors, and local people. Evenings we would often visit the ACAL hotel where two Spanish brothers made sailors feel welcome among their predominantly fisherman clientele: hot showers for twenty-five cents, phone calls at cost from a timer on the wall, hors d'oeuvres of salty olives, bits of spiced meat, or mild cheese free with the second thirty-five-cent glass of local brandy.

If I sound homesick for Puerto Andraitx, it is because I am. The harbor was safe and beautiful. The evening sun played exquisite tricks with the folding hills. The water was clean and clear for swimming right off the boat. Village people made us feel warmly welcome. We had all of the delights of living in a Spanish village and yet for a few pennies could take a thirty-minute bus ride into Palma when the lights and glitter of the big city called.

The two-pound package of mail we picked up our first day in Puerto Andraitx included one letter from Gingerlee Field, a friend from Newport Beach. "Linda and I are leaving for a six week art tour in Europe on June 30. Love to see you, call collect as soon as you can."

"What day is it?" Larry asked when he read the letter. "June thirtieth" I answered.

We waited until 2 PM, then placed a call at the ACAL hotel. We hoped the Fields would not leave before 5 AM, their time. "Check and see if that's the airport taxi," Gingerlee called to someone as she lifted her phone in California. When she found it was us she asked, "What country are you in?"

"Spain," I answered.

"What are you doing on the fifteenth and sixteenth?" she asked.

"No plans," I answered.

"Tell me a port, Linda and I will meet you for dinner one of those nights." We spelled out the name of Puerto Andraitx carefully and sure enough two weeks later on our way home from our weekly marketing trip, Gingerlee and Linda were standing on the sea wall looking for us. We had a wonderful three days together. The Fields had a room in Palma, so Larry and I took a day off to sail in and anchor in front of their hotel.

I learned something interesting about our cruising life from Gingerlee and Linda. The last day of their visit, I asked them to join me on a shopping tour of Palma's huge public market so I could choose the fixings for a paella dinner. Linda and Gingerlee had traveled in Europe before, so their amazed reactions to hens being slaughtered in the butcher stand, rabbits hung with their heads still on, and the bustle of open-market shopping made me aware of the special mode of touring a cruising sailor enjoys. Because we are not just one-week, restaurant-fed tourists, we learn the everyday realities of the countries

Linda Field found one of my favorite lounging spots on *Seraffyn*.

we visit. Since our needs cannot be supplied from a suitcase, we cruising sailors open the door to interesting and sometimes exciting encounters unprotected by tour guides and promoters.

The Fields' visit was like a breath of air from Newport Beach. As Linda played the guitar in *Seraffyn*'s breeze-cooled cockpit, we talked of friends we had not seen in five years. Both Larry and I felt a twinge of homesickness. And when Linda and Gingerlee left and flew on to Rome, we talked about how few friends really do come and visit when you go off cruising.

In five years we had had seven visits from friends and family. Most other cruising people we have spoken with have had the same experience. Dozens of friends at home will say, "Write and I'll fly out for a week or two." But when the time comes, expense, previous engagements, or business keep them at home. The farther you sail from your home port, the more true this becomes. Yet many people buy or build boats ten feet longer than they need so they will have good accomodations when their friends or family come to visit. Then they have to maintain the larger boat and handle it alone or search for crew. Annabelle Yates, a long term cruising friend, had her own solution to the guest question, "Save twenty thousand dollars by buying a smaller boat—just right for you. Then put your visitors in a good hotel and share their shower."

Since we were in Palma, where two large yacht clubs host about four hundred yachts, we took a stroll along their docks. When we got into conversation with a cruising sailor we had met on mainland Spain some months before, Larry happened to say, "If you hear of any delivery jobs for this winter, let us know." John told us about the fifty-three-foot ketch at the far end of the docks that was definitely headed for the United States in late winter. "Don't know who is coming for her but I hear the maintenance man doesn't know how to navigate and the owner can't afford the time off." We took a look at the heavily built wooden fifty tonner with its huge after cabin and long bowsprit, then I asked the manager of the yacht club for the owner's address. We sent a letter off describing our sailing experience and forgot the whole matter.

Palma Harbor is not the least bit attractive unless you are willing to pay ten dollars a night to stay in the yacht club and use their pool and moorings. The main harbor bottom is soft silty mud that does not hold anchors well at all. Sewage makes swimming inadvisable. So in spite of the delights of the friendly fifteenth-century walled city with its thriving night clubs and cafés, after a few days we headed "home" to Puerto Andraitx.

Our book project moved rapidly along. By the end of July we began seriously thinking about motorcycles, analyzing our budget, discussing all the reasons we could not splurge and all the other reasons why we should. In spite of our vacillation regarding money, we spent a lot of spare time thinking about motor bikes. Larry's previous experience riding them was limited to three or four times on friends' bikes. So we asked everyone we met, English, American, Spanish, or French, what they knew about motorcycles and touring. "If you want to go in the worst way, motorcycle touring may be it," one Texan tourist told us as he went on to rhapsodize over his last tour along California's rocky coastline on a powerful American-built machine. With our heads swimming with conflicting advice we spent spare afternoons riding around the island on various buses to see each second-hand motorcycle that was for sale.

The summer weather in Puerto Andraitz was always warm but frequently changeable. Some young people had asked permission to use a twenty-foot sailboat moored near us as a base for learning to use a surf-sailor. They offered to let us try the surfboard with its wishbone rigged sail, we offered them a cool spot in the shade of *Seraffyn*'s large cockpit—and a delightful friendship developed. Dave, a twenty-year-old American whose father spent his summers on Mallorca; Nicola, a tall, blonde Dutch girl; Pia, a curvaceous well-tanned Danish nineteen-year-old; and Chico, a twenty-year-old Spanish summer visitor, introduced us to the night life of the island. One afternoon, when gusty thirty-knot winds made surf-sailing too difficult for any of us, we set off in *Seraffyn* and beat outside the bay.

A few miles offshore the winds steadied to twenty-five knots, and Larry called, "Anyone for a swim?" We agreed immediately. Larry pulled the tiller to leeward, *Seraffyn* headed into the wind and, with the staysail down, assumed a comfortable, hove to additude lifting over each five-foot choppy swell but staying in position heeled about ten degrees. For safety we rigged a hundred-foot line off *Seraffyn*'s stern with two large fenders tied to its end like a buoy.

We need not have worried. *Seraffyn* moved so slowly hove to that I became confident about catching her even if I swam a couple hundred yards away. All of us shed our bikini tops and tee shirts. And in spite of our first apprehensions about diving into a windy, rolly seaway, *Seraffyn* soon became a diving platform in the middle of an endless sea. It was easy to climb back on board, the reefed mainsail kept her heeled so that if you timed the swells right, you could roll right over the bulwarks onto the deck.

Then one of the boys got a great idea. He climbed to the end of *Seraffyn*'s seven-and-a-half-foot-long bowsprit, waited until a large surge lifted the boat, then with absolute ease executed a perfect back flip tossed twelve or fifteen feet in the air by the wipe of the bowsprit. The scene reminded me of afternoons when I was much younger and at the public swimming pool with three boys (Larry included), each trying to outdo the other—swan dives, back flips, gainers—in a constant round-about procession. Pia tried a tentative simple dive off the lunging bowsprite end. On her next attempt she was goaded on by all of us. She climbed bravely out to the very tip, drew herself up to a spectacularly handsome stance, then arched her lean, tanned, full-breasted body into a back flip. Unfortunately her timing was off. The painful smack of a ten-foot fall into a belly flop made all of us wince. But Pia climbed back on *Seraffyn*, smiling through a few tears. When she stood up on deck we all broke into roars of laughter. The spectacu-

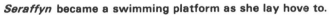
Seraffyn became a swimming platform as she lay hove to.

lar flop had left her body pink everywhere except for her perfectly aerodynamically shaped un-tanned bare breasts. Her next attempt at a back flip went far better.

Another day when we woke to thirty-five-knot gusts through the mountain canyons we worked till midafternoon then decided to try out the new set of reefs in *Rinky Dink*'s thirty-eight-square-foot sail. The six-foot eight-inch fiberglass lapstrake dinghy looked a bit silly with less than seventeen square feet of blue-and-white stripped sail set. But with one person seated in the stern, she surfed off the backs of two-foot wind waves and moved like a performance dinghy—if you kept her bow up. Larry and I took turns rushing through the moored boats and soon had quite a few spectators—cruising sailors bored with being confined on their boats waiting for the wind to quit. By late afternoon we had spent half an hour on each of eight different boats, lounging and drinking cocktails while the owners played in *Rinky Dink.*

We often left *Rinky*'s rig in place but took her centerboard and rudder out at night so that she would trail quietly astern. Then we would sail ashore or around the harbor rather than row. A forty-foot sailboat came in to anchor near us one day while Larry and I were taking turns sailing the dink. Two youngsters lay on the foredeck watching us scoot back and forth. "What's your dinghy's name," the blonde, serious little girl called. "*Rinky Dink,*" I called back. Everytime we sailed by the youngsters would call out, "Hello *Rinky Dink,*" as they lay slightly bored and obviously jealous in the afternoon sun. When we spotted their father alone on *Freebooter*'s deck later that day, Larry went over, introduced himself, and asked if we could take the youngsters sailing the next day. Dan Hobbel readily agreed. It took only one delightful day to teach eight-year-old Nikki and nine-year-old Yoni to handle *Rinky Dink.* Two days later when we planned a motorcycle hunting day in Palma we left the dinghy with the delighted youngsters and told them to use it but to stay inside the limits of the two headlands.

When we came back late that afternoon, there were two slightly bored looking younsters on *Freebooter*'s foredeck and no *Rinky Dink* in sight. Ten minutes later, Karin, their mother, sailed in around the breakwater from the outer harbor. "The kids seemed to be having so much fun I decided to try it," Karin called. "Nicest, quietest afternoon I've had in weeks!"

We often recalled those special days of sharing our dinghy with quick learning, exuberant Nikki and Yoni. Six years later an unexpected letter arrived which proved those days with a tiny sailing dinghy had meant a lot to them, too. Along with Dan's note welcoming us home from a ten-and-a-half-year voyage was this poem from a more sophisticated Nicola than we had known in magical Puerto Andraitx:

Seraffyn

The *Seraffyn*'s sails
Blow full and free,
Over the ocean,
Across the sea,
And wheels of foam
Crash against her sides
While overhead
The gulls all cry.

West and East,
North and south,
Through canals
And rivers mouth,
And still her sails
Blow full and free,
Over the ocean,
Across the sea,

—Nicola Hobbel, *1979*

CHAPTER 8

A Different Trip

By the beginning of August our book manuscript had been shipped off to New York. Like kids let out of school we celebrated by sleeping in, lazing around all day, and generally letting time slide by in a pleasant haze. Our motorcycle touring dream was up one day, down the next as we chased after each "for sale" ad in the two Mallorcan newspapers. With the limited size of the island and small permanent population, the only second-hand motorcycles we saw for sale were either lovely small dirt bikes, which were unsuited to our purpose, or really old beat up touring bikes we did not feel confident we could keep in running condition. A new touring motorcycle of any sort would have cost us over two thousand dollars because of local import fees.

Then one morning a note arrived from the owner of the big ketch in Palma. "I'll be on board Tuesday, August 18, please stop by and see me to discuss delivering my boat to New Orleans."

On our way into town we read the local Spanish ads. "Ducati 350, almost new," one read. With visions of a possible six-thousand-mile delivery to sweeten our cruising kitty, we went straight over to look at one last bike. The address in the ad was across the street from a motorcycle mechanic we had chatted with before. He had not known the bike was for sale but said, "Bring it over, I'll give you an opinion."

As soon as the motorcycle's owner opened his basement door, I saw the bike. Black, shiny, and almost like new, a clean-cut, unadorned, simple road bike stood in solitary splendor, slightly dusty but without a spot of oil beneath its aluminum engine. Using my deepest powers of careful observation, I instantly fell in love. "If it runs, I want it!"

I whispered to Larry.

Being his usual conservative self (thank God!) Larry asked permission to take the motorcycle to a mechanic. Two mechanics and two appraisals later, with the motorcycle owner riding along to protect his machine while I waited anxiously in a nearby café, Larry gave the go ahead and then tried to appear above it all while price negotiations went on. We left a fifty-dollar deposit and almost skipped the whole way to the bank, where we wired for nine hundred dollars more. Then we went to meet the owner of the fifty-four-foot ketch.

"I'm sorry to have troubled you," he said. "The other delivery skipper I contacted before I received your letter just wired that he'd take her across November first." When we learned the other skipper was Bob Sloan, the sailor who had originally taught Larry to navigate —and who had introduced Larry and I to each other twelve years before—we assured the owner he had made a good choice.

Even the lost delivery job did not deflate our bubblelike moods. In two days we would be proud owners of a one-year-old Ducati 350, single-cylinder, long-stroke touring bike with only six thousand kilometers on its odometer. The young Spaniard who had sold it to us was bound for two years in the army. His misfortune opened all of Europe to us. Who cared if we had just used one-third of all our cruising cash on a frivolous whim?

We rushed back to Puerto Andrait and rowed over to the shipshape twenty-six-foot cutter owned by a semi-retired Danish seaman. Sixty-year-old Ole Detlit had become one of our favorite visitors during the past six weeks. With the experience gained as a seaman on the cod ketches that sailed between Greenland, Denmark, and Spain forty years ago and refined during his years as a deck officer in the merchant marine, Ole was able to earn extra money to supplement his retirement checks. He rigged local boats and sewed flax sails by hand. He taught Larry a new and very efficient way to do rope-to-wire splices and offered his ideas to add to our bosun's knowledge. Ole's own boat was gaff-rigged, a warm cozy home with a wood-burning stove that we came to envy. "Sure I'll take care of Seraffyn for you," Ole said. "But I want to help you set the ground tackle so I know what's down there."

The next morning Larry and Ole moved Seraffyn as close as was prudent to a 3-foot shoal area on the far side of the bay. They set our twenty-five-pound CQR anchor to windward and then towed Seraffyn dead downwind with their two hard-rowing dinghies while I payed out chain over the anchor winch until 150 feet lay on the bottom, 20 feet below us. Larry attached a 150-foot-long mooring line to the chain, then he and Ole continued to play tugboat until all 300 feet of chain lay on the bottom. Then Larry set our thirty-five-pound folding fisherman anchor with a trip line and buoy on the other end of the anchor chain. He pulled *Seraffyn* back to the mid-point of the chain and rigged a one-half-inch swivel with two five-eighth-inch nylon mooring lines on thimbles. *Seraffyn* swung by the two mooring lines well clear of the main traffic of the bay and close enough to the shoal area that few larger boats would have any reason to come near her. Ole lived on his boat only fifty yards away. He agreed to accept a dollar a day to check the mooring lines and wash the decks with salt water twice a week.

So we forgot about boats, and our thoughts turned completely to our inland tour. A delightful new kind of shopping list filled the next four days: saddlebags, helmets, spark plug, chain links. Dave, our surf-sailor friend gave us a great gift—his old tube tent. This nine-foot-long, six-foot diameter, heavy-guage piece of polyethylene tubing created some real jokes later when we rendezvoused with three English friends near Valencia. They watched us tie a piece of clothes line around a tree, run it through the tube, secure the line to our motorcycle handle bars, then clip the tent in place with clothespins and spread our sleeping bags inside to form the floor. "Only an American would spend five hundred pounds on a motorcycle and sleep in a plastic bag," they quipped.

Four days after our bank draft arrived we set off on a heavily laden, newly named *Duke Moto.* Larry at 178 pounds, me at 100, two sleeping bags, one duffle bag full of three changes of clothes, wet-weather gear, a camera, two jugs—one for water, one for wine—two good books each, including *Zen and the Art of Motorcycle Maintenance,* plus a kit full of spares and tools for *Duke Moto.*

We learned one of the joys of European motorcycle touring almost immediately when we boarded the ferry from Palma to Barcelona. The fare for the motorcycle was one-fourth of what we paid for ourselves. Later when we took the Southampton ferry in England bound for Bilboa, Spain, a thirty-six-hour voyage, *Duke*'s fare was only five dollars.

As we wandered all over northern Spain, through the Pyrénées and into exquisite, miniature Andorra, we learned the second advantage of a motorcycle like ours—it ran ninety miles on a gallon of gas. With gas

Our plastic bag supported by a £500-motorcycle.

Our Michelin map helped us find this dirt cart road, which led us through a sparsely populated part of the Pyrénées toward Andorra.

costing $2.50 per gallon (1974) this really mattered. Throughout the trip along country roads that we chose by consulting the excellent Michelin touring maps, we found people friendly and anxious to talk. As we rode through northern France ever closer to Switzerland, villagers would ask in faulty Spanish, "Did you really ride all the way from Spain on that?" We never worried about theft, and local merchants always agreed to watch our luggage while we explored. One day when a rain storm caught us in a small mountain village, the owner of a local café motioned us in, led us to a table at the back, and turned the television so we could lounge back and watch a soccer match while the rain beat down outside; then he brought us each a steamy hot cup of coffee.

As we rode past vineyards and small farms we would wait until we saw someone in their yard, then ask in impossible French or sign language if we could buy a litre of wine. We were never turned down and often ended up buying wonderful slices of homemade cheese and heavenly garlicy, coarse pâtés to make up our lunches—along with long loafs of crips bread we carried, just like the locals, unwrapped and secured under the straps of our luggage rack. Farmers would hand us bunches of sweet, ripe, harvest-ready grapes when we stopped to watch and say hello. Blackberries ripe for the picking lined many of the tiny country lanes we rode over, and our only mishap came when I yelled "Stop!" when I saw one really prime bush. Larry slowed almost to a stop, put his foot down, and touched the handbrake; the front wheel skidded on some mud, and we both ended upside down in a grass-filled, three-foot-deep ditch with *Duke Moto* on top of us while we laughed like two fools. The only lasting damage was to Larry's jeans. They disintegrated into a holey mess the next time I washed them because of acid from the upside-down battery.

On nights when we chose to sleep in our tent, we ate breakfast and dinner at small inns or cafés. If we slept in a pension (boarding house), we bought cold-cuts and picnicked along the way.

Our only mechanical breakdown came on a Saturday afternoon in Switzerland next to Lake Lausanne, where we had hoped to visit François and Rosemary Greaser—two cruising friends we had made the year before in Gibraltar. When I telephoned from a pay box near our dismantled motorbike with its broken wheel bearing, I got quite a surprise. "Step outside the phone box," François said after I had described our location. Three hundred yards up the street, he was waving to me through his open window. We left *Duke Moto* where it was and spent three great days camped in the Greasers' spare room. François, a fine craftsman and talented marine architect, showed us the beautiful lines of a new boat they were building of teak and locust woods to replace twenty-six-foot *Kion Dee* (see appendix to *Seraffyn's European Adventure*), which had been their cruising home for three years.

Motorcycle touring had its drawbacks. We got caught in a rainstorm in the middle of France and only the sleaziest pension would give us a room. My rear end felt like lead after any day when we rode more than two hundred kilometers. Our limited baggage capacity meant putting on our wet-weather gear while we washed everything else. By the time we crossed the English Channel from Le Havre, France, in late September we had to wear our wet-weather outfits over our heavy jackets just to keep warm.

But for exactly the same amount of money that we spent living on *Seraffyn*, we toured for six weeks, covering six thousand kilometers of inland Europe. For only $120 per week we explored, met new friends, and saw much more than just seaports. We returned to *Seraffyn* eager for our own cozy bed but delighted by an adventure that could best be summed up by one tiny moment in a tea shop in southern England.

We had parked *Duke Moto* across the street and walked into the fifteenth-century, fire-warmed tea shop. A very old couple were seated at a cloth-covered table set with china. Their gloves and walking sticks were properly placed and every hair was perfectly turned. They watched as we cluttered the floor next to our table with helmets, mittens, wet pants. When Larry finished pulling my wet-weather parka over my head, the old man asked, "Is that your motorcycle?"

"Yes," Larry answered.

Then the rosy complected seventy-eight-year-old wife chirped, "I love motorcycle touring. Automobiles are such a bore." After tea and a delightful conversation that included a regretful explanation, "My doctor insisted we sell our touring bike when I reached eighty and my wife turned seventy-seven," we all went out to inspect *Duke Moto*.

When we finally rode down the valley toward Puerto Andraitx it was the middle of October, and *Duke Moto* was even more overloaded than when we had begun our trip. Yes, we both agreed, after touring on a motorcycle, cars are a bore!

The strangest thoughts came to mind as we rode along the last winding mile of pavement into Puerto Andraitx. What if someone had run into *Seraffyn* while we were away? What if she had dragged her mooring and was lying on the beach? This last-minute worry happens in my mind every time we come back after leaving her for more than a few days. She is all we own—our home, our toy. Inside are all the souvenirs and photos from years of voyaging, all our tools and clothes. To insure *Seraffyn* even for total loss while we cruise and visit foreign ports would cost us 3 to 5 percent of her replacement value every year. In 1975 that would have been equivalent to cruising funds for two and a half or three months. Insurance money would never replace our souvenirs or memories. So instead, when we plan to leave *Seraffyn* we search out a safe anchorage, set our own mooring, hire the best watchman we can, then go off and forget about her. We have done this a dozen times during our voyaging and every time when we are almost in sight of her on our way home, the same thoughts cross my mind.

As usual, *Seraffyn* lay contented and gleaming white. She was at the far side of the bay, just where we had left her. Ole happened to be on shore. So within minutes we had our knapsack in his dinghy and were rowing home.

We had just time enough to remove our helmets, unlock *Seraffyn*'s companionway, and survey our own little world when I noticed a two-ton racing boat headed into the bay. "Here's another Canadian yacht," I called to Larry. "Where's our flag? I'll put it up."

"Hey, they're from the West Vancouver Yacht Club, too. Where's our burgee?" I called before he had dug out our flag.

"Do you think they know there's a shoal here?" I asked when Larry climbed on deck. The powerful red sloop bore down on us under power. Their crew did not acknowledge our waves or shouts of warning. Only ten feet from our side, the red boat's skipper put his engine in reverse. A well rehearsed crew—all in sunglasses and watch caps—hurled mooring lines across *Seraffyn*'s deck, then pushed huge inflated fenders over their boat's side. "Surprise!" six voices yelled. We rushed to secure the lines, still unsure of the reason for this invasion. Six watch caps came off. Six pairs of sunglasses came off, and all of a sudden we recognized a boat full of friends from Vancouver, Larry's hometown, including two of our very favorites: Richard and Susan Blagbourn, whom we had last seen three years before in Virginia.

"Tracked you two down through the grapevine," Richard told us. "*Kanata* was shipped over from Canada to race for the Admirals cup then cruise for a while in the Med. Vladimir Plasvic, her owner, offered me a chance to skipper her on this cruise."

"But how can you take the time off?" we asked Richard, who had been working as an architect last time we saw him.

"We've sold everything including our house," he answered "We're taking two years and looking for a cruising boat to buy in the Med. This trip on *Kanata* is the perfect way to start looking."

It took us a few days to celebrate the surprise visit. Then we lifted our mooring, cleaned the chain, and spent a day storing all the tackle away. On the fourth day after our arrival home we took Richard and Susan for a gentle autumnlike, day-sail.

We were ghosting up the fiord on the last zephyrs of a dying breeze when we heard the steady stroke of someone rowing a boat coming closer through the dark. "Larry Pardey, *Seraffyn*," an unfamiliar voice called. A retired English sailor who lived in a cottage on the cliffs near the entrance to Puerto Andraitx pulled alongside. "Bob Sloan has asked me to watch for you and tell you to come over and see him in Puerto Soller as soon as possible," Kieth Taylor told us and then rowed away into the night.

The next day we rode our motorcycle along the beautiful coast between Puerto Andraitx and Soller, enjoying the twists and bends tremendously now that we were familiar with our old friend *Duke Moto*. When we reached Soller it was not hard to find Bob. He was halfway up a mast with a varnish brush in his hand. He yelled down to us, "That ketch in Palma isn't seaworthy. The owner didn't know that his standing rigging needs replacing before it can leave port. I don't have the time or equipment to do it. I've told him I'd ask you to give him a price to make her ready. Then if you want to take her across the pond, you've got your work cut out for you. I've got another delivery lined up. I'm taking this boat and leaving Saturday for Antigua." Then he went back to work putting an extra coat of varnish on the forty-footer's mast.

Bob Sloan, who works full time delivering boats anywhere in the world, has built up a reputation that keeps his office phone ringing. But to earn a good full-time living moving power and sailboats across oceans, he has to have an answering service and be available on the spur of the moment to fly off and inspect a boat. Even for experienced cruising people, long-distance, money-making deliveries usually come along only by chance. When you have no telephone and no regular mail delivery, it's a case of being in the right place at the right time.

Through the years on *Seraffyn* we have been able to find about one delivery a year, usually moving boats 1000 to 1500 miles and charging an average of one dollar a mile (1975) plus fuel and return air fares for an appropriate number of crewmen. (As of 1980, fees on the United States west coast are almost two dollars a mile.) This would be a real honey of a delivery job for us: 5800 miles to New Orleans.

With the fee plus charges to re-rig and repair the boat, we would earn enough money in seventy-one days to last us a year of cruising. That sounds great but one day I happened to break it down to man hours. For over two months both of us were totally involved and committed twenty-four hours a day with only three afternoons off to lounge and be away from the ketch. Our hourly pay averaged just two dollars. But we did end up with a lump sum that we could not spend at sea; we had the experience of handling one more different type of boat at sea; and we learned a lesson that scared the pants off us.

As we rode *Duke Moto* home to *Seraffyn* we felt like we had won on every count. We had had our motorcycle tour of Europe. Now we had our winters work to refill our cruising kitty. And to top it all, we could afford to visit our friends and family for the first time in three years without sailing over halfway around the world on *Seraffyn*.

This big ketch would help us top up our cruising kitty.

〜〜〜

CHAPTER 9

A Winter's Work

When we arrived at the yacht club in Palma the next day the maintenance skipper was on board the ketch. We asked him to show us through the boat. "Engine needs a top job, transmission seals are blown, and the generator only works in port," the gruff middle-aged man snapped. Then he walked off the boat, and we never saw him again. We later learned he was furious that an outside delivery skipper had been called in, even though he could not navigate and knew little about ocean voyaging.

A two-hour cursory survey showed that all of the main standing rigging—cap shrouds, forestay, backstays plus the bobstay—had to be replaced. Six years previously, when the boat was built, iron commercial bridge type swage fittings and been used on the one-half-inch stainless steel wire. The two metals had set up a reaction, and now several of the end fittings were badly rusted.

The main cabin, a huge salon with a seven-foot-by-nine-foot bed or "rompetorium" as we came to call it, stood open and clear of obstructions sixteen feet wide and twenty-five feet long. The mizzen mast was stepped on deck, but we could see no structure inside the main cabin to counteract the downward thrust of the mast. Three deckbeams were already cracked. Larry opened the floor boards and found an excellent mast step. Overhead there was all of the proper blocking for mast partners. "Looks like someone forgot to put a compression post in. We can build a good temporary one for the voyage, then the owner can decide if he wants to leave it in place permanently," Larry said. The main 453 GM diesel started well, and the steering worked—as did the generator. But a glance overboard showed three inches of barnacles and coral growth on the rudder and propeller. The boat had been sitting for two and a half years without a haulout. So our final estimate included new main rigging, a compression post, hauling, scrubbing, and bottom paint, plus the delivery fee.

We telephoned the owner then went home to *Seraffyn* for four pleasant days until a bankers draft for one-third of the total fee was wired to Palma.

"Sure I'll take care of *Seraffyn,*" Ole said with a bit of indignation in his voice. "You have been home a week and never once washed her decks. I've been watching, she needs it." That solved one problem. We had heard of the gusty winter storms in the Med. But under Ole's eagle eye, *Seraffyn* would be safe.

"Of course I'll hold your mail," the postmistress snapped. "Don't you think I know you'll be back?" Our only other problem was finding crew. For a boat this large Larry wanted at least one other experienced sailor plus a fourth person to stand watches. This was easily solved by a sailor's grapevine that spreads gossip like wildfire.

Palma is one of the four main crew pickup and trading places in the Mediterranean. Gibraltar, Palma, Malta, and Rhodes, Greece, are ports where charter boats stop for their final stores on the seasonal migration between the Med and Caribbean. These ports are a constant scene of musical crews. Three hours after we had carted all of our rigging tools from *Seraffyn* into the city, cashed the bankers draft for the delivery deposit, and bought a three-hundred-foot coil of one-half inch galvanized seven-by-nineteen wire, potential crewmen were coming down the dock and yelling, "This the boat that's headed for the United States?"

It took two days to splice new rigging for the boat and two more to provision for the trip, with the help of a local chandler recommended by the yacht club manager. During that time we interviewed five potential crewmen and checked what references they could provide. We have tried to select compatible, neat, eager-to-learn crew each time we have delivered a boat. Our averages have been pretty good considering we have had to make most choices based on very little . information. Professional references, such as RYA captains papers or coast guard sea-time records, do not seem to count for much. One of our worst crewmen had hundreds of hours documented on his official-looking records. Age or occupation does not seem to matter either; the best crewman we ever had was sixty-year-young Rod Pringle, ex–vice president of Shell Oil Company, who was willing to work like a Trojan for the miserly six dollars a day we could pay. It was personal references of any sort that got us all of our best crew. A ragged looking skinny, long-haired wanderer came up the dock while Larry was sixty feet above the deck attaching new cap shrouds to the mast. I was on deck trying to guide the cantankerous coil of wire up to him. "Hear you might be looking for crew," Richard yelled. "I came across the Atlantic on an eighty-foot powerboat four months ago. Been wandering around the Middle East and was supposed to meet the boat here ten days ago. My plane from Athens was held up. Missed the boat by four hours. Don't know anything about sailing." I asked where he was staying and said to come back later that evening. Then I rushed to get Larry a wrench.

In the late afternoon we were in town near the shipyard where the eighty-foot charter ketch, *Stormvogel* was undergoing a re-fit. Richard was staying on board so we asked to see her skipper. When I asked him about having Richard as one of our crewmen, the skipper answered, "He's been living on board for nine days. Neat, easy to be around, works hard. If I had room for another crew I'd take him along."

Larry asked my impression, "He sure had dirty feet," was all I could remember. That evening we hired Richard at a dollar a day plus keep. I am glad we did. He arrived with a bulging five-foot-long duffle bag, a ready smile, and a desire to learn everything he could. A week later I fleetingly mentioned, "Wish I had a teapot." Richard disappeared into his mammoth and battered duffle bag and handed out a chased brass Egyptian teapot. In the trade winds a month later Larry said, "All we need now is a hammock to string between the shrouds." Minutes later Richard appeared, hammock in hand. When Larry told him about my comment from our first meeting, it became a family joke. If I stepped on board the wet white decks and left even a hint of a footprint Richard would use a stage whisper to quip, "She's a pretty nice gal, but she sure has dirty feet."

Another crewman we picked up later in Antigua was champion Australian sky diver. He had jumped out of airplanes with twenty-five other men at 25,000 feet. Then all twenty-six would hold hands to form a star while free falling thousands of feet. Less than 1500 feet from the ground they would open their parachutes. Our new crewman claimed heights never bothered him. He fell head first down the ten-foot companionway ladder time after time. At first we would rush over, pick

A Winters Work

him up, and sympathize over any bruises. By the fourth time one of us would just turn and say, "What's wrong Ken? Forget your parachute?"

Before stores or crew came on board Larry and I searched the boat from stem to stern, opening every locker, bunk board, and floor board, looking into each nook and cranny with a powerful flashlight to make a general inventory list of each locker. This way not only did we know where each through hull fitting was, where the wiring and pipes went, and what was on board, but also we hoped to find any illegal goods the owner had inadvertently left on board. When we had previously moved boats out of Mexico, every professional delivery skipper we met warned us, "Search for drugs. The owner of the boat sitting safe in his office won't go to jail when you sail into customs with a stash of his marijuana on board. If you find anything, dump it at sea." We knew of sailors who had languished in foreign jails shouting their innocence when drugs were found on boats they had moved for other people.

We were very tired by the time we had spent two days inspecting every locker and each drawer in three private staterooms, a huge engine compartment, beneath six water tanks, and in 119 cubby holes, a report of which now filled my seven-page inventory. We found the boat to be solidly built and well equipped, luxuriously fitted out but heavily dependent on the large onan generator with its dicey reputation. At 2130 on the second day we opened the heavy bunk boards under the seven-foot-by-eight-foot rompetorium mattress. Four large cardboard boxes labeled "Genuine GM parts, filters" were arranged in this huge locker. Two of the boxes were right up behind the steering quadrant. It would have been a struggle to get at them, we would have needed to remove the huge mattress and all the bunk boards and then climb past the greasy steering cables. Besides, they were identical to the ones closest to us and were still sealed with brown tape. The two boxes near us were open and contained fuel and oil filters. "I'll check when we're underway and see if she needs her filters changed. Probably never been done, since there are so many filters here," Larry commented. Then we flopped exhausted into the second stateroom aft, our home-to-be for the next two months.

When our crew moved on board the next day we tried to be as diplomatic as possible about our concern for drugs. Richard had several Middle East stamps in his passport so we knew any customs

103

official would be suspicious of him first. Larry took Richard aside and suggested, "If you have any hash or marijuana in your bags, drop it overboard after we leave port. I'll have to search everyone's bags before we reach the next port. I'm the one that will get nailed if any drugs are found on board." Since both Richard and our other crewman, Chris, openly invited us to inspect their lugguge, we never worried that they might have illegal goods with them.

Two days later we powered the ketch around to Puerto Andraitx, setting each sail to check it over in the light breeze. She behaved well but even at 1800 RPM her barnacle-encrusted propeller barely pushed us four and a half knots. After a haulout, scraping, and fresh bottom paint, she moved six knots at only 1400 RPM.

Ten days after we received our delivery deposit, we were underway—sure of the ketch and her equipment and pleased with our two crewmen. In Gibraltar Richard helped us pull a fun trick on our old racing friends Sandy and Chris Bunney. He telephoned their home and in his most formal voice said, "The Pardeys have sent a package for you. Please pick it up as soon as possible from the last boat on the marina dock." An hour later we let out a shout of "Surprise!" that almost sent Sandy and Chris off the far side of the dock. We soon had a reunion party planned for the next evening.

Our second crewman, Chris Edwards, an English Sandhurst graduate and ex–army officer, had once served under the present governor of Gibraltar. He called and invited Governor Sharp and his wife to our reunion. They in turn insisted we be their guests for hot baths and dinner at the governor's palace our last evening in port.

We spent the next day shopping for fresh stores and all of the engine parts we had not been able to find in Palma. When we came back from one more shopping tour late in the afternoon, we were discussing the hors d'oeuvres for that evenings open house. There was no sign of our crew. We had told them to take the afternoon off, so we were not surprised. Richard had been in Gibraltar before on the eighty-foot powerboat he had helped bring across the Atlantic, and he had mentioned some friends he wanted to visit. We were not prepared, however, for the sight that met us when we climbed down the companionway ladder into the main cabin. In a wonderfully staged act, seven handsome eighteen- and nineteen-year-old, dark-haired, dark-eyed Gibraltarian girls were ripping the clothes off skinny, scraggly haired Richard while he lay giggling in the middle of the rompetorium. We collapsed into gales of laughter, especially when Chris, who is a Greek god of a man with sleekly combed black curls and flashing blue eyes, walked into this noisy scene and complained, "I couldn't even get a local girl to talk to me."

The next day we all worked on the boat—checking rigging, cleaning lockers, and replacing impellers on each water pump. By evening we were really ready for those promised baths. A very scruffy crew gathered fresh clothes and bathkits then walked to the marina gate where we had been told a car would be waiting at 1800.

We were not prepared for the fully uniformed chauffeur and polished limousine, and we could see the chauffeur was not prepared for us. Four greasy, scruffily dressed sailors walked up to him. Chris drew to attention, shifted his bundle of clothes, then saluted and stated, "Major Edwards here." The chauffeur looked Chris up and down from untied sneaker shoelaces to grease-stained pants to the frayed rope belt, shook his head, then remembered his training and saluted as he opened the car door for us.

The whole scene sent the four of us into convulsions of laughter; when we arrived at the hillside mansion and had the same shocked greeting from the uniformed majordomo who opened the car door, it was hard to keep straight faces.

Lady Sharp loved it all. She hustled each of us off to a separate mammoth bathtub where warm towels and drinks of our choice were waiting on tubside tables.

At dinner both the uniformed waiter and the chef had a hard time performing their jobs with dignity as the Sharps fell in with our hilarity. Chris broke everyone up when he described coming into the main cabin of the boat and seeing Richard surrounded by beautiful girls, "He was just like a rabbit in a lettuce patch! He didn't know which girl to grab first!"

By the end of the wonderful evening all of us were lounging on the thick carpet in front of the blazing fire. Every once in a while Governor Sharp's handsome and proper English-lady-of-a-wife would repeat, "Like a rabbit," and we would all break into fits of laughter.

When we finally cleared the Straits of Gibraltar we found the first winds stronger than ten knots. Larry steered the ketch as close to the wind as possible, we lowered her ten-foot-deep centerboard and sheeted in all sails until she boomed along, ports awash. I took over the helm while Larry inspected the masts and rigging, first on one tack, then the other.

After two hours of hard beating, checking, and testing we all felt confident. The new compression post, which Larry had shaped out of a six-inch-by-six-inch piece of mahogany, took every bit of movement out of the mizzen area. The ketch pointed quite acceptably and footed well. Her steering felt good and she took on very little water. So we eased off on a beam reach for Madeira.

We averaged 186 miles a day, reaching in twenty knots of wind right into Funchal Harbor. We were the only yacht there and found shopping for fresh food and wine excellent. We had to top up our water tanks from a barge. For four hundred gallons of water they charged us a carton of cigarettes.

The trade winds never seemed to fill in properly as we headed WSW for Antigua in the British West Indies. So we had to power almost half the way. Because we had been warned about the main engine, Larry scrubbed it clean one calm day at sea. Then he watched to see where the oil was leaking from. The GM diesel ran wonderfully, so we were not surprised to find all of the dirty oil was being thrown over the engine by the leaky transmission.

The next day Larry asked me to find the owner's manual for the Borg-Warner hydraulic transmission. I located it in a folder along with two different receipts showing that the rear seals on this unit had been replaced every two years. I found a comfortable spot to sit in the engine room while the ketch reached briskly along on a comfortable sea; Larry climbed around the transmission, checking each part. "What's this?" he would ask. I would turn to the diagram, search for something that looked right, and call out a name. Everything seemed to please Larry until we came to a corroded-looking aluminum cap on top of the transmission. "What's this?" he asked again. "It's called a pressure release valve on this diagram," I answered. "Do they say what it's supposed to do?" Larry asked. I thumbed through the manual while Larry fought to remove the small fitting. Salt water had been spraying over this part of the transmission from the lifting cable hole in the steel centerboard trunk. I read the instructions from the manual, showed Larry the diagram, and he solved the transmission problem. This tiny fitting was supposed to equalize the oil pressure when the transmission warmed up. Its internal spring had seized up from the aluminum corrosion and kept the fitting closed at all times. Larry scraped the corrosion away, cleaned the spring, then reassembled it. With the pressure release valve working properly, the transmission oil consumption dropped from one quart every six hours of running time to one-third of a quart every twenty-four hours—since no more oil was being forced out the rear seal.

During the quiet sailing days all four of us pitched in to clean the boat thoroughly and put fresh varnish on the cap rails and cabinsides. The work helped fill our days and made us quite proud of the ketch's appearance. Chris quickly caught on to wire splicing and made up new life line gates. I sewed a snug new mast boot from some waterproof canvas I found on board. Richard became a trustworthy helmsman and seemed ever eager to put up more sail, and Larry got his fill of tinkering with engines.

Larry had worked for a year as a diesel mechanic's helper in the Canadian logging industry fifteen years before. So when the generator did start giving us trouble he quickly decided it was starved for fuel. Making deductions like a Sherlock Holmes (to me motors are still a complete mystery), he found the problem: the main fuel intake line had an air leak which only became apparent when the fuel in the main tanks was half gone. No mechanic had been able to find the problem because in port the tanks were always topped up. Ten minutes later our worries about electricity to power the running lights and drinking water and to keep our fresh stores cold were all taken care of.

Our final engine-room problem on this delivery looked insurmountable at first. Eight days later, when the cooling jacket on the water-cooled muffler of the generators rusted through and began spraying geysers of hot salt water right across the engine room, I began counting my canned food and searching for spare flashlight batteries. We had over a thousand miles to go. Maybe someone in Antigua, our next stop, could weld up a new jacket. The day was completely windless and hot. Larry suggested stopping the main engine while the crew had a swim overboard on the absolutely smooth Atlantic. When he set to work removing the muffler our prevoyage search and inventory paid off. I knew where there was an old aluminum pot exactly the same diameter as the muffler. Larry remembered where to find a sheet of cork gasket material. An hour later the muffler was back in place proudly sporting an aluminum patch held securely in place by silicon sealant and self-tapping sheet metal screws.

English Harbor, Antigua, held some very pleasant surprises. It seems this is a favorite as a cruising man's Christmas rendezvous. Every time we turned around we met another old friend. Derek and Vita Simpson, racing friends from Vancouver, were there with the ketch they were sailing home from England. Nick Skeates with *Wylo* was in the back bay eager to share the cruising stories he had collected since our last meeting in Dartmouth, England. Jim and Erica Leech on thirty-five-foot *White Water* spotted us immediately. We had last seen them in Gibraltar a year before. "Where's *Seraffyn?*" Erica called. "Let's have dinner together." Eric and Susan Hiscock were in port on board *Wanderer IV* celebrating one last English Harbor Christmas before they set off for a permanent home base in New Zealand. We enjoyed afternoon cocktails on their neatly kept forty-nine-footer and marveled at the nimbleness of this couple in their mid-sixties.

Since we felt obligated to deliver the ketch to its anxious owner as soon as possible, we planned only a two-day stop to replenish stores before the last two-thousand-mile voyage across the Caribbean and around Cuba's western end. But we had over one thousand dollars cash still in our pockets from the delivery deposit, and since we would miss the huge pot luck dinner planned for Christmas Eve, we decided to throw our own party.

We located the resident Calypso band, started an invitation along the grapevine, and bought a good supply of rum, ice, and Coke. By 1030 the wide decks and huge main cabin of our temporary home were lost under the feet of forty or fifty dancing, singing sailors. The band was lousy but their beat was contagious and so were their smiles. By 0300 most of our visitors had found their proper boats. At 0900 when we woke to get underway, the scratched state of the varnish in the cockpit and on the coamings—plus sensitive heads—reminded us that Mount Gay Rum should be served in moderation.

The normal boisterous trade winds never showed up this year. So we had plenty of time to refinish the varnish as we powered across the Caribbean. We had called the ketch's owner from Antigua to tell him we were on schedule and to give him the final delivery costs so he could have the payment ready. He surprised us by saying, "Don't sail into New Orleans. I'd rather have the boat closer to home in a small port near the Mississippi-Alabama border. You should find a chart somewhere on board that shows it. I'll pay for the extra mileage."

With the Gulf Loop Current behind us we averaged almost nine knots as we approached the Mississippi Delta bound for the wide gulf between New Orleans and the Alabama border. All of us were anxious to be ashore. We had been responsible for another man's vessel for over two months. We had had only a few afternoons to relax off the boat. Since the owner wanted his boat at home to use for the winter season, we felt obligated to turn on the diesel every time our speed dropped below four knots, so for the past 5500 miles we had not really had the joy of sailing. All of us worked hard cleaning the boat inside and out as our days position fell to less than 300 miles to go.

Sixty-seven days after we had taken charge of the forty-nine-ton ketch Larry announced, "Our noon position shows less than seventy-five miles to go. I don't want to attempt the channel at night since our charts are pretty small scale. We'll hold at five knots until midnight, then slow her down to two and go in at day break. How about a fancy dinner for the crew?" I agreed wholeheartedly and set to work making an angle food cake with thirteen of our last twenty eggs plus a huge casserole—using almost all of our remaining fresh vegetables. Then I began packing our dufflebags.

Richard came in from sunbathing on the white foredeck before it was his turn at the wheel. "No wind yet, but its turning cooler," he commented as he went forward for a sweatshirt. By dusk a yellow haze cut visibility over the glassy sea to about two miles. Sunset was yellow and if we had not been so happy to be within a few hours of port, I think one of us would have made some comment on the weather.

By midnight we lay hove to in fifty-knot winds, less than thirty-five miles from our goal while the temperatures on deck dropped to eighteen degrees Fahrenheit. None of us had the proper clothes for this weather. To keep a man on watch even close to comfortable we had to donate all of our spare clothes and wrap his hands in two or three pairs of socks. With the wind blowing offshore we felt safe lying hove to. The ketch rode comfortably—her mizzen sheeted in flat, centerboard down, and wheel tied to leeward. By morning a thick fog formed in spite of the strong winds. For three days the temperatures stayed below twenty-four degrees in the foggy, stormy weather. I cursed that angel food cake and fancy dinner as we made do with canned food, potatoes, and onions.

During the second day the fog cleared for a few hours. All of us were below trying to warm up in the main cabin. The butane oven was on full and the engine thumped over with the engine room door open to add its warmth to our blanket-covered crew. I went forward to the radio room and tried to get a weather report, since the atmospheric disturbances had made reception impossible the previous day. Chicago reported sub-zero weather, Montana was having blizzards, Miami was having snow. Then finally I found a local station which immediately blurted out, "Small craft warning, waterspout alert! All vessels within a fifty-mile radius return to port and be prepared to take evading action." I wrote down this complete report and the announcer's suggested actions for evading a waterspout. Then I pulled out our own chart. Even allowing for drift and current with the fifty-knot offshore wind, we were still within the fifty-mile radius.

Larry listened to my report, his eyes growing bigger with every word. He grabbed the assorted pile of warm clothes that lay next to the companionway and started pulling them on as he rushed up into the cockpit. "God damn, come look at this!" he called down. All three of us wrapped blankets around our shoulders and stumbled into the cockpit. The ketch rode comfortably in the angry turbulent gray-green sea, gray storm clouds rushed past in low streamers, steamy fog rose from the seventy-degree Gulf Loop Current water into twenty-three-degree Canadian-style winds, and all across the horizon was a line of black, vulgarly undulating funnel-like waterspouts. Six slowly bowing, twisting devils danced across the water while we watched in silent awe. Larry had his hand on the throttle ready to put full power to the engine and turn beam to any twister that came directly toward us so that we could try and steam out of its path.

The twisters marched downwind a half mile away on either side of us. Within an hour they had dissipated into black spots in the tumbling gray clouds. Seventy hours after the temperature had dropped to eighteen degrees, the skies above us cleared and Larry was able to get a round of star shots. By early morning the low fog was mostly gone, and our decks were free of ice. Forty knots of wind had also left so we had a nice sailing breeze in the forty-five-degree sunshine. We powered down the long narrow channel into the small fishing port just before noon with some new lessons under our belts. Never again would I plan the last meal of any voyage until the breakwater was on my beam, even if there was a good engine on board. And never again would we underestimate the ability of the weather to surprise us.

We had to wait three hours for the combined customs, health, and immigration official to drive out from a local airport. Meanwhile the café on the pier willingly gave us dockside service of whopping hamburgers and thick milkshakes so we could stay on board. When the uniformed official finally arrived he sat down for a cup of hot coffee and asked point blank, "What do you have on board that you want to sneak past customs?" Larry laughed and admitted, "Four bottles of Spanish champagne and four of Mount Gay Rum."

"That's okay for the crew you have," the inspector said "Sign here, have a nice stay in the United States." Then he hurried off to meet an airplane coming in from Jamaica.

We were surprised when we called the owner and were told to move the boat to yet another place—a small marina down the coast. But by now the weather was clear, and we could get in before dark. When we did get there we found an excellent restaurant that provided all of us with a steak-and-lobster dinner.

It was midafternoon the next day before the owner showed up with his girlfriend. He had the final payment but said he worried about carrying so much cash so brought us half in bills, half in a personal check on his bank. He was very pleased with the condition of his boat and after reading through our log of the voyage, gave us a five-hundred-dollar tip; then asked us to join him at a special restaurant he knew of nearby. Since he was driving a two-seater sports car, we called a taxi. I rode with the owner and his girlfriend while Larry and the crew went in the taxi.

By this time I felt fully relaxed. We were finished with our job. A years worth of cruising funds lay hidden near our luggage in the ketch. The owner seemed delighted with our care of his boat and kept asking for more stories about the tiny, crazy incidents that happen on any long voyage. His new lady friend, a fashion model from the East Coast, was fascinated by the whole situation: an afternoon on a very large yacht, the sea stories, and the fancy sports car. When the owner said to me, "Hope you felt free to use the rum and the stash," I asked in all innocence, "What do you mean?" "The hashish," he replied, "There are two boxes full of it under the big bunk in the stern. There must be at least three or four cases of Mount Gay Rum under the false bottom in the locker under the book shelves."

My immediate reaction was, this is a hoax or he is bragging to further impress the elegant woman seated next to me. So I let the whole subject drop and enjoyed the evening, which included a superb gourmet southern-style dinner of lobster à la Louisiana surrounded by blackeyed peas, hot cornbread, sween corn, and buttered collard greens.

When we were back in the private cabin on the ketch, that conversation in the car kept haunting me. I could not sleep, so I woke Larry and told him. I was not prepared for his violent reaction. "The bastard," he hissed. "Do you realize we could be in jail right now? We could be up for eight years! If the customs men had found that, we'd have been blamed. How could we prove we hadn't brought it on board? Let's turn him in."

"But Larry," I protested, "we searched the boat in Spain. We didn't find anything then." Larry reminded me about the four cartons of filters. We had only used filters from the forward boxes. "Hell, there could be a hundred pounds of hash in those two boxes behind the steering quadrant," Larry said. My immediate reaction was, "Let's go look."

"No," Larry answered. "We don't want our fingerprints all over them, that would make matters worse. Let's just check on the rum." We went into the main saloon, removed the books, and once again looked through the locker at the head of the rompeterium. We had found nothing but newspaper-wrapped seashells and odd souvenirs when we checked this small compartment before our departure from Palma. This time we removed everything. Sure enough, the bottom of the compartment could be juggled loose and bottle after bottle of Mount Gay Rum gleamed in the beam of our flashlight. "We'll he wasn't joking about this," Larry stated with a worried glance toward the place where those two boxes of "filters" were stored. "Let's get off the boat first thing in the morning, go to the bank, cash his check, then we'll decide what to do. Now I understand why he didn't want us to stop in New Orleans. One of the charter skippers in Antigua told me the customs officials in New Orleans use dogs to search any yachts coming in from the Caribbean."

We spent a sleepless night and early the next morning paid off our crew. We hitchhiked into town, cashed the check, then boarded a Greyhound bus for the long ride into New Orleans. There we found a hotel room near the river front section of the old town and enjoyed some fine jazz while we waited for a car to deliver to California. We spent a lot of our time discussing the ramifications of this frightening situation. Because of another man's total disregard we could have lost the one precious thing that gave our lives their special charm: freedom.

On the other hand, maybe there had been no drugs at all on board, we had never seen them. It could have been just a practical joke on the owner's part. I know I project an innocent, almost square image. Maybe he had just been trying to fluster me in front of his very sophisticated lady friend.

As we tossed the whole situation around we decided we only had one course of action open to us—forget the whole matter. "If we call the narcotics agents anonymously and turn him in, he'll just put the blame on us," Larry reminded me. "Besides, he has probably removed the evidence from the boat by now."

Through the years as we wandered ever eastward on our own boat, this moral dilemma and our own final decision was something we discussed with other cruising sailors. We were just a bit shocked when we sailed through the Far East and saw the cavalier attitude some yachtsmen took toward carrying marijuana and sometimes heavier drugs on board. Then we began to hear of underfinanced sailors who had turned to amateur drug smuggling and were now languishing in the jails of Singapore, Thailand, Australia, and Indonesia—their boats impounded and rotting away. We had learned our lesson the easy way. Drugs and boats do not mix. And as a delivery skipper Larry cannot waive any of the traditional responsibility of a ship's captain. It is up to us to be sure each time that our search for drugs is thorough and complete before we leave port—not after we have endangered our whole future.

~~~~~~

CHAPTER 10

Starting Eastward

When we flew back to Palma, Mallorca, on the first of March 1976, we were eager to use our floating home. The delivery had topped up our cruising funds, and we had had a chance to visit all those people we missed in California. We had joined other, more recent sailing friends in New York, and we had missed all the worst of the Mediterranean winter storms.

Seraffyn had been based in Puerto Andraitx for over eight months, and we had come to feel like part of the village—even though we spent five and a half months of that time away on our motorcycle tour and delivery trip. Now it was time to see more of the Balearic Islands, free from the concerns of having to write or of a depleted cruising fund.

Ole had taken excellent care of *Seraffyn*. He had kept her decks and varnish work glistening with careful washdowns. His sewn leather chaffing guards left our mooring lines looking like new. Inside, the boat smelled sweet and fresh from frequent airings. But on her bottom was a one-inch thick accumulation of barnacles, weeds, and the coral growth that is peculiar to boats left sitting in Mediterranean ports—no matter what kind of bottom paint you use. Since we had to sell *Duke Moto,* the delay for haulout and clean-up time did not bother us so much.

Mike and Frankie were in port on board *Scarab;* when Mike asked if we needed help, I was surprised and delighted to hear Larry say, "Let's hire Mike to scrape and sand the bottom. We owe ourselves that treat. The rest of the work is fun in comparison." Mike was glad to have the work and I have never seen anyone move more efficiently. He seemed to care about our boat as much as we did. I loved being free

Frankie's and Mike's twenty-four-foot *Scarab*.

of the one really dirty job of haulout time. Since then whenever local wages make the cost of hiring a person to scrape and sand the bottom less than the cost of a lay day on the slip, we have hired the help and considered it money and time saved.

Selling *Duke Moto* was a pleasant surprise. During our winter away, the same type of motorcycle won the European concourse for the second year running. So fortunately for us, a For Sale sign on *Duke*'s handlebars found us several interested young buyers within a week. Even though she now had six thousand kilometers extra on the odometer, we received ten dollars more than we had originally paid for her.

As we began our final round of good-byes in Puerto Andraitx, a familiar yacht came through the harbor entrance and dropped anchor less than 150 yards from *Seraffyn*. Dale and Betty Nordlund had built fifty-foot *Aegean* in Victoria, British Columbia. We had met them shortly after *Aegean*'s launching. Their sturdy, high-powered motor sailor was designed with a fish hold forward, since Dale intended to supplement his savings by fishing as he cruised. But his excellent boat building skills were what earned him most of his cruising funds. Six months out of each eighteen Dale, Betty, and their sixteen-year-old daughter, Shelley, left *Aegean* in a safe port and went to work for the United Nations. He was regularly sent to an underprivileged nation to teach boat building skills to the natives. The most challenging part of Dale's job was adapting his ideas to fit the locally available materials and supplies. We had seen *Aegean* moored in Gibraltar while the Nordlunds were in Mozambique. But this was the first time we had met up since a pleasant afternoon in Victoria several years before.

Aegean's wheelhouse galley was complete with a Dickerson diesel cook stove. This wonderful device served as a fine cooker and cabin heater for the northern climates where the Nordlunds usually cruised. Even in the cool of a Mediterranean spring, its steady dry heat was appreciated. But for the tropics or summertime cooking Betty carried a small butane stove, since the diesel cooker threw off far too much heat and needed twenty-five to thirty minutes to warm up enough to heat coffee.

Larry and Dale disappeared into the vast engine room soon after we rowed out to greet *Aegean*. Betty set to work warming a pot of tea. She and I were just beginning the usual cruising sailor's round of "Have you seen? Did you meet?" when I heard the sound of an electric bilge pump from the forward cabin. Betty climbed quickly down into the forward area and much to my surprise came out carrying a foot-and-a-half-tall bright green parrot. Perfect Jabsco bilge pump noises came from this brighteyed bird. Betty set him on a perch in front of the steering station. "We found him in a bar in Costa Rica. He imitates any noise he hears," Betty commented.

The parrot began a slow series of "Thurunk, thurunk, thurunk."

"That's the engine," Betty said as she set out a plate of shortbread cookies.

The parrot saw the plateful of goodies, spread his wings, jumped from foot to foot, and began squawking, *"Puta, Puta, Puta!"* Betty tossed a cookie onto his tray, shook her head, "Dumb bird forgot every Spanish word he ever knew except that one. It's Costa Rican for whore!"

When the men joined us for tea, the parrot and his antics filled our conversation. "He loves noise, any noise. The louder it gets, the louder he gets," Dale told us, then he and Betty kept us laughing with stories about how this three-pound bird had charmed customs officials, scared visitors, and been snuck into airplanes. When the Nordlunds tried to fly from Tangiers into Gibraltar after their stay in Mozambique, they were told that no animals were allowed in the passenger compartment. The airplane had no pressurized luggage compartment, and the next ferry was a week away. Finally a stewardess offered to carry the caged bird on board and let him stay in the spare pilot's seat. Halfway through the very bumpy flight across the Straits of Gibraltar the stewardess came out of the cockpit, laughter and shrieks filled the air before she could shut the door again. Then she stumbled back to the Nordlunds to tell them, "That parrot is a scream! Pilot is having a hard time flying straight. You should hear his gyrocompass sounds."

Meanwhile this green wonder gobbled and chuckled to himself on his perch ten feet away while we enjoyed our reunion.

The next day the Nordlunds lifted anchor. From 150 yards away we could hear that parrot calling and laughing as the hydraulic anchor winch ground the chain in. Dale headed over to yell something to us. The parrot went wild, letting out jungle screams, motor noises, and cackles so loud we could not hear a word Dale yelled. Betty took over at the wheel and steered within twenty feet of *Seraffyn* while Dale yelled as loud as he could. But the raucous imitation laughter from that eighteen-inch-tall bird drowned every word.

Finally Dale signaled that he would write us a letter. *Aegean* steamed toward the open sea. The parrot's perfect imitation of an unmuffled diesel engine slowly faded into the morning breeze, and we broke down and roared. "I want one," I choked through the tears that ran down my cheeks. "Imagine sailing into port with a parrot like that on the spreader yelling, *'Puta, Puta, Puta!'* " Larry gasped.

We never did get our own parrot. Practical considerations like limited space got in the way. But I still think one could be the perfect addition to a cruising home.

Once again we started our rounds of good-byes. But when we reached the post office there was a telegram from Susan and Richard Blagbourne. "Wait for us, we bought a boat, leaving from Almería today, be in Andraitx within five days." We were really excited about this, since Richard's parting words when we sailed out of the Chesapeake Bay three years before had been, "Don't worry, we'll come cruising with you, some day." Now we would have a chance to be together with our favorite friends while we cruised toward the oldest parts of civilization in the Med.

Two days before Richard and Susan arrived, a gale blew across the island. Forty-five-knot gusts of wind sent boats rearing back on their anchor rodes. Six yachts lay at anchor. Three dragged and caused real confusion and some scratched paint as their owners struggled to lift fouled ground tackle then reset it again in a safe spot without hitting one of the local fishing boats or the twenty yachts tied at the town quay.

We stayed on board to fend off any possible dragger while the wind gusted first through one canyon then another, and we noticed an interesting comparison emerge. Three boats dragged: a forty-foot sportfishing boat, a fifty-foot ketch, and a thirty-foot sloop. Each was using a Danforth-type anchor with combination chain and rope rodes. We watched while for a second time an around-the-world voyager lifted his dragging Danforth anchor and found a lump of mud stuck between its flukes and stock. It had pulled loose when the wind shifted direction and now it could not reset since the mud kept it locked in one position. When the voyager broke the mud loose, he was able to successfully re-anchor. But the other two draggers tried several times then went alongside the already crowded quay and tied to other boats. The three yachts that did not drag had CQR anchors with rodes made entirely of chain.

When Susan and Richard arrived on their newly purchased thirty-two-foot fiberglass sloop, we made a final round to say good-bye. The postmistress promised to return any late mail to our English bank, which handled our post. "But don't worry," she said. "You'll be back, and I'll still be here!" The tobacco shop owner treated us to a glass of summer wine, "You'll be back," he said. "Andraitx won't change but the rest of the world will." As we finally sailed out of the safe, cliff-edged little port, I felt as though we were starting on a brand new cruise—the same feeling of an unknown future, the same tears at leaving a comfortable home, the same excitement over the adventures that lay ahead.

When Richard eased the sheets on *Taganita* and headed south, we followed suit. The cliffs soon hid the entrance to a place that had been almost unreal and certainly had created a mood that filled some fine months of our lives.

Richard and Susan on *Taganita*.

CHAPTER 11

Two Friends, Two Boats

In 1963, when Larry was twenty-three, a sailing friend returned to Vancouver a voyage to Panama with a story that was probably the cause of our whole cruising life. "You should have seen the gorgeous thirty-foot steel cruising cutter a Panama Canal pilot sold for only four thousand dollars," Richard told him. "He picked it up from some cruising guy that got tired of sailing when he reached the canal. The pilot fixed it up then decided he wasn't going anywhere with it—sold the boat to the first guy who had cash."

Larry spent the next year selling his racing sloop, saving his money, and getting every bit of sailing experience he could. Then he hitchhiked south from Vancouver to San Francisco to start his search for what turned out to be the mythical "perfect cruising boat going for a song in a foreign port." He wandered along the California coast and signed on as firstmate on an eighty-five-foot schooner bound for the Hawaiian Islands. After six months he came back and went to work as a charter boat skipper in Newport Beach. His search was ended by the decision to build his dream boat, since buying it seemed impossible.

All during the time we spent building *Seraffyn* and in almost every country we have visited since we launched her, dreamy-eyed sailors we met would tell us, "I heard there are some real cruising boat bargains if you've got cash in Spain [Mexico, England, Malta, Singapore . . .]". The port or country seemed to change every few years.

We did occasionally meet people who had been in the right place at the right time. Lou and Joannie Siegel were crewing for a friend when they bought a run-down, rusty-looking hulk of a steel sloop for only a few thousand dollars in the British West Indies. With some tremendously hard work and several thousand dollars more they spruced the boat up until its hidden beauty and charm came through. After a year of work and another of cruising, they turned a profit of close to twenty thousand dollars.

Sandy and John Price, an Australian couple we met in Spain, had flown to England with their two children to take a six-month touring holiday. One day they happened to be talking to an English sailor in a waterfront pub. He offered to sell them his twenty-eight-foot fiberglass Holman and Pye sloop for a ridiculously low price if he could have the cash within a few days. So Sandy, John, and the two children (aged twelve and fourteen) ended up with a year of cruising in the canals of Europe and through the Balearic Islands. Then they sold their boat for a handsome profit and flew back home.

But when the person who had started Larry on his quest actually sold his home in Vancouver and came to Europe with his wife to try and buy a boat that was already located where the cruising seemed exciting, we learned some of the problems inherent in this scheme.

Richard Blagbourne had searched the "boat for sale" ads in both English and American yachting magazines before he left home. Then he had chosen Spain as his main searching ground, first because the Mediterranean cultures fascinated him; second, living costs there are generally among the cheapest in Europe; and finally, the ads showed a lot of low-priced cruising boats for sale in Spanish ports.

The first thing Richard and Susan learned about their search is that it costs money to look for boats—hotels, trains, taxis, buses. Living in a town was one thing, but traveling from port to port was draining their funds. So they bought a cheap Volkswagen camper van, which not only cut costs but made getting around easier. As they checked out each ad and lead, they were amazed at how much traveling was involved. They would spend a few days camped near each harbor, get to know some sailors, and hear about another possibility only 150 miles away. They soon found that everyone seems to be looking for a good small cruising boat. We know there are far fewer real bargains in boats under forty-five feet now than there were in the early 1960s. The reason is simple. Many more people have been able to sell their homes at highly inflated values so they have the money to fulfill their desire to go cruising. By the time Susan and Richard had been looking for six months, they were tired of living in a camper and anxious to be afloat before the best sailing months of the year came and went. So when they finally found a boat that looked safe, clean, and reasonably priced, they gave up their search for a bargain.

Then the real problems of buying a boat in a foreign country became apparent. There are no yacht surveyors in Spain. Though Richard is an experienced sailor, his inspection of the English Rival 32, home finished, fiberglass sloop failed to show up some of its basic mechanical problems. The owner allowed Richard to have the boat hauled out for his inspection. A surveyor would have caught these problems while the boat was out of the water, then made some arrangement to have the owner either correct them or adjust the sale price so that the repairs could have been done right then.

One of the more frustrating problems Richard encountered was the transfer of funds. Because the owners wanted their payment in English pounds and Richard's money was in Canadian dollars, the Spanish bank made some real foul ups. Then there was the problem of deposits. With no broker or bank manager to arrange an escrow period and formal contract, there were hard feelings between both buyer and seller long after the boat changed hands.

When it came time to start outfitting the boat, Richard found he desperately missed the tools that would have been too heavy to bring from Canada. He missed a workshop of some kind and the gems of knowledge from old friends and craftsmen he could trust. Every small job he needed done by local craftsmen became a tangle of translation problems—complete with drawings and a dozen trips back and forth when a misunderstanding occurred. In spite of the friendship of local Spanish sailors and a half dozen foreign cruising sailors, Richard found information on sources for supplies difficult to get. That is the biggest difficulty when buying a boat in a foreign port, very few of which have marine stores such as you find in major yachting centers in the United States and England. People who outfit a boat anywhere in the Far East try to sail to either Hong Kong or Singapore because they are the only places where supplies are available. In the Med, most people do what Richard finally chose to do. He made a shopping list that included everything from stainless steel screws to charts to spinnaker pole fittings and a windvane. Then he flew to London and stayed with a friend while he spent three weeks shopping.

When he came back both he and Susan were anxious to get cruising. They were tired of the hassles associated with getting their small floating universe and all of its basic systems cruiseworthy. They were worried that we were impatient at being kept waiting in Andraitx, and, besides, April was at hand with wonderful spring weather and fresh breezes. So they set off to join us with a five-page list of unfinished items—from a half-built ice chest to a stern bearing and packing gland which had shaken loose.

Richard and Susan's foreign boat buying experience is pretty typical from what we have seen. The only real bargains we hear of now are found by people who are crewing on other peoples' boats and can hear the local gossip firsthand while they live almost free from the expenses of room, board, and transportation. They sometimes find a boat that is badly run down or damaged—even to the extent of being holed or dismasted. Then by using imagination and by working hard, they end up with a bargain. Other people who are planning a long holiday in a foreign country do sometimes end up with bargains just by including tours of the local yachting scene. Even if they do not find any boat that interests them, they end up with interesting new friends and experiences, since people sitting on their boats on a nice sunny day are far more likely to open a conversation with passers-by than people sitting in a hotel lobby.

As a general rule, the people who are most successful at searching for, buying, and enjoying outfitting a boat in a foreign country are couples who share the same desire to go adventuring. If one partner really enjoys overcoming a dozen small obstacles daily and excells at organizing details, while the other partner has some basic woodworking, rigging, and mechanical skill, you might end up with a bargain and a good time besides.

We spent the first week of our cruise with Richard and Susan in Cala Pastilla, just southeast of Palma. This private harbor nestles right in the center of some of Mallorca's finest beaches. Lovely outdoor cafés line the sidewalks just one block from the harbor. Street vendors sell everything from fresh watermelon slices to pin-stripped shoelaces.

Richard had planned this stop to haul *Taganita* and repair his badly thumping stern bearing. Since a bus ran directly into Palma from the corner of the harbor, Susan and I rode into the city each day with a new shopping list while the men pulled *Taganita*'s engine and shaft. In the evenings while we waited for a machine shop to extend the torque tube which had been installed improperly by its original owner-finisher, we enjoyed the nightlife of Palma. But we all felt as if we had been let free when Larry and Richard re-launched *Taganita* with a now clean bill of health and we sailed away from the bright lights, evening strollers, and mooring lines of the marina.

Impromptu races developed between each anchorage we visited. The early spring weather was delightful—warm sunny days with enough breeze to make each days sail successful. The anchorages at Isla Cabrera and along the southeast coast of Mallorca were almost deserted since the normal cruising season didn't start until June. The Mediterranean waters were too cold for swimming, evenings were chilly enough so that the four of us planned dinners together below decks. The late ride home to our own boats were starlit and crisp enough so the cozy double sleeping bags felt especially welcoming.

When we reached Cala Petro, a lovely tree-lined bay with a small village on one shore, we decided to stop for a few days while Richard and Susan located the money that their bank had supposedly wired to them from Canada over two weeks before. Classic signs of impending bad weather appeared in the sky our second morning there. Long thin streaks of cirrus reached from west to east. By evening when we rowed ashore for a hot shower at the small local hotel, the sky was covered with clouds and the sun was only a dreary yellow patch in the west. The next morning rain began to fall. A cold front moved in with fresh

The breaking surge coming into Cala Petro.

gusty winds which drove the rain away. Larry rigged *Rinky Dink* so we could all take turns rushing back and forth across the bay.

By morning northeasterly gale force winds were blowing. For some reason the shape of the island and the points at the entrance to Cala Petro deflected each breaking sea into the almost land-locked harbor, where it became a rolling surge. Each hour our anchorage became less comfortable. Both boats lurched and rolled until life on board became unbearable.

The day before, Larry and I had sailed *Rinky Dink* into the tiny unfinished inner harbor being built for fishermen right in the middle of the village. Now when we looked across the rolling, surging mile-wide bay to the perfectly smooth water inside that seventy- by one hundred-foot stone cove, we decided to move—even though the entrance was only one inch deeper than our draft.

Taganita powered slowly in just ahead of us and ran aground. We tacked over and reached back and forth with our staysail and double-reefed main while Richard backed down and then got across the bar ten feet to starboard. We followed him in, headed into the gale force wind, and came alongside the unfinished stone breakwater, which still had pieces of steel reinforcing bar sticking out like daggers every four feet. There was just enough room for the two boats to lie alongside the more finished part of the breakwater. Below us there was ten feet of water. We felt wonderfully safe and comfortable once our lines were secured and fenders tied in place. I remember feeling quite smug as Larry and I stood on the breakwater head watching the bay fill with ever larger waves until it looked like a bathtub stirred by a mischievous child. Then Susan and I—each bundled in two sweaters plus a sailing jacket—set off to explore the wind-whipped village, while Larry greased *Seraffyn*'s turnbuckles and Richard cursed *Taganita*'s outboard motor.

The sight that met us when we walked down the main street of the friendly, sleepy town two hours later sent me running full speed. For some reason even the tiny inner harbor with its fifty-foot-wide entrance was filling with surge. Larry and Richard were scrambling around tying anchor rodes and mooring lines right across the one hundred-foot-wide harbor, trying to keep our boats from grinding against those rough stone walls. Thank God we carry a three-hundred-foot-long spare anchor rode, a two-hundred-foot warp, plus four hundred feet of assorted mooring lines. We used every one to position

The tiny new port at Cala Petro.

Seraffyn and *Taganita* five feet away from the walls.

Life on board the next two nights was not comfortable. Lines squeaked and groaned. Chaffing guards both ashore and on board had to be checked every four hours. Getting ashore meant loosening off a spring line, pulling the boat closer, and then timing your jump so you missed any surges that swept a foot over the top of the stone pier. Spray broke right over the ten-foot-high outer wall and pelted our decks at high tide. Glasses could not be left unattended or they would fall over, cooking called for searails. But both boats rode safely while the gale roared for thirty-six hours. For twenty-four hours after that the surge continued, so we left *Seraffyn* bucking about on her tethers and walked along the shores of the bay to explore a deserted Club Mediterranee site and watch the waves breaking forty feet high at the rocky points.

Spring returned bright and calm the next day. It took us two hours to sort out mooring lines before we set sail. Outside the bay a still lumpy sea made for slow progress on a warm southerly breeze. Then an early afternoon squall sent us roaring past *Taganite,* much to our delight. Even though *Taganita* was eight feet longer than *Seraffyn,* our huge spread of canvas got us moving at six knots as soon as the wind reached twelve.

After two days in Puerto Colom we said good-bye to Richard and Susan. They were planning to leave their boat in the care of a small local yacht club while they flew to Italy for a three-week reunion with Richard's family. We were bound farther east; our next stop would be the least populated, least advertised island in the Balearics: Minorca. We all agreed to try and rendezvous again either in Puerto Mahón, which we had chosen as a mail drop, or in November in Malta.

As we reached clear of the narrow entrance to Porto Colom, Larry and I waved until the point cut off our view. Then we settled into the rhythm of a reaching sea and started discussing the pros and cons of cruising in company. We had enjoyed having friends along who thought the same North American thoughts we did. It was great knowing you were really communicating when discussions turned deeper than "Isn't this pretty, tasty, helpful?" Because we had been able to pool our resources and ideas, we did more on shore in the way of exploring of archeological sites and museums than we would have alone. We rented cars together and splurged on dinners out. Richard had been able to rebuild *Taganita* more easily because of the extra tools and supplies we had on board *Seraffyn*. His different experiences as an architect had shown us some new ways of solving old problems. On rainy days the extra company on board made life less dreary as discussions and card games were expanded to include four people. In addition Richard felt that my experience and enjoyment of cruising had made Susan feel less nervous about the adventure, which had been new for her.

But all of this had to be balanced against some definite disadvantages. Every decision any of us made had to include the plans of four people. Instead of choosing the next port just by whim once we were actually out sailing, cruising in company meant we had to decide before we left in case we got separated. The difference in boat speed presented other problems. Since we had no engine, we were occasionally delayed when the winds were light and we had to wait for a shore breeze to fill in; Richard and Susan would then worry about us. Similarly, when they did not catch up with us soon after we left a port, we would sail back to check and see if their anchor had fouled or engine failed. This concern for the other boat has led some cruising people into compromising their own safety just to keep up with their companion boat. When one sailor decides to take a risky shortcut, such as behind a reef at night or across a poorly charted shoal area, his companion boat's skipper is under the pressure of appearing to be either a poor sport or a chicken if he decides to take the longer, more prudent route.

Differences in income or savings create problems for some families who cruise in company. I know of one sailor who spent two years cruising funds in less than seven months because he never wanted to say he couldn't afford the meals out that his friends could afford. I know we found ourselves treating Richard and Susan when we felt like eating out at times when they did not.

Boat problems become joint problems as do personal problems. I know that when I got a skin allergy Richard felt he had to help find a doctor. Similarly, when Richard and Susan's bank lost their money we felt we had to help locate it. This also goes for any marital problems which might exist on either boat. We have heard of couples who broke up their own relationship by trying to help the couple on the boat that was in company with them.

Far more likely than this, cruising in company—especially by people new to voyaging on a small boat—keeps individual couples and families from forging the strong, wonderfully interdependant relationship that grows out of normal cruising situations. When two couples are together most of each day, the men turn to each other for decisions on mechanical matters, and the women end up going shopping or doing the laundry together. Discussions in the evening split up into women's or men's things. Instead of teaching your wife to be your back-up when you repair the engine, you ask your male cruising companion; your wife or crew does not get the chance to learn about machinery or repairs. Your wife does not ask you to come along on a search for some fabrics or parts for the boat, so you miss out on a day in town which might have made you more aware of the local customs and culture.

But the main reason we have tried to avoid cruising in company for more than a few weeks at a time is that two boats arriving in the harbor together and four people going ashore as a group present a self-sufficient appearance that keeps outsiders from feeling necessary. Because you appear to have most of the entertainment you need, you miss out on what we consider the main reason to cruise off to a new country—the chance to meet and get to know local people who can share their lives and ideas with you. People who cruise in company get to know fewer cruising people, since fellow sailors are less likely to yell hello to four laughing, chattering people headed ashore in a dinghy than they are to two. I know we would be less likely to invite four people over for lunch than we would a couple. In the month we cruised with Susan and Richard our evenings and days were so full that we did not meet one outsider beyond the local merchants, and even there we didn't spend any time chatting once our purchases were made.

Meeting favorite cruising friends at a selected rendezvous and then spending a week catching up on the past months adventures is one of the delights of cruising. A tentative statement such as "I plan to haul in Malta this November" or "I'll be cruising the Greek Islands in April" is all you need to insure exciting reunions. And just the general flow and wind patterns will almost always insure that the longer your cruise, the more often you will wander into ports where one or another of your favorite cruising friends just happens to be. The well worn cliché "It's a small world" is absolutely true for cruising sailors.

CHAPTER 12

~~~~~

Caves and Bank Robbers

Our trusty barometer indicated unsettled weather. Soft, thin clouds confirmed its report. Though it was sunny and warm as we cleared Mallorca and headed east toward Minorca, gray clouds covered the sky within an hour. We needed sweatshirts and jeans to be comfortable on deck. But what a sail! A southwest wind filled our small genoa and full mainsail as we ran wing and wing over an amazingly smooth sea at six knots. Occasional gusts sent our taffrail long spinner turning at up to seven knots. Since there were now thick clouds which blocked the sun, we spent a lovely day on deck. Coffee cups nestled behind jib sheet cleats never spilled a drop, midafternoon snacks stayed on the plate, and Minorca grew from a shadow to a reality at an amazing clip.

We made lists part of the afternoon: boat-maintenance lists, photos-to-take lists, people-to-write lists. But mostly we lay back and reveled in one of the most beautiful days of sailing we had had since we entered the Mediterranean. Just before I was ready to serve dinner we reached the far eastern corner of the island. The wind had been swinging to the south for about an hour, and we had readjusted steady old Helmer three times already. Now a simple jibe brought us right on course, running wing and wing again after changing eighty-five degrees from our afternoon course.

For the next hour Larry and I discussed the pros and cons of changing our spinnaker pole handling arrangements. Because of her long bowsprit, *Seraffyn*'s J measurement (the distance from the front of the mast to the headstay) is sixteen feet. Therefore, the most efficient length of spinnaker pole, or whisker pole, for both cruising and racing efficiency is sixteen feet. This is a long pole for one person to handle alone on the rolling foredeck of a twenty-four-foot boat. Larry could usually manage to set or take the pole down by himself. But the only time I could handle it alone was on days of a very light wind and calm sea. Otherwise the varnish work, my toes, and the mast were in jeopardy from my clumsiness and lack of strength when that sixteen-foot spear with bronze end fittings came free of its mast front ring.

In England we saw a wonderful pole arrangement on Dan Bowen's cruising sloop *Romadi*. His pole worked on a slider controlled by a sort of endless clothesline with a topping lift so the pole never had both ends loose at one time. All we needed to buy to convert our pole to a similar arrangement were nine feet of bronze track plus some bronze screws. So out came our shopping list.

The well-lit mouth of Puerto Mahon started opening to port. We got the pole down while *Seraffyn* rushed through the water as if she were trying to race the quickly failing light. By now the wind was due out of the south. In the smooth water of the three-mile-long bay, light gusts of wind sent us scurrying along at top speed on a beam reach. Larry steered as I took the oil lamps below and lit them. When I came on deck, soft shore sounds added to the lovely rustle of water against our bow. Each navigation light in the island-cluttered bay came clear right on cue. Cows mooed, a small fishboat putted out to sea, a singing voice carried across the water. The dim lights of the small city of Mahon glowed off the bottoms of fluffy, wet-looking low clouds, and exactly ten hours and sixty-two miles from where we had lifted our anchor in Puerto Colom, we let it fall again—into sixty feet of water just in front of the deserted little yacht club on the towns edge.

Just as we finished putting the cover on the mainsail, a spattering of rain came down. We laughed as the same words came from both of us. "*Seraffyn* was trying to beat the rain."

The island of Minorca was captured by the British in 1708. At that time Spain was only a loose confederation of warring states. This low, hilly, and arid rock of an island is over 150 miles away from Barcelona —the nearest port on mainland Spain. So the British had little interference as they turned Minorca's only deep-water and fully protected bay into the headquarters for their Mediterranean fleet. For a hundred years Minorca's exquisite three-mile-long maze of coves and islands was improved and adapted to the needs of massive sailing ships. Water catchments were built along its shores and on the roofs of each house to supplement the extremely meager supply of underground water. Admiral Horatio Nelson lived here while he organized his fleet for the Mediterranean campaigns that culminated in the fateful battle of the Nile. Lady Hamilton borrowed a friend's home on the northern shore of the bay so she could be with Nelson. But by 1802 when France and her growing expansionism threatened England's home shores, a more strongly united Spain offered friendship to the British people in exchange for Minorca. The island's wild splurge of importance was over and it soon reverted to being a pleasant but almost ignored Spanish outpost.

We sailed into Puerto Mahon and found Minorca to be a cruising sailor's dream. History was everywhere apparent—from stone warping bollards, scarred by huge hemp lines and cast-metal rings sunk into boulders on the shore, to old stone quays and handsome brick island armories, which stood as silent reminders of the days when ponderous sailing warships came here for provisions and repairs. English-style homes with elaborate fluted chimney pots were alongside white-washed Spanish homes with their decorations of wrought iron. A few English descendants of sailors who had fallen in love with this change-able climate and quiet atmosphere still lived along the shores. But only a few tourists came to visit this outpost of Mediterranean Spain. Although there were over a dozen lovely ports to gunkhole in and out of, there were almost no beaches. The only way to reach the island was by ferry from Barcelona or Mallorca. So package tours did not exist, and the few foreigners who did come to spend the summer tended to come back year after year to rent some local family's back room or stay in the small inns which offered bed and breakfast.

The lovely clean town perched along steep stone streets on half a dozen hills. The foot of each street ended at the stone quay that wound around the edge of the upper end of Puerto Mahon's undulating bay. Small grocery stores and a well-stocked farmers market plus the friendly attitude of each person we met, made us decide to provision *Seraffyn* right to the brim.

We have found it really adds to our cruising life if we keep the boat stocked with long-lasting vegetables and dry and canned food—just as if we were planning an offshore passage. Even when our immediate plans are for gunkholing, this two- or three-month supply leaves us free to change our plans: to hole up in some hidden spot miles from the nearest town for two or three weeks or to create an unexpected company dinner for eight or ten without a rush to the market. So for our first few days in Puerto Mahon, both Larry and I left the boat early each morning with page-long lists, found a rendezvous café, then went our separate ways to hunt down everything from fifty rolls of film to forty liters of wine, from eight dozen eggs to ten canned hams. Then we rendezvoused for our taxi trek back to the boat. Later events confirmed our faith in this "keep her well stocked" axiom.

While we were loading our mornings purchases directly into patient *Rinky Dink* from the taxi that had brought us from the upper part of town one day, a handsome Spanish-looking couple began asking us questions about our boat and life aboard. Marja was Minorcan born; her husband, Tim, a transplanted Englishman. Since they could see our fifty-pound block of ice slowly melting in spite of the cloudy weather, Marja suggested, "Don't stop now, meet us back here at eight o'clock. We will take you to a very special cave." This chance meeting led to some of the finest evenings we have ever spent.

As we rode away from Mahon in the rickety car with Marja and Tim, lights started winking on—some electric, some oil, some candles. The houses gradually pulled back from the streets then thinned quickly until the winding, dipping road ran through brush-covered rocky fields. Six or seven miles later we turned back toward the shores of the main bay and entered a small fishing village clustered on the cliffs around a three-hundred-foot-wide cul-de-sac. From the edge of the cliffs we could see the lights of Mahon—and *Seraffyn*'s anchor light about a mile to the right. To the left, the main navigation beacon flashed two miles away.

We climbed down one hundred worn stone steps set into two-hundred-year-old walls. At the bottom of the cliff under white-washed homes, a stone quay wound completely around the little bay. Small wooden fishing boats rode on long mooring lines strung from bollards right across the bay. (A later check of our chart showed two hundred feet of water in the center of this tiny cove.) Caves had been carved into the foot of the cliffs. As we walked along the quiet shores toward the open water we could see fishermen's supplies and un-used boats stored in each opening. The last cave we saw was completely different. Light poured from the makeshift door, guitar music spurted out to mix with the murmur of water lapping the old stones and gently surging boats. We walked into a handhewn ten-foot-high, twenty-foot-wide, one-hundred-foot long, domed cavern. A tiny bar took up most of the entrance, two waiters shoved their way past burly fishermen with trays held high above their heads. Just past the bar thirty or forty tiny tables and wooden handmade chairs filled the rest of the space except for a five-foot-by-five-foot spotlit area in the farthest corner. In spite of the crowd, complete silence reigned while a single guitarist pulled tears from his battered instrument and sang of the death of his childhood sweetheart.

During the enthusiastic applause that followed, Tim spotted a friend seated only two tables from the singer, then pulled us through the maze of feet, tables, and rushing waiters. Somehow room was cleared for the four of us. The evening flew past as bar regulars joined the blue-eyed, curly dark-haired guitarist, who owned the café. Sometimes four would play their instruments while five or six deep mellow voices joined in, other times two fishermen with well-matched but not always true baritone voices sang arias from Puccini operas. Late in the evening, the low solid stone ceiling amplified the sound of a seventy-year-old, grizzled carpenter whose flamenco songs seemed almost too large for his age-darkened guitar.

As we prepared to leave Tim called one request. Almost half the audience of roustabouts, fishermen, and net and boat builders joined in to sing "Minorca, Isla del Amor." During the long climb up those steep quiet stone steps, its strains rang out and Minorca did seem like an island of love.

We returned to that unnamed cave several times. But when we did, we rowed down the still bay in *Rinky Dink*. One very special evening when two old cruising friends arrived and anchored nearby, the four of us found a front row table by arriving early. Halfway through the particularly boisterous evening our favorite old flamenco guitarist claimed his complimentary drink and came to the tiny spotlit corner. His slow mournful music soon gave way to the infectious rhythm of a sensual fandango. Dozens of hands clapped out the intricate themes. Across the tiny open space two men sat with their arms tightly around each other's waists. An argument seemed to be going on between them. Then the heavy-set one nodded his head. His slim, carefully groomed partner jumped into the open space. He posed for a second on the balls of his feet, eyes closed, while his snapping fingers slowly adjusted to the guitarist's beat. Then black, snuggly fitted trousers flashed while the green-sweatered torso became a graceful weaving invitation to dance. From the first, calls from the audience goaded him on. My whole body ached to be up there with him, and somehow Larry sensed my desire. "Go on," he whispered. "Dance for us, don't be shy."

My momentary shyness and my doubts about the tiny dance floor and strange partner fled before that wild rhythm. Memories of late-night Spanish movies and the touring dance groups my mother had taken me to see came rushing through my mind. I knew nothing about flamenco dancing or in fact any dancing, but the lovely calling, weaving strains wrung from the guitar by that old carpenter taught my feet as the time whispered past. The audience called and clapped. The two of us filled the tiny open space yet never seemed to leave our self-made trance. Over and over the guitarist played his haunting melody and cried his flamenco love words.

When the music stopped I realized how breathless I was. My partner threw his arms around me, pulled me close, kissed my forehead, and yelled over the clamorous crowd, "Oh, I wish you were a man."

Larry hugged me tightly when I fell into the seat next to him. Then he proudly accepted the two complimentary glasses of wine the club manager rushed to our cozy table.

Our British cruising guide packet had one especially intriguing chart. Where our regular navigation chart showed a long narrow swamp piercing the northern shore of Minorca, Bobby Somerset, a long-time Mediterranean cruising sailor, had drawn a detailed sketch of a deep-water lagoon with a maze of shoals at its mouth, high hills on each side, and no town or city nearby. We ran fifteen miles from Puerto Mahon until a chain of three rocky islets opened into a gulf with five white-washed fishermen's houses and a tiny pier. We lay in on the chartlet's recommended course of 180 degrees toward a water tank on a hill. One hundred feet to port breaking waves smashed against a reef that was just barely submerged. To starboard, shoal patches showed dark green in the early afternoon sun. Eight or ten knots of easterly wind slowly drew forward as the houses grew larger. When we were able to put the center house dead on our stern on a course of 167 degrees, we tightened our sheets and heeled sharply to the gusts of wind which were sneaking around the outer islands. I stood on the foredeck, chartlet in hand, eyes shaded as rough-looking rocks glared at us fifty feet away on each side. When the inner islet and a small point were exactly in line, we eased our sheets to run down a shoal-lined channel past two more houses. Then steep hills surrounded us on both sides. Trees and bushes grew right to the edge of the water, the sea and every sign of civilization were cut off from view as we skirted a steep small island and glided into a fully enclosed, enchanted mile-long lagoon. A whisper of wind found its way over the hills, and the sound of bird calls and cicadas carried from the shores. Small shoals of minnows scattered before our bow wave. We anchored in fifteen feet of clear, cool water and spent a busy week of solitude in Puerto Addaya.

One afternoon we rowed to the small point indicated on our chartlet. There we found the promised footpath. We followed its curves and bends till we reached a white-washed ancient farmhouse. Cows called from the barn, which had concrete walls and a thatched roofed. Fifty chickens and three children ran to announce our arrival. Three lazy dogs barked while they walked up to have their heads touseled. The farmer's wife immediately invited us in. Her Spanish seemed heavily accented to us, but still we were able to communicate. (We later learned many Minorcans speak an old style of Spanish tinged with French and Arabic.) She made us sit down for a snack of thick coffee and sweet cakes while she ran to get her husband. The ten-pound pure white rounds of cheese our chartlet had promised lined the kitchen shelves.

We spent the whole afternoon there, admiring huge breeding bulls and watching another thirty cheeses pressed into shape. Our hosts took us to the edge of their stone patio, and through the trees we could see *Seraffyn* riding calmly five hundred feet below.

When we finally strolled down the well-worn path, we carried a round of fresh cheese we had bought plus a jar of tart apricot jam the farmer's wife had presented to us as a gift. "Spread that on slices of my cheese, that's the Minorcan way." We tried it as soon as we were home. The dry, slightly salty cheese did blend wonderfully with the flavor of her homemade jam.

When we finally sailed from Puerto Addaya we had finished a bit of varnish work on deck, done a bit of letter writing, and lazed most of the days away. *Seraffyn* glowed from bow to stern, but *Rinky Dink*, who trailed docilely behind, was scarred and weathered from being dragged over dock edges and up rocky beaches.

Our chart showed that a large bay with a stone breakwater at a small village called Fornelles would be just twelve miles farther west. With luck we could tie to the pier and give our eleven-year-old fiberglass dinghy some tender loving care.

Fornelles was one more delightful surprise. The village on shore was quiet and totally Minorcan. Stone streets, red tiled roofs, a small café, a butcher shop, one small grocery, and a restaurant made up the whole main street. A large breakwater stuck straight out from the shore to break the surge that could come into the wide mouth of the bay during northerly blows. Behind the breakwater, fifty small, shoal-draft fishboats filled most of the basin. Only the last sixty feet of the outer quay had water deep enough for *Seraffyn*. But we were the only yacht or deep-draft vessel in all of Fornelles. We set our large anchor off our stern and tied our bow lines so our bowsprit just cleared the stones. We moor this way when we tie Mediterranean-style so we can have some privacy below decks. With our stern to the quay any stroller can see right through the companionway and into the whole interior of the boat.

All afternoon the wide walkway on our end of the quay stayed quiet. Not a soul came to say a thing, not one official strolled out along the long sea wall. But as evening drew on with its lovely shading light, strollers from the village livened the streets, and fishermen came out to sit on the quay and mend their nets. When one barrel-chested fifty-year-old man in a badly abused Greek seaman's hat stopped by *Seraffyn* and said, *"Buenas tardes,"* we asked if he thought our dinghy would be in the way while we sanded and painted it on the quay next to our bowsprit. "Of course not," he replied, then he called to a strong-looking housewife who was sitting on the sea wall a few yards away and confirmed his answer. By the next evening we were just one more part of the village.

Enrico came to admire our work each evening. When it was well along, he said, "If you need fresh water, bring your jugs to my house." The same lady was close enough to hear him. "No! Bring your jugs to my house," Elena shouted. "My cistern has sweeter water." Enrico yelled back, "I just refinished my cistern. They should drink my water." The two of them got into a shouting match which only ended when we brought a bottle of local wine into the cockpit to share. The next morning Enrico came sneaking down the long quay just after we woke up. "Bring your jugs, I've got a wheelbarrow to help," he said. So we surreptitiously topped our tanks with sweet rain water. The wheelbarrow was really welcome because Enrico's house was five streets away, and he insisted we top up—which took four trips with two five-gallon jugs. That evening when Elena came by to admire a glowing white-and-teak *Rinky Dink,* she did not say a word about water, but she also did not say a word to Enrico.

Larry was resetting our stern anchor the next day because of storm clouds which traced across the sky as forerunners of a summer mistral wind. Our five-eighths-inch mooring line lay right across the main entrance to the boatbasin as he rowed the dinghy hard to pull the anchor farther out while I worked on deck paying out the anchor rode. I caught a startling glimpse of two masts rushing past the breakwater. A glorious fifty-foot, freshly painted yawl came speeding around the corner—its diesel roaring, its mizzen sail still set. It turned into the harbor at close to five knots. The startled skipper just missed Larry and the dinghy. Then he headed right across our anchor rode. Larry tossed the anchor over the dinghy's stern, and it quickly pulled the rode to safety. Then Larry started shouting, "Slow down, there's no water in there!" The flustered helmsman throttled back, but the boat was out of control and wind shoved against the strapped-in mizzen. She smacked broadside into the two fishboats, then the engine stalled. Another man came on deck and together they got the glamorous yacht alongside two fishing boats next to *Seraffyn.* Larry rowed over and suggested they set a bow anchor to hold them away from the rocks, since the fishboats they had tied to were on very small anchors.

The skipper walked forward, unclutched the anchor winch, and dropped his anchor right off the bow. Then he rudely told Larry, "We don't need any help."

Larry and I finished resetting our stern anchor. Then I walked over to look at the yawl while Larry scrubbed bottom mud out of the dinghy. The skipper answered my questions in broken English. "We've just come from a voyage down the Dutch canals," he told me.

When I went back to *Seraffyn* I said, "That yacht's been stolen." "What makes you think so?" Larry asked. "There's no name on it, no flag, there are dinghy chocks but no dinghy, spinnaker pole chocks but no poles." I ticked off each item in my mind. "The burgee they are flying is from a French yacht club, and with that kind of handling they'd never have made it this far without scratching the boat."

"There's your chance," Larry told me, pointing toward a uniformed man coming along the quay. We both went ashore and met him next to *Seraffyn*'s bow. "I'm the port captain," he told us. "Enrico said that boat almost hit you." I used my most careful Spanish to describe why I thought the yawl was stolen. The port captain called to the man on deck, "I want you to fill in this entry form." Five minutes later the port captain was back to whisper, "I've called the guardia, those two didn't even know what their registration numbers were."

Ten minutes later sirens filled the air. Four cars full of police, customs officials, and the high-powered Guardia Civil rushed down the small main street to the end of the breakwater. They all climbed on the yawl. The two men were soon led off in handcuffs while a massive search began on board. Just as the first car left with the befuddled pseudo-sailors, the local policeman came roaring into town on his motorcycle. His eyes immediately turned to the crowds and cars on the sea wall. The departing squad car startled him, he lost control of his motorcycle, and his sidecar hit the one tree in the small open space at the harbor's inner end. An ambulance soon added its siren to the excitement that had almost everyone of the town's two hundred inhabitants crowding the harbor walls. The sorry, broken-legged policeman was carried of on a stretcher amid the cheering words of his friends and family.

Two hours later all was quiet, and the only sign of the excitement was a uniformed guard toting a submachine gun and sitting in the yawl's cockpit. Enrico came rushing down the next morning. "I just heard it on the radio. They robbed a bank in France. Then they stole this boat from a shipyard in Marseilles. It belongs to the president of the university there. They got in a storm and got lost. Remember when they asked Elena where they were and when she told them Fornelles they asked what country? Well, they thought this was Sardinia."

Enrico was thrilled with this break in the quiet life of Fornelles, "First you come to visit. Then a bank robber comes!" he told us.

The next morning seventeen Spanish naval ratings and officers piled out of two buses and trooped down the quay while we were eating lunch in *Seraffyn*'s cockpit. We both winced as seventeen pairs of black polished, hardsoled shoes leaped five feet onto the yawl's exquisitely scrubbed teak decks. A fat, red-faced gaudily uniformed man with enough gold braid on his shoulders and cap to make him an admiral, began shouting orders. Sailors rushed to cast off mooring lines and haul in the bow anchor that Larry had convinced the bank robbers to let him set just before the police came the first day. The naval ratings had almost 150 feet of heavy chain to pull on deck while the "admiral" stood in the small helmsman's cockpit shouting orders.

When the anchor actually broke loose, he finally ordered the helmsman to start the engine and give her full throttle forward. The rest of his shouted orders were lost to us because of the roar of the diesel engine. Nothing happened. The yawl barely inched forward.

Larry shouted, *"Transmisión hidráulico!"* but no one heard him over the motor sounds and shouted confusion. He turned to me shaking his head, "Until the transmission has time to build up pressure, the prop will barely turn. They should have let the engine idle before they lifted their hook."

Just as Larry finished these words, the yawl shot forward with a jerk. The "admiral" staggered back a step. The edge of the cockpit caught him right behind the knees. He fell over backwards. His gold-covered hat rolled toward the stern. Sixteen spanish sailors struggled to keep straight faces as they steamed toward the Mediterranean. But Enrico and Elena were on the breakwater laughing delightedly. Then Enrico called, "First you, then the bank robbers, then the navy!"

To this day we wonder about being compared to bank robbers by an old fisherman who was reputed to be retired on the proceeds of his smuggling efforts. But our photo of Enrico, the man people in Fornelles called *Lobo del Mar* (Wolf of the Sea), reminds us of a month of fine days on the smallest Balearic Island, Minorca—the island of love.

Enrico, the man locals called Lobo Del Mar.

CHAPTER 13

~~~~~

Not Far from the Crowd

Mistral clouds laced the sky as we set sail from Minorca. These high-level mare's tails are the usual forerunners of fierce northerly winds which blow across France and blast the western Mediterranean through the Gulf of Marseilles. Cruising friends who have sailed through the French canals tell us of three-week sieges of fifty-knot chilling winds when the mistral blows. But by the time these spring and summer gales reached the center of the Mediterranean, most of their fury is spent. On the other hand, the sea they kick up travels fast and takes days to disappear, so our log of the voyage from Fornelles east to Sardinia is a three-day saga of rough seas but only moderate-to-fresh winds.

Seraffyn was still well stocked from our shopping spree in Mahon. We only needed some fresh meat, tomatoes, and lettuce from the tiny shop in Fornelles—plus a block of ice from the fish storage plant—to complete our supplies. As soon as we cleared the land Larry insisted on getting out his optimist line, a fishing setup consisting of lures, weights, and a one-hundred-pound test line led to a shockcord which was supposed to set off an equally haywire alarm: a tin can with half a dozen nuts and bolts inside. We had dragged this same line for over a year of sailing with absolutely no success. It had once tangled with the taffrail long spinner to create a mess that took most of an afternoon to untangle. Larry bought new lures in every port, talked to local fishermen, and added different weights. Still no fish. I was not too disappointed. The idea of leaping, scaly, slimy fish spreading their blood and guts across the scrubbed teak decks and cockpit did not interest me at all.

Our second night at sea we were running wing and wing at close to five knots. The sea was still lumpy, and that line trailed aft bouncing and submerging. I was on watch, all was going well. I sat in the cockpit reading a good book by the light of our kerosene anchor lamp cum stern light. Every few pages I would get up and check the horizon for ships and the sails for their set and then returned to my comfortable cushion-padded spot. A particularly snappy wave jiggled the bolts inside Larry's fish alarm. The proverbial light flashed on in my mind. I tied a light line to the shock cord, quietly led it forward, then sat down against a sailbag as if I had been there a long time. Giggling all the while, I jerked the line and kept pulling it. That tin can jumped and danced, setting off a cacophony of sound that brought a shout of joy from Larry. "Fish, finally caught a fish!" he yelled. Then I heard him hit the overhead, curse a stubbed toe, and scrambled out of the bunk halfway into the cockpit before he got free of his sleeping bag. My uncontrollable giggling gave the whole game away. Larry gave me a disgusted look, retreated below, and started climbing back into the bunk mumbling all the time. "Your watch in five minutes," I called as I came back to the cockpit. "Serves you right for that mud in Puerto Andraitx!"

I brewed up a cup of hot chocolate for both of us before getting ready for my three hours in the bunk. By the time I was comfortable in the bag, Larry stopped grumbling, kissed me, and then hooked up the lee cloth. As I started to doze off, I heard him out in the cockpit lockers mumbling through his fishing lure collection in search of another possible combination to end our fishless existence.

Although the Mediterranean is a favorite cruising area for people from all of Europe plus a growing number of North Americans and Australians, we were surprised to find many areas where we were either the only cruising sailors that year or one of only two or three. It seems that most cruising people stick to well-traveled routes chosen by reading other sailors' books and guides or by planning to avoid overnight passages. Though harbors on the south coast of mainland Spain and France are full of yachts, we found wonderful hidden coves and harbors along the southern shores of Sardinia and around Sicily. We found crowded harbors at the well-publicised ports of Malta, Rhodes, and Corfu, yet almost no cruising boats at all in the outer islands or Adriatic. So during our two years in the Mediterranean it was easy to enjoy a variety of situations: quiet coves where local people eagerly invited us into their lives; yacht clubs now and then in big cities; and week-long rendezvousing with cruising sailors whenever we wanted to exchange tales.

We chose our route along the southern shore of Sardinia to rendezvous with Richard and Susan. When we beat up the coast of Isla San Pietro into the huge harbor at Carloforte, which is only a small fishing village, we were delighted to see not only *Taganita* but also three other cruising boats owned by people we had met in Mallorca. Our arrival turned into an evening full of boat hopping and catching up.

The Shotts were real favorites of ours. Sue and Mike had sold their small home in an English village and fullfilled a life-long dream by buying a thirty-six-foot Hillyard Ketch then leaving for the French canals with their two sons—Jasper, fourteen, and Lucas, aged ten. The boys loved their cruising life, and now an aura of sadness hung over the party because the Shotts had reached the point of no return as far as their funds went and were turning homeward. We corresponded with them as they sailed north through the Canal Midi back to England, where they sold their beloved *Ashnai*, bought an old farmhouse, and settled down to save up for yet another cruise someday. One touching letter from Jasper arrived a year later, "No one here is interested in my sailing adventure," the wistful youngster wrote. "All they want to talk about is the drought and the soccer games." We laughed at the time, but through the years as we met other people who had returned to normal community existences after a year or two of freedom, we learned of their disappointment when shore-bound friends asked one or two perfunctory questions and then ignored what had been the adventure of a lifetime. We came to call this frustration, which is part of the life of many returning voyagers, the "Jasper Shotts complex."

Richard speaks Italian, but even so when he powered by on *Taganita* one morning and yelled, "Come on, they've got two hundred tuna trapped in a net outside. The fish weigh five hundred pounds a piece." We figured some fisherman was putting Richard on. The whole cruising crowd was on board *Taganita*, so we grabbed our cameras and joined them for a pleasant ride out of the harbor and north along the coastline into the mouth of the wide channel that separates San Pietro from Sardinia.

Two miles north of the island a mass of buoys and net floats pointed toward the open sea. Local fishboats were busy ferrying every able-bodied man in town to four huge wooden barges which formed an open square at the far end of the nets. (We later learned that young men return from school early each year to earn money by joining the *matanza*.) We eagerly boarded the pilot's launch, which came over to point out a safe mooring buoy in the two-hundred-foot-deep water.

After we had scrambled up onto the scarred and leaking barges we tried to stay out of the way of over one hundred fishermen ranging from eighteen years old to over seventy. They sang as they heaved on the heavy net with its two-inch-square openings and three-quarter-inch diameter rope edges. Slowly the four barges drew closer together as the net piled up along their sides. One older man stood in a heavy fourteen-foot wooden launch right in the center of the square. He was covered in foul-weather gear and shouted orders at each team of net haulers while his rower propelled him from edge to edge of the diminishing square.

One of the fishermen explained this was the death chamber at the end of a maze of nets that stretched for over three miles. Four hundred anchors, each weighing at least fifty pounds, held the maze in place across half of the main pathway used by giant migrating tuna who come from the Canary Islands into this part of the Mediterranean each year to breed between May and July. When the tuna hit the maze, they follow it until they reach this chamber—the only one with a floor. A diver came out each day to count the fish in the death chamber. He had been the one to report there were over two hundred trapped tuna to haul up that day.

For close to an hour we saw nothing at all as the square of barges slowly closed and sweating men took turns sipping from a bottle of red wine before they returned to their stations to haul again. One of the younger men stopped and explained, "This is the only chance we have to earn extra money to go to university or buy a new fishboat or pay for our weddings. Our families own these nets and maintain them all year just for this six-week season. The cannery owns the barges. We split the profits and make sure our nets don't trap too many tuna. Every year our catch stays about the same. Last year it was fourteen hundred fish, forty years ago my grandfather said they caught fourteen hundred tuna."

Huge, darting black shapes became fish as the floor of the death chamber netting grew clearer. With unbelievable suddenness the two hundred-foot-wide square erupted into a mass of ten-to-twelve-foot-long leaping, pounding tuna. I have never seen such huge fish. They flashed silver and panicked blue in the churned waters. Shouted, relayed orders and the nets were belayed. Blue water turned to blood red as long gaffing poles were tossed to the men, who began slamming them into the sides of the closest fish trying to get a grip so they could haul the terrified tuna into the barges. Thrashing tails and pounding eight hundred-pound bodies turned the huge solid barges into quaking platforms. I ran for one of the launches to hide from the sight and sound of the slaughter.

When the wildness of the initial kill was over I went back to watch the now drenched headman herding the last of the slowly dying fish toward the gaff men on the barges. Some of the largest tuna weighed over nine hundred pounds. Up to a dozen sweating men teamed up to spike these monsters; each man was armed with strong short-handled gaffs. The headman yelled encouragement. All twelve gaffers heaved and groaned in unison. Slowly the huge fish were inched up the four-foot-high sides of the barges until they tettered on the very edge. Then all twelve men threw down their gaffs and leaped clear while the wide tail flukes whistled past and the tuna fell into the barges to join the quivering mass of dying fish that filled the bottom.

By noon all was quiet as the net was lowered back into position and a pilot's launch came out to drag the laden barges into the cannery. A scuba tanked diver climbed into the cold waters to check the nets and we rode back into Carlo Forte quietly discussing the unusual sight we had seen.

Later that afternoon Richard, Susan, Larry, and I walked along the rocky shore to the cannery, two miles outside of town. Richard explained some of the simple changes in pronunciation that make it possible to convert our growing Spanish vocabulary into a reasonable facsimile of Italian. If you want to learn a language to help add to a cruising way of life, I recommend Spanish first, French second. With a working knowledge of English and Spanish you can communicate in almost 70 percent of the countries a cruising man is likely to visit. Since Portuguese and Italian are very closely related to Spanish, with some local help you will be able to pick up enough words to be comfortable in Brazil, Portugal, and Italy within a few weeks. French is only helpful in a few Polynesian and Caribbean islands and parts of Africa and of course mainland France.

With Richard's assistance, our tour through the primitive cannery

was fascinating. Every net puller was there getting his ten-pound share of tuna head meat from the 212 tuna caught that day. Butchers separated the entrails, roe, intestines, and sperm in glistening piles. Then the headless fish were hoisted onto conveyors which ran into the canning shacks. We were amazed to learn that the fishermen were paid only by sharing in the sale proceeds of the offal and tuna heads. We watched at the auction as bidders from all over Sardinia heatedly drove the price of tuna roe up to twenty-five dollars a pound. The sperm, packed in wooden crates and covered with ice, sold for twenty-two dollars a pound. Each male tuna had up to thirty pounds of sperm; the females, twenty pounds of roe. To my amazement even the intestines were auctioned off at over four dollars a pound.

When Mario, a retired fisherman and bachelor who had become our unofficial guide, noticed our curiosity about the high prices for fish innards, he invited us to his home to taste these regional delicacies. His barbeque pit warmed the small flower-filled garden of his simple, one-room stone house, and the fragrance of tender grilled tuna steaks and fried potatoes filled the air that evening. The hors d'oeuvres of roe sautéed in olive oil and garlic had been tasty, the sperm boiled in milk was interesting, but the shriveled blackened intestines which Mario plucked off the barbeque in five-inch-long tubes and chewed on with obvious delight were nearly beyond the limit of my gastronomical tolerances. We each dutifully sampled an inch-long piece. Leatherlike casings held mild-flavored, paté-textured paste. Then we asked for more of the moist, tasty tuna steaks.

We headed farther east a week later—bound toward Cagliari. Richard and Susan set off for the Greek Islands; the Shotts, for France and home; and the other two cruising families turned north toward the fabled Costa Esmeralda, where the Aga Khan had created a pleasure port to host royalty from all of Europe later that summer.

As we gunkholed along the almost deserted coastline, our H. M. Denham guide livened the rocky coves and bays for us. His historical asides told of the days when Admiral Nelson pushed his weary fleet in pursuit of the elusive French, who had by then conquered most of Europe and were trying to take over Egypt and expand their empire down the Red Sea toward India.

A fearsome southerly gale struck the English fleet as it sailed past these same rock-strewn shores. For five days it howled, and *Vanguard*, Nelson's flag ship, was completely dismasted. The wicked motion of the mastless, uncontrollable ship threatened to dislodge the guns and ballast and eventually cause a capsize. Then two days later in an amazing show of seamanship, Captain Ball of the ship of the line *Alexander,* spotted Nelson's helpless hulk and floated a towing line to her eager crew. With careful skill, Ball set enough sail to keep a strain on the towing cable that held both ships hove to facing the growing seas. Since their ship was no longer rolling gunnel to gunnel, the men on Nelson's *Vanguard* were able to repair some of their damages. By the fourth day, the sound of breakers could be heard to leeward, and Admiral Nelson sent up signal flags, "I demand to be cast off." His hope was that the *Alexander* at least could be sailed clear. *Alexander*'s captain risked courtmartial and refused, signaling back, "I feel confident that I can bring you in safe. I will not slip my tow line, I will not leave you now." Slowly he set more sail and at the agonizing creeping pace of one half a knot, towed *Vanguard* away from the rocky shore and breaking seas into a deserted cove near the present site of Carloforte.

In an even more amazing show of the self-sufficiency that helped give the British Navy its successes, the sailors on board the four ships that made up Nelson's fleet were able to round up enough spars, spare timber, and sailcloth to refit *Vanguard* right at anchor. Within four days, all four ships set sail toward the fateful battle of the Nile. We spent hours pondering this example of how simple and repairable a basic sailing ship can be, especially if you eliminate things like swagged rigging ends and exotic hard-to-work metals—which require shoreside machinery and sophisticated training for repairs or modifications.

The weather we encountered on this history-laden shore was delightful. When we reached past Pula, a low spit of land which darts a mile out into the Gulf of Cagliari and is crowned by the ruins of a Roman city, fresh winds caused us to shorten down to reefed mainsail and staysail for a twenty-mile beat. Then the normal evening calm slowed our progress so we did not sail behind the craggy breakwaters until almost midnight. The confusion of city lights, lights from ships at anchor, lights from dredges, and lights of the small fishing boats which darted here and there made navigation inside the huge harbor almost impossible. So we worked in close to a quiet dredge, Larry took several soundings with our lead line and then he let our anchor down in fifteen feet of water over a soft mud bottom.

Early the next morning we were lifting our anchor to sail around the five-mile-long harbor and find a better place to moor. Our charts gave no indication of a good place to look. Our Denham guide warned against the Cagliari fishboat basin near the customs house because its high walls cut off every breeze and the crowded docks were covered with strollers from early morning to late at night. So when a thirty-five-foot racing sloop with an Italian flag steamed by bound away from the center of town, we set sail and followed. Behind a small shipyard, past a handsome park, and over a mile from town the yacht turned to enter a basin protected by a low rock breakwater. Bright-colored floating plastic docks were lined with a variety of racing dinghies and about twenty larger keel boats. We prepared to come alongside the open area at the farthest dock. A watchman came running out the undulating floats yelling the Italian words for "No foreigners allowed." It was too late to stop *Seraffyn* or turn her away, so we came alongside the dock then prepared to get underway again. But before we could turn *Seraffyn* around, the owner of the racing sloop came running up, "Don't go away, wait just five minutes while I make a telephone call!" he said. Then he lead the watchman down the docks and across the street to a clubhouse.

Paula del Vicardo took us for a closer inspection of the Roman ruins at Punta Pula.

When Georgio Sanna came back ten minutes later he explained, "Five years ago a French yacht came here and we made the owner and crew welcome. Three nights later they left after stealing everything they could from our boats. The winches had been removed. They took sails, flags, even cleats. So we closed the club. But now it has been so long, and you're not French, and your boat is too small to be a problem. So please stay. The commodore agrees too."

We did. And by that afternoon a dozen people had come down to greet us. Our evenings and afternoons were soon filled by our new friends. Swimming parties at the club pool, lovely dinners at private homes (cheese and caviar, lemon linguini, ravioli, roast wild kid, berries, and molded ice-cream topped with cognac), barbeques on the beach, rides in the country, and tours of Roman, Greek, and megalithic ruins. One special morning we were woken at 0530 to join Steve Gongaries, a dental student working with a local clinic, and his wife, Renée, an artist, for their normal morning exercise. Along with the Gongaries and the horse trainer we exercised thorobred horses on the soft sands of a nearby beach. We galloped home on powerful handsome horses while the sun rose over the distant hills.

A week later when a sixty-foot American ketch spotted our flag, they powered into the yacht club too. Without one bit of hesitation they were made welcome, and our parties simply expanded to include Maryly and Gordon Martin while they waited for new crew to fly in from Italy.

We did manage to get in a few mornings of work. We had found the flat bar stock we needed to extend our spinnaker pole track nine feet up the mast front. One of our new-found friends was head of the industrial arts college less than three blocks from the yacht club. He enthusiastically arranged for Larry to use a drill press and put screw holes and lightning holes in the nine-foot strap. Since everything seemed to fall into place, we decided Cagliari was the place to set up our spinnaker pole arrangement. So we dug out our electric Skil screwdriver-drill and the small but heavy step up–step down transformer we carry to convert the local 220 volt electricity to 110 volts. We have had this same drill since we started building *Seraffyn* and now, fourteen years later it has been around the world and is one-third of the way into building our new boat. To protect the drill from the ravages of life at sea, we spray it with WD 40 then wrap it inside an old cotton rag. This is sealed in two separate plastic bags. Though the drill has not been stored in the driest spot in the boat, this procedure has proved to be sufficient protection. It also keeps the drill from scratching the inside of our locker.

After only one and a half days work Larry wowed not only me, but every one of our Sardinia Yacht Club friends with a pole that set itself. An up-haul–down-haul line takes care of the inboard end; our staysail halyard working as a topping lift controls the outboard end. (For more complete details, see our book *The Self-Sufficient Sailor,* published by W.W. Norton.) I have rarely had to wake Larry to jibe or set a sail wing and wing since we converted to this instant pole arrangement.

A week after our arrival, the final galleys of the book we had finished writing in Puerto Andraitx arrived. It was exciting to see these typeset pages. We spent three mornings going over them word for word, correcting spelling errors, and delighting in the idea of something as permanent as a book with our name on the cover.

When we sent the galleys back to our publisher we decided it was time to move on if we wanted to see Tunisia before the hottest season of the year dissipated the lovely winds we'd been having.

Our new Italian friends planned a special farewell party for us. We spent the day on board Pier and Paula del Vicardo's thirty-seven-foot racing sloop designed by Sparkmen Stephens and anchored alongside another boat full of club friends—all of us watching the European Lightning class championships. Our on-board picnic lunch included rice salad, three kinds of pasta, cold spiced pork chops, fruit and cheese washed down by chilled white wine. Then the owner of the matching thirty-seven-footer next to us challenged us to a race, twelve miles back to the club. Pier appointed me helmsman; Larry, tactician; and his four sons and their two friends, crew—eager in spite of occasional language foul ups. Both crews enjoyed trading tacks as the wind grew from a fluky nine knots to over thirty-five. I loved the power of that stiff racing hull, but the destroyer-type wheel took some getting used to. I missed the feeling of balance I had learned to depend on with our tiller. I couldn't tell if we had weather or lee helm. And the tension of being helmsman even in such a casual race soon got to me. Just before the finish, when I no longer needed to look over my shoulder to see our competitor's bow, I yelled, "You take over Larry." He did, but we still tied up five minutes after our competitors.

We had a surprise waiting for our warm Italian hosts. Marly and Gordon immediately started their taffrail barbeque going onboard

Larry at the helm in our impromptu match race.

Katrina C, and together we spread out a good old American dinner to thank everyone for a two-week binge of hospitality. Twenty-five Italians joined in to eat the two gallons of chili and beans we had made early that morning. They devoured the coleslaw, french fried potatoes, and hot dogs that the Gordons had provided—along with a bucket of iced beer. Music, friendship, and invitations to return flowed that warm, still evening. We got out our guest books so we could have the names and addresses of our newest friends when we set sail the next morning.

When Cagliari slipped away behind us, we were headed for a tiny cove Paula had sketched for us. Carbonara is right at the southern tip of Sardinia. From there we were bound for Africa and the fabled city of Carthage.

CHAPTER 14

Another World

A blue lagoon ringed by tropical forests and crowned by the tiger-
toothed peak of Bora Bora; barges on the Thames River at old
wooden piers shadowed by London's ancient Tower; the rugged volcanic ring of Post Office Bay in the Galápagos—each image evokes
some sailor's dream of far off lands and the perfect anchorage. The tiny
bay of Carbonara formed by a hook at Sardinia's very tip will always
be my idea of perfection, even when cruising is only a memory for me.
High mountains drop suddenly down to form a long white beach
which wraps around in a horseshoe and encloses crystal-clear water
broken by occasional haphazard jumbles of granite. A short, weather-
beaten stone breakwater juts out from shore to stop any northern swell;
it provides perfect protection for five or six fishboats. An unpaved road
leads off across the hills to a village that must be there though no sign
other than that ribbon of smooth dirt tells of its existence. And right
next to the shore, less than one hundred yards from where we anchored, wind and waves had carved one pillar of granite into a perfect
whale's tail, its flukes spread wide and arched as if the mammoth rock
were trying to sound and avoid yet another century of erosion.

Four colorfully painted Italian fishboats lay tied stern to the low
breakwater. Their graceful wooden hulls with flared bows and
rounded sterns were little bigger than dories. But two fishermen lived
on each boat. When we rowed ashore for an evening stroll we noticed
that their small propane stoves set on top of tiny deckhouses were
roaring under pots of what smelled like fish stews. As we headed back
toward *Seraffyn* an hour later boisterous shouts from all eight fishermen drew our attention. When we rowed alongside the outermost

Carbonara.

boat, one man handed us a glass of coarse red wine while a second one reached down, grabbed *Rinky*'s painter and offered me a hand up.

We tried to get the eager, friendly men to slow down, explaining again and again that we did not understand much Italian. But each time we would ask a somewhat properly worded question, the fishermen would avalanche us in Italian explanations. We lounged back against a pile of nets and laughed at what seemed appropriate times, hummed along on a few local songs, and watched the first stars breaking through above our heads. Then all of a sudden it seemed as if we were being hustled off the fishboat. *"Arrivederci"* rang in our ears. Larry shook his head and said, "I think we're going fishing for lobster at 0330, but I'm not sure."

We had no need for an alarm to wake us. Shouted Italian greetings and the throb of a slow-speed, diesel engine came closer as our new friends, Mario and Georgio, brought their rough, metal-protected fishboat carefully alongside *Seraffyn*. We grabbed warm jackets and climbed into their boat, which had a low deck and high bulwork. Then we settled on a canvas arranged in a nest of drying nets for a two-hour ride around the tip of Sardinia and north along the coast.

Some special cross bearings on shore must have been very familiar to Mario because he did not once look at his clouded compass yet unerringly found a foot-long black float over three miles offshore. He and Georgio started their powered winch and a mile-long, open-weave net slowly lifted off the bottom and ground in bringing an occasional large crab, a small shark, and a few clawed lobsters. Each lobster had to be carefully extracted from a ball of netting because one broken claw reduces the value of a lobster by 50 percent. We helped set and retrieve four nets during the next two hours, trying our hand at carefully untangling snarls caused by fish, lobsters, and twigs. Then Mario shut his motor down; as we drifted over an almost windless, glasslike sea, he swung open a large hatch in the bridge deck and cockpit area, climbed in, and grabbed the double-burner propane stove, a huge pot, and two five-gallon jugs of wine (one red, one white). After flinging them all on deck he set to work in his open-air galley that had full-standing headroom. He proceeded to create a gourmet's delight for breakfast. Georgio filleted the two-foot shark, broke up two large crabs, and removed the meat from a dozen small conch. A small halibut was cut in pieces and the meat from a one-legged three-pound lobster was added to the pile. Mario quick-fried the lot in a generous amount of olive oil, added a dozen garlic cloves, four large spoonfuls of tomato paste, a handful each of fresh oregano and rosemary from the bushes near Carbonara Bay, plus a cupful of sea water. Then he decanted two cups of white wine, poured it into the steaming kettle, and shut the lid. We munched on crusty chunks of coarse white bread torn from two-pound mounds Mario had extracted from his magic locker and sipped potent coffee. Ten minutes later Georgio dug out four dirty enameled tin bowls from a place next to the engine, scrubbed them overboard, shook off the excess water, and held each one out for Mario to fill. The unnamed sea-food stew we ate in the slowly warming morning air still makes my mouth water. The last drops of the soup flavored bits of bread.

Then we all dozed contentedly for an hour before the relentless throb of the dirty but dependable engine started again. We helped pull in the last three nets along our ten-mile route. Seven miles of netting yielded only fourteen perfect lobsters and four damaged ones. Yet Mario slowly explained that catches like this were very good. If they continued at this pace both Mario and Georgio would be able to afford

Breakfast at Mario's.

to fly from Cagliari to their homes on the island of Ponza two hundred miles away to spend every other weekend with their families. They would still have enough profit left to take four months off each year. "We'll sail for home at the end of the season, haul the boat, mend our nets, then tease our wives," Mario told us. "But come spring we'll be eager to return and spend our mornings hauling nets and our evenings saluting the whale's tail."

By the time we set sail south for Tunisia we were pretty excited. This was the ancient home of the Carthagians and the stepping stone for Phoenician explorations that stretched as far as South America's Brazilian shores. Ahead of us lay a land of desert oasis, nomads, and Arabs; it was untainted by an overabundance of oil wealth yet was listed in our world almanac as one of the most advanced Moslem nations in the world. We had heard very little about Tunisia among the cruising community, in fact, we had never met anyone who had been there. No cruising guide mentioned the harbors shown on our charts, so we were doubly anxious to explore a land so close to Europe in miles yet so far away in culture.

When we were less than eight miles from the north coast of Tunisia approaching the huge port of Bizerte, we learned the first reason this area is far from a cruising man's Mecca. We had been careful with our navigation and knew our taffrail log was accurate because we had taken a distance check only two weeks previously, yet no signs of land appeared over the clear horizon. We sailed on toward shore until we felt we should be within three miles of the coastline. The water under us seemed to change its rhythm as if it were feeling a shoaling bottom, yet still there was no sight of land even though it was a bright sunny morning. Since this is a gradually shoaling sandy shore line where we could anchor safely if we got close and ran out of wind, since we were beam reaching on a seven-knot wind which gave us plenty of maneuverability, and since our visibility seemed almost limitless, we continued toward shore—convinced that we had made some errors in our calculations. Exactly one mile from shore we burst through a band of thick haze only two hundred yards wide. The breakwaters of Bizerte lay in front of us right on schedule. We found this band of haze along the whole northeastern coast of Tunisia during the next weeks. You cannot see it until you sail into it, but the fog wraps the land from view and, according to local fishermen, lies in place from early May to late September in spite of the strong northerly winds that blow almost every day of the summer.

Bizerte was definitely the wrong place to get a feeling of the real Tunisia. It was built by the French during their seventy years as protectors of this agriculturally rich country. But when Tunisia became independant in 1956, the French navy and army left Bizerte. Now it is a slowly decaying city with only one-third of its previous population and only a few old tourist hotels on the white sand beaches a few miles from town. We were made to feel welcome by the easy going customs officer. His flower-covered cottage was just behind the seedy remains of an almost deserted yacht club in the center of a vast unused harbor. We took a horse-drawn cab out to one of the hotels to change some money, since the banks were closed for a week, and walked through the local casbah, where we bought a pair of leather sandles in one of the tiny shops that lined its mazelike alleys. But for some reason the city seemed to have very little of interest for us. So our second morning in port when the wind, which was almost gale force, started building up a three-foot chop by blowing across almost a mile of open water, we were glad of an excuse to move somewhere else.

Our chart showed a wide river that ran right through the center of the port and led into an eight-mile-by-eight-mile deepwater lagoon. Along the shores of this river were several neat bays where we knew we would find an anchorage protected from the gusty north wind. Our British coast pilot stated there was good holding ground anywhere in the river, so we set our double reefed mainsail and staysail and ran down the river past a small naval base, past almost deserted commercial docks, and out into an area with yellow, grass-covered slopes just like the hills of southern California in late summer. Three small fishboats were tied to a small wooden pier in a lovely protected bay three miles from the main port. On the hillside a shepherd in flowing white robes walked through a flock of brown sheep and settled in the shade of a clump of trees. We rounded into the wind and set our anchor about one hundred yards from shore. Since there was no one in sight for miles, other than the shepherd, who soon walked away over a hill, we got out our quarterberth cushions and put them into the cockpit, where they form a wall-to-wall, double bunk. Then we shed our clothes to sun-bathe and enjoy ourselves—sheltered from the strong wind by *Seraffyn*'s deckhouse.

Within twenty minutes the sound of roaring engines disturbed the peace of our cockpit world. Larry peered over the bulwarks and said,

"Better slide below and get a bathing suit on for a few minutes. Some sort of navy launch headed this way."

The fifty-foot vessel came within calling range, and their loudspeaker blared out a string of French. Being of the, "when in doubt, smile a lot and look dumb," school, we called back, "No French!" Larry held up our Canadian ensign, which we had removed because of the strong wind. The launch roared away, and we settled back into our little haven.

Less than fifteen minutes later, engines again grew closer. Larry propped himself up on his elbow—"This looks serious!"

A 120-foot naval vessel was steaming toward us. This time the voice on the loudspeaker spoke English loud and clear, "Canadian yacht, you are under arrest! Start your engine and follow me immediately." There were guns on that ship and at least three dozen uniformed men. Larry tried yelling, "We have no engine, what is the problem?" But the wind and the roar of their engines drowned his efforts. Finally Larry indicated he would row over to their ship in *Rinky Dink* while I stood in clear view on *Seraffyn*.

I tried looking nonchalant and nonaggressive under the guns and eyes of that ominous gray ship. I had no idea what was going on, the only thought I remember was, "Nobody in the whole world knows where we are right now. No one is going to miss us for a long time." When Larry came down the boarding ladder after what seemed like hours, he was followed by a Tunisian naval officer. They rowed across the gap to *Seraffyn*, the officer seated gingerly in the stern of our bobbing 55-pound dinghy. Captain Hamad bowed politely when he climbed on board and introduced himself. His holstered pistol was very obvious. Larry told me, "We seem to be really under arrest, but no one will tell me why. They want us at the navy base, and I told them we would rather sail there than risk being towed by a ship as large as theirs. Captain Hamad is our escort. He speaks excellent English. We had better just keep cool, it can't be too big a problem."

As soon as we had our anchor up and sails set, the patrol ship headed back toward port. Our armed guard sat quietly on the after deck. I was bursting with curiosity and not just a little concerned, but the relaxed mood of our Tunisian captain did keep me from panicking. As soon as the naval ship was out of view Larry suggested, "How about a stiff drink?" Being ever the hostess, I asked Captain Hamad, "Would you like a glass of whiskey?" He frowned, paused as if to think of the right words to say, then replied, "You realize Moslems don't drink alcohol," then a smile spread across his dark, handsome face, "but if you put it in a coffee cup, no one will know." That broke the ice. Hamad had never been on a sail boat before and he loved it all. As we took yet one more tack away from the base to gain weathering, Captain Hamad pointed toward the patrol ship just tying up at the pier a mile to windward and asked, "Do you think they know what we are doing?" "Did you know before you came on board?" Larry asked. "No," our guard answered. "Do any of them have training on sailing ships?" Larry asked. Captain Hamad laughed at the thought of Tunisian naval officers having sail training. Then he made a decision, "Since they won't know the difference, let's do some more of this. It's a lot more fun than the work I should be doing."

So we fell a bit farther off the wind on each tack to lengthen our voyage into the naval base that was to be our jail. The reception we got a half hour later was much more serious. Three armed guards stood on the dock, a destroyer lay astern of us, another lay ahead, and seventeen different uniformed men inspected inside *Seraffyn*, opening each

Our arresting officer, Captain Hamad.

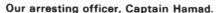

locker, bumping into each other, banging their heads, and asking us questions. We even had to unroll our neatly packaged sun awning. After an hour of polite but insistent questions all of the officers left with our passports, our ship's papers, charts, and coast pilot. But the armed guards remained.

We still had no idea of what the problem was. We had been assured our embassy in Tunisia would be contacted if necessary, but no one told us when. Everyone had been polite, but the whole situation was uncomfortable to say the least. The nearest American or Canadian consulate was in Tunis, fifty miles away. We had seen no foreign faces in the whole city of Bizerte.

As the hours of the afternoon passed, Larry and I tried to keep occupied by reading, answering letters, and working on little rigging jobs around the boat. Dark slowly crept over the docks, and still no one came down the pier other than the three men who replaced our armed guard. I lit *Seraffyn*'s cabin lamps, poured us another stiff drink. Just as I started to think about some dinner, an officer from the destroyer behind us spoke to our guards and brought us a tray with a dozen deep-fried six-inch-long fish surrounded by french fried potatoes. He sat on the edge of the dock while we ate. His questions about our little sailing ship relieved the tension, and I poured him a cup of hot coffee while we relaxed after the surprisingly tasty dinner. An hour later we were all startled when three obviously high ranking officials came toward us, charts, pilot, passports, and ship's papers in hand. "You are free to leave, either now or in the morning," the oldest one said. Then they all turned and left, taking our armed guards with them.

The officer who had brought us dinner suggested, "Stay for the night, we'll fill your water tanks." Only when Larry had followed him toward the water tap to get a hose and when they were well out of sight and hearing of anyone on the two destroyers did he say, "You chose to anchor within 150 yards of the main underground ammunition depot for all of Tunisia."

By the time we sailed clear in the morning the humor of the situation had started to appear. *Seraffyn* was no worse for the wear other than scuff marks on the decks from dozens of hard-soled shoes jumping and climbing around. Our water tanks were full, our charts had "restricted area" boldly written on them, and we had had a good nights sleep. But we did not feel like staying in Bizerte one minute longer than necessary. So we beat up the river and across the huge bay then eased sheets in the thirty-five-knot wind to run south toward Sidi-bou-Zid, the gateway to Carthage.

In spite of the fine sailing winds we found all along the Tunisian coast and in spite of the safe harbors and low-food costs, we became more uncomfortable with each day we spent in this predominantly Moslem, North African country. Officials were always polite and seemingly educated. The ruins of old Carthage stretched for over ten miles along the sandy shore and were exciting to behold. The Bardo Museum just outside Tunis is probably the finest archeological exhibit we have ever seen. The luxurious homes on the hill overlooking the well-run marina made a delightful view. But armed guards and high gates made it clear that the foreign diplomats and business executives who lived there wanted no visitors. The delightful old train that chugged along the shores from this luxury area, past old ruins, and then through the port of Tunis into the main street of the capitol seemed to burst through a curtain in time. On one side was Sidi-bou-Zid with well manicured lawns, underground sewers, and paved streets. On the other was the real Tunisia: a land of garbage on the side of dirt roads, people squatting to defecate right on the street or beach.

This is only a small section of the old city of Carthage.

Goats grazed on sparse grass right off the main street of the capital. We saw no beggars, but children in rags swarmed around the street corners looking underfed and scarred by running sores.

I know our poor impression of this whole country was probably caused by our lack of a common language. Because I dressed in light summer tops and Western-style clothes the street urchins who came up and pinched me and the men on the buses and trains who nudged me knew I was a foreigner. All of this made Larry so uncomfortable that he felt compelled to accompany me even to the local market. There we found poor quality produce and meat but excellent seafood. Yet the dirt and smells made shopping of any kind a real chore.

Added to all of this was the fact that we had followed the Mediterranean cruising custom of having a months worth of mail sent in one package addressed to us, care of the port captain of Tunis. When we sailed into Tunis, there was no port captain. We visited over twenty offices and the kind people in charge of each one found someone who spoke English. Yet no one, including the head of the main post office, could decide where our package would have been delivered. Though we searched for two weeks, we had no luck. (We later learned the package had been returned by sea to our English bank almost immediately, marked "no such address"). The package reached us seven months later. We also were told that it is best to address any mail care of Poste Restante, Port of Tunis—or whichever port you happen to be visiting. (Poste Restante is the name used throughout Europe to designate General Delivery.) Your mail will be held for thirty days under your name.

We decided the problem was that we were too close to a big city. So we set sail for the tiny resort island of Zembra, thirty miles east of the Port of Tunis. Once again a veil of haze similar to the one we had encountered on our way into Bizerte played tricks with our navigation. It took us two days to find the island, heaving to for the night and sailing slowly along until the steep-to island finally popped into view in full sunshine two miles to windward.

The miniscule rock-enclosed bay in front of the small, modern hotel complex was deserted except for a neglected sloop. The hotel had two Arab caretakers; a shepherd was the only other inhabitant on this rocky island, which stands right in the entrance to the Gulf of Tunisia.

Just after dark we heard the sound of babies crying. Both of us climbed on deck, and the eerie sound crescendoed until we felt surrounded by the sorrows of every sailor who had drowned when his fragile ship foundered on these fog-shrouded rocks. As the moon slowly rose, its silver light climbed down the sides of the cliffs and revealed numerous cave openings. Thousands of cony shearwaters flew along the shore crying and calling as they fished. It was their calls, magnified by echoes from the sheer wall of cave-riddled stone, that gave Zembra its mournful sounds.

A strong mistral wind blew across the cliffs just after we secured our lines. For three days fifty-knot gusts screamed down the canyons. We explored the hilly paths and tried skin diving but had little success. Roman lead anchors and broken remnants of huge urns stacked under the old hotel stood as silent reminders of the thousands of Phoenician and Roman galleys which had failed to reach Carthage. Their remains ringed this rocky island.

When a small ferry came in the second day to bring food for the caretakers, we found that the captain spoke English. He explained that a French consortium had planned a skin diver's paradise on this island. But Tunisia's independence frightened away the tourists, and the unskilled local labor could not meet the demands of maintaining and running the hotel, so after only three years the project had been abandoned. The neglected, cold-molded thirty-foot sloop next to *Seraffyn* was a remnant of a once proud fleet of charter boats owned by the hotel group. "Yes, the hotel corporation would be glad to sell it cheap," the ferry captain told us.

We spent part of the next day surveying the sloop. It had a damaged area on the hull and needed hundreds of hours of refurbishing. But for someone with very little money and lots of patience, that boat could have been a bargain. Especially since it could be towed to Malta, about two hundred miles to the east, where supplies and boat repair services were available.

When the strong winds eased just a bit we were glad to be under-way bound south for one more try at enjoying mainland Tunisia at the small "oasis" towns along its eastern shore. As Zembra slipped into its cloak of haze behind us, I shuddered involuntarily. The whole island had seemed a place of death and decay, held in eternal sorrow by the heartrending cries of the birds that owned its cliffs.

In the fine harbor at the small port of Kelibia we found the same uncomfortable cultural differences we had met in Tunis. Here gowned women giggled and pointed at me even though I now wore a dress or

long pants to go ashore. We decided to take one last trip into Tunis
to scout for our mail. After a two-hour bus ride we had no luck, so we
left a forwarding address with the postmaster and headed back for
Seraffyn. The crowded bus stop presented another less than pleasant
glimpse of everyday Arab life. When the bus arrived, fifty men and
women screamed, shouted, and shoved to get in first. Larry was bodily
shoved out of line. He would have lost his temper except all around
us the same thing was happening. He put his arm out to protect me
from the crush and we managed to get two seats. But the rough ride
and strong smells in the bus made us decide to hitchhike when we
reached our transfer point in a small village twenty miles from Kelibia.

The very first car that passed stopped for us. "Do you speak English?" its driver asked. "Yes," Larry answered. "Then climb in," the
driver said introducing himself. "I'm Nadir, the head of water sanita-
tion for all of Tunisia. Next month I go to a conference in New York.
So I want to practice my English." He insisted we come spend the next
day with him at his family's country home in Korba, just eight miles
from the port. We were delighted at the chance to finally get to know
something about Tunisia other than what we had learned from the
kind officials who had tried to handle our mail problems.

Yet lunch the next day just deepened our awareness of the gulf
between us and the Tunisians—the people who proudly call themselves the world's most advanced Arabs. As soon as we arrived at the
large stucco and tile home set in a small garden on the main street of
the village, Nadir took us for a tour of the marketplace. In this little
village every woman wore a chada, or robe, and many wore veils
completely covering their faces. In the cool of Nadir's home, we were
shown through the kitchen where an old lady sat on the floor cleaning
vegetables for a traditional lunch while a large pot of a grain called
cous cous steamed on top of a Primus one-burner stove. Water stood
next to her in a large tin basin. Her chopping board was the concrete
floor. Nadir's sister Sonia served us strong coffee and tiny sweet cakes
made from dates and sesame seed while we lounged on an overstuffed
sofa to wait for lunch. Sonia was a graduate of the University of
Munich and spoke five languages well. She spent much of her day
teaching French and English at the regional secondary school. Together she and Nadir told us of their country's efforts to educate six
million people, 70 percent of whom preferred a nomadic life. "There
are only three hundred college graduates in our whole country, so it

is a slow process. Especially since half of the bright young people we send abroad for the final education, don't want to come back. Until we can give college-level educations right here in Tunisia, we'll never get ahead!"

Nadir led us into a small dining room where only three places were set on a bulky, carved mahogany table. Sonia laid out all of the courses for a traditional cous cous and mechwi (mesh-we) dinner, then quickly left the room. "Isn't she going to join us?" both Larry and I chimed. "No," Nadir answered. "Sonia will be more comfortable eating with my mother." Larry asked, "Where is your mother?" "Oh, you saw her," Nadir answered. "She was the one cooking the meal."

After a very flavorful dish of boiled lamb and potatoes served with cous cous, we went out on the wind-cooled front porch, where Sonia had spread several handsomely woven wool rugs and a pile of cushions. She joined us as we lounged and chatted the enjoyable afternoon away while sipping iced lemonade. Less than twenty feet in front of us the village life presented a kaleidoscope of passing goats, sheep, camels, and from time to time a car.

Just when we were preparing to leave, Sonia decided she had to find us a special sweet she had been describing. She ran into the house, then came out with her hair and modest European-style sundress completely covered with a white wool Arab gown which reached to her ankles. "I'm not allowed outside the gate without this," the twenty-five-year-old European educated woman explained as she ran toward the market.

When we sailed from Tunisia less than three days later the thought of Sonia and her mother eating on the kitchen floor while we sat on cushioned chairs in the dining room, still haunted me. We had planned on spending the whole summer in Tunisia. But after less than four weeks we pointed our bowsprit eastward. As the first swell from a southeast breeze passed under us, Larry set the self-steering vane, turned to me, and said, "It feels good to be leaving. I never once felt comfortable and I could never figure out what we were doing wrong."

Out of over thirty-five countries we eventually visited during our voyaging on board *Seraffyn,* there were only two we wished never to visit again: Tunisia and Egypt, both predominately Arab countries. When we arrived in Malta five months later, we met Frankie and Mike on *Scarab.* They had sailed into a tiny river on the north coast of Tunisia, a river where only their shoal draft boat could fit. The villagers included both Frankie and Mike in every aspect of their lives. When a local wedding was planned, the ladies made five-foot-ten-inch Frankie a special gown to wear since no other woman in the village was over five feet tall. Mike was invited to go hunting and fishing. They had planned to spend two days on the river but stayed a month. We discussed the glaring differences between our two experiences and came up with some possible explanations. Frankie speaks excellent French. So language was not too much of a barrier as almost half of the villagers spoke some French they had learned from working with the navy or army. The people of the village had never been nomads; their forefathers had been fishermen in this same spot for centuries. The nearest city was several hours of driving or sailing from the river and not one resort had been built within fifty miles of the village. Finally, Frankie and Mike had been the first foreigners to visit the village for several years.

One of the main goals of our cruising life has been to learn as much as possible about other countries and their cultures. We probably should have spent the rest of the summer trying to find the one Tunisian port where we could break through the cultural barrier and relax. But our decision to leave left the best sailing time of the Mediterranean year open for a tour through the friendliest country in the world.

CHAPTER 15

Italy's Island Outpost

Before we set sail from Cagliari, we had been given a copy of a book called *Ulysses Found*. It was written by Ernle Bradford, a retired British naval officer who had spent twenty years exploring the Mediterranean on board his forty-foot yawl. Bradford wrote several excellent guidebooks for this area that has such a wealth of history. But his real fascination lay in trying to pinpoint the route of Ulysses' odyssey. Using the seaman's logic gained sailing a small boat, he voyaged through the Greek, Italian, and Spanish Islands with Homer as his guide. Then Bradford wrote his conclusions backed by careful discussions of the unique weather and currents he encountered. Both Larry and I were so intrigued by this new type of adventure book that we searched for secondhand copies of Homer's *Iliad* and *Odyssey* in the one book store in Tunis. We then read them aloud. What had once been boring reading assignments for school became living history as we came to know the changeable Mediterranean. I had a hard time, however, believing that any sailor as skilled as the man described by Homer could have wandered and been lost in such a small sea for ten years.

Then as we sailed eastward and encountered the strong currents plus the fierce winds and day-long calms caused by the ever-higher mountain chains and ever-wider deserts edging this restless inland sea, I became a believer—especially when I again read the description of Ulysses' fragile, open boat, held together with animal sinews. It carried a single square sail that could only be used to run before the wind. Its only other power source was from oars that could become almost useless to a boat pitched and buffeted by the short chop left by quickly passing squalls.

Our voyage from Tunisia toward the Italian island Lampedusa was a case in point. As is usual in the Mediterranean, there was a good breeze blowing as we cleared the land. But a high steady barometer should have been a warning to us. Forty miles from the nearest land, we ran out of wind. All night we lay absolutely becalmed. By mid-morning a fickle breeze filled in and danced around the compass until dark, when it quit completely.

The next day was the same, but by then we had worked within thirty miles of Lampedusa and Linosa—two islands whose mass attracted the day breeze, which was much steadier. Our round of sights held a shock for us: we had been set twenty miles north of our course by currents. In a fresh breeze we would have been making five knots forward, and the passage might have taken twenty-four hours or so. A current of less than one-third of a knot per hour would have made little difference. But drifting as we were for over two and a half days, it added up to cause a dramatic shift in direction. So when Linosa Island appeared that afternoon, we changed our plans and eased sheets to reach toward an anchorage on its western shore.

I know someone is thinking, "Didn't you wish you had an engine?" Strangely, the more we sailed in the fickle Mediterranean, the more we came to enjoy the challenge of moving without auxiliary power. In this land of ancients it seemed to put us in touch with the past. We had seen other cruising people with auxiliary power rush from one historical harbor to the next, trying to see every museum and each recommended archeological site, concerned that the season was too short to properly "do" one country or one area. They were constantly on the move, powering over windless seas or bucking into headwinds, and only getting their sails up when the afternoon breezes filled into at least eight knots. And eventually they were tired by the confusion of so many overlapping civilizations—so many Greek ruins remodeled by the Romans then destroyed by the Vandals and built on by the Moors to be overrun by the Goths.

The wind and sea edited and shaped our plans. If there was no wind to enable us to sail toward some new port, we would relax and spend another day exploring where we were, or swimming or skin diving or puttering around the boat. If we got becalmed at sea, we did everything a person at home on a Sunday afternoon would do with none of the disturbances of a telephone or passing traffic. When a gale caught us offshore, we were probably more comfortable than sailors whose boats have engines, as we had learned to cooperate with the sea and sail *Seraffyn* with properly shortened canvas until prudence and discomfort told us it was time to heave to. Just when the frustration of trying to catch a stray breeze or trim sheets to yet another wind shift caused me to wonder why we were out there, Larry would remind me of the joys of having a well-designed, modern sailing boat, "Think of how Nelson would have given anything he owned for ships that could point as close to the wind as we can. His crew would have traded their souls for the comforts we have on board." Then I would go below to an ice-box full of cold drinks and fresh fruit and see our dry, well-cushioned bunks and laden bookshelves—every thing that makes *Seraffyn* my home—and I would realize the main reason we were out there was for the sheer sport of sailing. Remove an engine from today's modern sailing yacht and cruising becomes one of the most exciting sports there is. It has only one rule, seamanship. Each challenge is one you choose. Each voyage has a definite beginning and a definite end so you can count your successes right here and now knowing they are absolutely and wonderfully personal. You planned the voyage, you prepared your ship and surveyed its gear, and you worked the ship to gain advantage over your only foes, which are also your only allies, the wind and the sea. No other sport allows you the chance to form a completely coordinated team consisting of just a man and woman or a man, wife, and their children and then compete without defeating any other team. This is in complete contrast to the competitive and scheduled world on shore, controlled by human beings and having undefined goals and uncertain successes.

The hardest thing for people to understand about the whole concept of engineless cruising is that once you accept your boat as your home and once you eliminate schedules, you become absolutely free. Add an engine, and it would be like allowing the shoreside things we resent most right back into our wandering life: noise, controls, and schedules.

The black sheer cliffs of the inside of a volcanic cone formed the only safe anchorage on Linosa. The sea had breached on the side, forming a crescent with a black volcanic sand bottom that was clearly visible through thirty feet of water. The anchorage was completely calm, and once again cony shearwaters cried and moaned through the night from their nests along the volcano's time-riddled sides.

We had failed to check our butane gauge in Tunisia, where most of the towns had refill tanks at the gas stations, and had run out of butane for cooking. There would be no way to fill our bottles in Linosa, since the only village consisted of ten fishermen's homes. So we got out our back-up primus kerosene stove and clamped it in place and set sail on the first of the morning's breeze to head for Lampedusa again.

Our first sight of the southernmost Italian island was less than thrilling. A tilted flat rock of limestone stretched in a straight line five miles long. From the north there was nothing to be seen except sheer cliffs and a large radio transmitter on the westernmost tip of the island. It was after dark when we glided along the southern shore and identified each of the navigation lights leading into a well-protected harbor. We anchored right in the center. Not another yacht was in sight, but the gently bobbing fishboats and winking lights from the town made us feel safe and welcome.

The next morning we rowed into the stone pier at the foot of a flight of steps which lead up to the tidy town perched on the southern slope of the limestone island. Larry shouldered our empty butane tank; I carried our transfer tube plus three stretchy nylon shopping bags. There was absolutely no one to be seen until we reached a small central plaza where several children played on a swing set. In the first shop that displayed hardware our embryo Italian plus sign language got unexpectedly fast results. The shopkeeper called his son to take over the counter and then led Larry, with his tank, down the street. "Do your shopping and I'll meet you over there as soon as I can," Larry called, pointing at a small, cheerful-looking café across the plaza.

I found some lovely fresh food in the dozen small shops plus several small items we needed, such as sewing pins, paper towels, writing paper, and the inevitable *Time* magazine which seems to be available in even the smallest European village. Then I went into the café, dropped my bags in the corner, ordered tea, and sat down to read last weeks news. A few minutes later someone tapped my shoulder. A tanned, conservatively dressed, fifty-year-old Italian man said in English, "It is rude for a lady to sit alone in an Italian café." I was almost ready to ignore his advances when he continued, "My wife has asked if you would join us at our table."

By the time Larry was deposited back at the café by the same shopkeeper, our butane tank had been filled and returned to the dinghy and I was able to introduce Mario and Maria Corvo. Maria was a city administrator and Mario, the mayor of Ancona—a large city on the Italian shore of the Adriatic. They were in Lampedusa for their yearly visit with Mario's brother Franco, a local fisherman.

That evening we met Franco when everyone in his family powered out to see this tiny boat that had sailed from America. "Welcome to Lampedusa," they all called as Franco maneuvered alongside. Then we were presented with a freshly caught five-pound red snapper. The Corvos shared drinks and hors d'oeuvres on board *Seraffyn* and made plans to fill our next three days.

We quickly learned that all Italian recreations center around elaborate, leisurely meals. A cruise around the island on Franco's fishboat was really an excuse to have morning coffee and exquisite pastries along with a swim at a sandy cove four miles up the south side of the island, then a six-course barbequed fish dinner on a hidden rock landing on the island's north shore, and finally wine and snacks when we arrived back in the harbor—salty and tired seven hours later.

Eating carefully prepared meals is such an important part of Italian village life that even this community of only one thousand people had four cafés, three regular restaurants, and a gourmet restaurant. One evening we tried to find Tio Micheales, a restaurant Mario described as impossible to miss. We followed his directions—landing on the rocks at the bay's western side and then walking toward the first green house until a flower garden appeared on our left. We followed a small dirt path until it dwindled at a garden gate. Feeling absolutely lost, we retraced our steps until we found one home with a light on inside. Its owner led us right back to the garden gate and on through past two more houses and around onto the back porch of a house just like all the rest. Three families were seated at kitchen-style tables lit by candles. The owner of the house, Uncle Micheal, came and invited us into the steaming, old-fashioned kitchen. He opened the lids on each kettle and pot and showed us a display of seafood in his battered refrigerator and a table full of desserts and fruit. Under his direction we carefully planned our evening meal, surrounded by the savory aroma of the Italian equivalent to a menu.

We could see *Seraffyn*'s anchor light from Uncle Micheal's back porch. A handsome tiny garden framed the view across the quiet bay. We ate a superb dinner topped off with a lovely white wine called

Porto Palo and bottled on Sicily's southern tip, and we laughed about a project we had finished that day. Three months after launching *Seraffyn*, we added a linen locker across from the forward bunk. Then we installed our English Sestral sextant in the best part of the locker —its mahogany box screwed securely down but easy to remove when we went on a delivery. After over seven years of cruising, our writing supplies had nibbled away at that linen locker until towels had to be kept in with Larry's clothes. That morning, when Larry reached for a tee shirt and came out with a dish towel he simultaneously came up with a brilliant idea. He measured the space between the deck beams over our chart table. Then he drilled three screw holes through the top of the sextant box and into the underside of the teak deck and inserted three one-inch number 10 bronze wood screws. We then had a new home for our sextant. The bottom could hinge down when we needed it and stay out of the way when we didn't. My linen locker suddenly grew larger, and again we were reminded that cruising boats are never completely finished, they just keep evolving.

We left for Malta with invitations to Mario's home in Ancona, two cases of the modestly priced Porto Palo wine, and twenty kilos of pasta. We had been told that Maltese wines were expensive and poor quality, that's why we bought so much of the wine. The huge supply of linguini, spaghetti, and lasagne noodles was a two-party gift to someone we had never met. Marly and Gordon Martin had refitted their boat in Malta the previous winter. Sally, the wife of a small restauranteur in Malta, had gone out of her way to assist the Martins, when they tried to find a way to repay her, Sally had asked, "If ever you come back, please bring me some Italian pasta. My husband hates the Maltese ones." So before we left Cagliari the Martins had given us twenty dollars to buy noodles—and with it, a letter of introduction that eventually added a whole new dimension to our view of Malta, the Mediterranean's finest cruising man's crossroads.

CHAPTER 16

~~~~~

The Middle of the Med

We had excellent five-knot sailing as we reached toward Malta and from our first sight of the three islands that form this country of 350,000 people, we were delighted. The only building material naturally found here is creamy yellow sandstone. So local customs, reinforced by high import tariffs, have kept the sailor's view of the islands as it must have been hundreds of years ago. New villas and resorts made of sandstone blend right in against the weathered fortresses built during the Crusades. The imposing walls of two thousand-year-old Valletta and the eight-hundred-year-old fortress on Manuelo Island frame the entrance to Marsesmett Harbor. Once inside, you can see a wonderful array of over three hundred cruising boats and charter yachts that lines the sea walls in front of the handsome old homes of Sliema.

Within one day of our arrival we had met a dozen voyaging sailors from all points of the globe, including some of the first yachtsmen to sail through the newly re-opened Suez Canal. We explored the excellent local shipyard facilities, which included a huge dry storage area for visiting yachts, met the owners of three different yacht chandleries, and discovered a good English library and seven movie theaters where single admission to English and American films cost less than $1.50. Local buses ran frequently to every point on the island for less than ten cents a ride, and the Maltese all spoke English along with their own dialect—which seemed to be a combination of Italian and Arabic. Then we delivered the twenty kilos of pasta.

Sally squealed with delight when she realized this was a gift from the Martins. Her husband came running from his tiny restaurant kitchen to see what the commotion was all about. *"Que Buono!"* he exclaimed as he rummaged through the forty packages of noodles. He insisted we be his guests for lunch. Sally spread a lovely set of old china at our table next to the window. The restaurant only seated twenty-five people, so she had time between her chores as the only waitress and dishwasher to tell us the delights of her small country. "Come back this winter and you'll see what I mean," she said.

"What are the chances of renting a reasonably priced place to live for four months if we do come back?" Larry asked.

"No problem," Sally answered. "The summer visitors are gone by October. So I'm sure I can get you a good place at a Maltese price. Can you afford fifty dollars a month?"

Her answer along with a tour through the well-stocked local groceries (where Australian sirloin sold for $1.50 a pound, pork chops for $.90, and English cheddar cheese for $.80) convinced us. Malta would be our winter goal. There would be lots to do; with a safe harbor, we could move off *Seraffyn* for a while to make working on her interior for the first time in three years much easier. Over three hundred yachts were already on the harbormaster's winter mooring and storage plan.

At a small café by the harbor.

Local labor laws were lax, especially if you confined your work to foreign registered yachts. So we were sure there would be lots of work available to refuel our savings account.

With this decision made, we avoided touring beyond the edges of the port. We wanted to save the rest of this tiny country for leisurely winter excursions. But our days were filled to overflowing by the interesting people we met right in the harbor.

We put up a note at the Camper Nicholson Yacht Agency where we had our mail sent. "Will trade charts of Western Med. and English Channel for Eastern Med. Charts." (The agency is located right across from the mooring area and gave us excellent service; write and ask before you use their mail holding service. Tell date of arrival and yacht name. Address: Camper Nicholson Yacht Agency, Ta'Xbiex, Malta).

By afternoon three cruising sailors from different boats came to where *Seraffyn* lay at anchor with bundles. John Kylie, who was sailing a Tahiti ketch named *Josepha*, delighted us by sailing his tiny dinghy downwind with his trading charts held like a square sail. We ended up with every chart there was from Malta, through the Adriatic, Aegean, and on to Turkey. They ended up with all our charts and navigation pilots. The afternoon slipped away as each new friend told us about favorite anchorages, good diving spots, bad currents. We poured over the charts and marked each bit of local knowledge with penciled explanations. That evening Larry and I got out our chart catalogue and tried to organize the mixed lot, which included not only English charts but also Italian, American, and German ones.

Since it is expensive and difficult to try and buy charts all from one source, we have finally found a good way to catalogue and arrange our mixed bag of charts. We select one catalogue, either United States or British, then mark all of the charts we have on board in the catalogue. If the area covered by an American chart is not exactly the same as that in our British catalogue, we mark its corners in the catalogue and then put its number next to the penciled corner. If it is exactly the same, we just renumber the chart so it coincides with its English counterpart. Then we put a check next to that chart on the printed list of charts and pencil around the edge of the catalogue diagram. We fold the charts so they will fit under our bunk cushions and mark the number that corresponds to our catalogue so it can be seen with the chart folded. Then we try to put them in an approximate order for the general route of our next few months of sailing. We store the charts

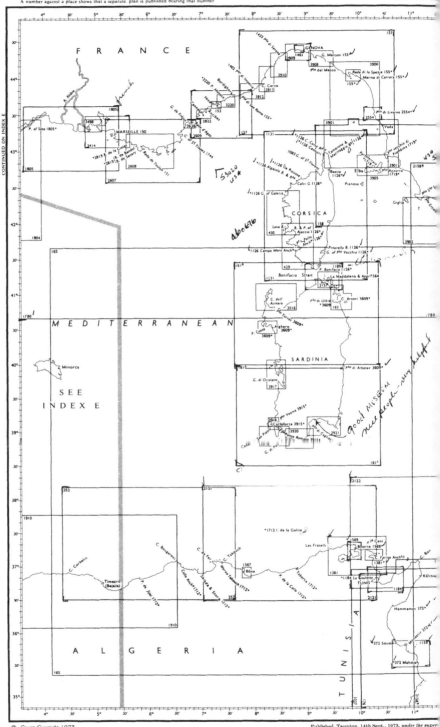

*2819 indicates that a plan is shown on sheet Nº 2819
A number against a place shows that a separate plan is published bearing that number

CENTRAL

Published, Taunton, 14th Sept., 1973, *under the super*

This is a page from the actual chart catalogue we used during our voyage.

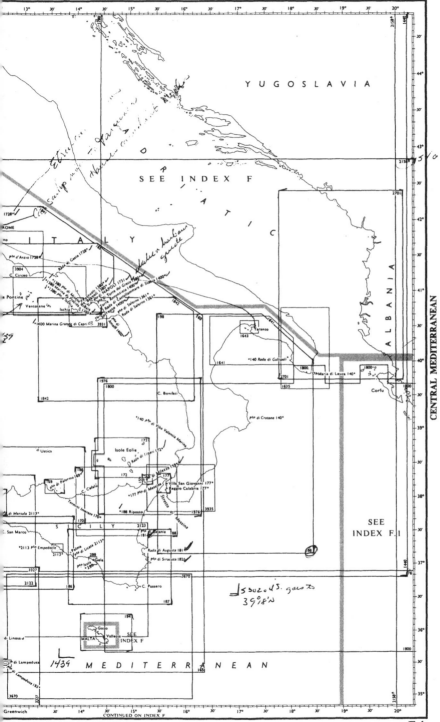

ral G. P. D. Hall, C.B., D.S.C., *Hydrographer of the Navy.*

we plan to use first under a quarter berth, the rest go forward under
our double bunk cushion. In Malta we ended up with close to eighty
charts, which would have raised our forward bunk cushion about six
inches. So we took the ones we wouldn't be using in the next few
months and rolled them compactly into extra strong plastic bags (we
got these from the local fertilizer dealer), sealed them well, and stored
the bundles in a rarely used area under the dockpit. A quick glance at
the chart catalogue shows us what we have and, with luck, we can find
the next chart we need just by glancing under the quarter berth cushion. Even with a proper chart table and storage drawer some system
like this is necessary, since the charts just for the Mediterranean make
a pile over nine inches thick.

Phineas Sprague—who had sailed *Mariah*, an Alden designed sixty-
five-foot schooner, from New York, west about through the Red Sea
—noticed Larry's hand-spliced wire. "My bobstay is starting to fall
apart," he mentioned. "Could you splice it before you leave? There is
no one here that has swaging tools or nico press fittings for wire over
one-fourth inch." Larry said he would teach Phin to splice his own
wire. The next morning when Larry set up his rigging vise on board
Mariah, several other sailors came over to watch. Larry spliced Phin's
three-fourth inch bobstay wire. Then Phin and the interested observ-
ers each tried making one splice each. The next day Phin started
replacing each piece of rigging he had been concerned about. For over
a year the cost and unavailability of large mechanical rigging ends had
made this impossible.

Although tests show splices to have only 85 percent of the strength
of wire and swaged ends 95 percent, we have never met anyone who
has had a reasonably well-spliced rigging end fail. In the long run,
especially under cruising conditions, spliced ends with properly sized
thimbles are more dependable. Splicing costs nothing but the price of
a thimble and one foot of extra wire; once you learn the simple proce-
dures, you can do them yourself anywhere, anytime. The tapered
splice has no hard spot to bend and fatigue your wire. Visual inspection will show any potential defects.

Since you can't see what is going on inside swages, Norseman or
Tru-lock fittings, they require polishing and machine X-rays once a
year for a true safety inspection. They each put a crimping hard spot
where the wire enters the fittings. This will eventually cause work
hardening. Each one presents a shoulder where water can collect and

Phin and Larry splicing wire on board _Mariah_.

start corrosion. Besides, especially in the case of swaged ends, you are putting your complete trust in some machine operator who may or may not have a hangover and who may or may not be properly trained. One extra pass of the roller can weaken a swage. One too few can cause it to slip under load.

Modern racing yachts need the extreme low stretch of 1×19 wire and the reduced weight of rigging just sufficient to hold up their mast. But for cruising boats 7×7 wire is more forgiving and has low enough stretch to be handled by a good set of turnbuckles. The extra weight of wire with three times the minimum strength factor for your type of rig will not slow you down enough to be noticed. So you can more than account for any lower initial strength ratings when you use hand splices.

With open-hand splices and proper toggles we would carry the same stainless steel rigging wire for as long as it showed no signs of pitting and as long as no single strands parted when the wire was bent to a radius ten times its diameter. This can be twenty years with real non-magnetic stainless steel wire. (Test it with a small magnet when you buy it.)

On the other hand, swaged fittings must be replaced either at the first sign of a crack in the polished swage or every three years to guarantee safe ocean voyaging and to meet Lloyds' standards for insurance. We have seen swages start to crack within one year in the tropics.

Phin's case was a classic one. In our experience even the more sophisticated yachting centers outside the United States rarely have the fittings or dies to do your particular size of wire. (Inch-sized wire and millimeter-sized wire each require their own tools and fittings.) But you can always buy some type of wire that can be spliced and thimbles. Then you can create your own rigging right on board. Swages are fine for the guy who is racing his boat within calling distance of his local rigging shop. But for long distance voyaging wire splicing is the cheapest, most reliable, and most practical way to keep your mast up.

We received a huge bundle of mail a day after we finished our splicing party. One exciting letter came from our publisher in New York. "Printing date for your book *Cruising in Seraffyn* is August 1st." We had seen the typeset page proofs in Cagliari. But this would be the real thing. Another long roll attached to our mail package contained drawings that eventually changed our whole future.

Lyle Hess had sent us the preliminary lines plan of a twenty-nine-foot-nine-inch version of *Seraffyn* drawn to our specifications. We had enjoyed sailing *Seraffyn* so much during the previous eight years that we realized we would never trust anyone but Lyle to design us a boat that was not only sea-kindly but also weatherly when it had a good cargo on board. Our small smuggling adventure in Gibraltar had furthered this feeling. What other twenty-four-footer could have carried all our worldly possessions plus almost a ton of cargo and still handled so well? We also knew that wood was Larry's forte and that if some day we decided to live on a boat, "for the rest of our lives," we would want one built of hard woods. Lyle had built yachts out of wood at his own shipyard. In our minds we were far from ready to build a boat to replace *Seraffyn,* but (and maybe it was foolish) we worried that Lyle might get run over by a truck or retire from drawing yachts if we waited too long. Besides, we anticipated the pleasure of having a dream boat slowly evolve to suit our personal needs and desires during the next four or five years.

"We want the beamiest thirty-footer you can design that will still go to windward well. Give her the biggest rig she can carry so we won't need overlapping genoas. Cargo carrying capacity is important and so is a long flat area on the bottom of the keel so she'll stand on a beach with her own legs. And of course we want her handsome," Larry and I wrote. Then we went on to give our dream ship's mythical construction as, "Teak planked on locust frames, bronze floors, internal lifting eyes, lead ballast, and solid teak decks."

This lines plan had arrived at least a year before we had expected it. The drawings were beautiful to our eyes—exactly what we had dreamed of, similar in appearance to *Seraffyn* but with subtle changes to make this a powerful downwind machine with flatter buttocks and a fine bow to drive her to windward in a chop. Every visitor we had the next few weeks was subjected to that lines plan along with a discourse on how, "We're too busy enjoying ourselves right now to build it. Probably won't get around to stopping for ten or eleven more years."

When we left Malta, our lockers were full of canned and packaged foods from England, America, and a dozen other countries. Our bilges had three cases of duty free whiskey and sherry in them. Our minds were full of new ideas, with dreams of a winter in Malta and then the next summer in the Greek and Turkish Islands. Now it was the begin-

SERAFFYN'S MEDITERRANEAN ADVENTURE

ning of August and we had heard of the World Half-Ton Regatta planned for September 12 in Trieste, Italy, right at the head of the Adriatic. Using that as a goal, we had lots of time to explore the Dalmation Islands of Yugoslavia.

We set our spinnaker to catch a light southeast breeze when we were just north of Gozo. It was a warm sunny afternoon, visibility was very good, and we could count half a dozen ships passing back and forth through the twenty-mile-wide channel next to Sicily. Helmer was steering, the spinnaker pulled us proudly along at four knots, and we lay on deck keeping watch and talking about all there was to see in the Mediterranean.

A freighter was coming toward us from the west. Larry had first noticed him when the three hundred-foot ship was four or five miles away. Since we were headed perpendicularly across his path, with a one thousand-square-foot blue and white stripped sail rising thirty-five feet in the clear sunny afternoon air, we did not worry that he might not see us.

But that ship plowed steadily toward us, its bow always pointed dead at our side, just like we were a huge magnet. The ship's course was erratic, so we could not decide which way to sheer off to give him a bit of room. "Someone just wants a closer look at us," Larry concluded; we had often had ships alter course to come closer and exchange greetings. But this one kept plowing straight at us, its bow wave seeming to grow taller and wider. When it was less than one fourth mile away, both of us were still unsure of its exact course—but Larry was definite on one thing, "We've got to gybe that spinnaker fast and reach parallel to his course or we'll never be able to maneuver out of his way." The gybe that followed was not one of our best. By the time we were reaching as close to the wind as we could with our huge running chute, that ship passed within fifty yards of us. There was absolutely no one on the bridge of the Greek registered freighter.

Both of us were more than a bit shaken as we cursed the advent of auto-pilots on commercial ships. Sure they saved fuel for shipping companies, but they also meant the man on watch could go away from his post and make a sandwich or read a book. Why didn't they invent some kind of auto-pilot that required the man on watch to always have his hand or foot on a lever of some kind that would release the auto-pilot as soon as pressure came off? That way he would have to stay on the bridge. If a three hundred-foot ship would run through the crowded Malta Straits at close to twenty knots without a helmsman or watch keeper, what did they do at sea? Our decision to keep a watch at all times was reinforced.

As we wandered from port to port along the Sicilian and Italian coastline someone in each anchorage would come up and say, "I have an uncle in America" or "I once lived in America," and we would be invited home for lunch, a dinner, or a tour. Italian and Sicilian hospitality from the smallest village tot he largest town was warm and homey. The restaurant owners were eager to tell us the best dishes to try and the best sites to visit.

Syracuse wore our feet out. History surrounded us from the moment we landed at the three-thousand-year-old shipyard in the original Greek port. Plato had lived here, there was a Roman amphitheater, and an Helenic temple that had been built into a Catholic church was right in the center of today's town. We found excellent, inexpensive family-style cafés on sidestreets and alleys by asking local police officers where they ate their meals. This whole area of southern Italy is full of good harbors, fine well-preserved ruins, and excellent museums. Yet we never met another foreign cruising yacht here. During the next four months when we sailed from Sicily in the south through the whole Adriatic to Triest, including the Dalmation Islands south to Split and back to Malta, we only saw two other visiting yachts.

CHAPTER 17

An Introduction
to the Adriatic

Crotone is a modern industrial city nestled in the instep of Italy's boot. Rather than make a 240-mile passage straight from Sicily to the tiny port of Tricase just inside the Adriatic, we decided to stop here—though both our pilot and Denham's guide made it clear there was little of interest for the tourist.

We approached the stone breakwaters at Crotone running five knots wing and wing under just staysail and double reefed main. It was almost 2200 and very dark. Not one navigation light made sense. Larry pulled down the staysail to slow our approach, while I checked our three-year-old British Admiralty chart again. This had to be Crotone, there was no other city or even village within thirty miles. "Shall I heave to?" Larry called down. "We're only two miles from the first lights, a green five-second flasher seems to be right behind a red fifteen-second light." I got out our brand new light list for the Med, found the listings for Crotone, and called back, "Got the answer. Red light is on a new extension to the moll. Clear it to port then reach into the main harbor."

Twenty minutes later we were anchored, sails stowed, anchor lamp in position. I made a late snack of cheese and crackers with a glass of wine. Larry proposed a toast to that light list. "Without it we would have spent the night hove to, watch on watch, instead of comfortably anchored and sleeping together."

Light lists are imperative if you depend on trading charts instead of buying new ones each year from one of the authorized dealers who have a chart correcting department. Only these dealers update charts to correspond with the notices to mariners which are used by nations

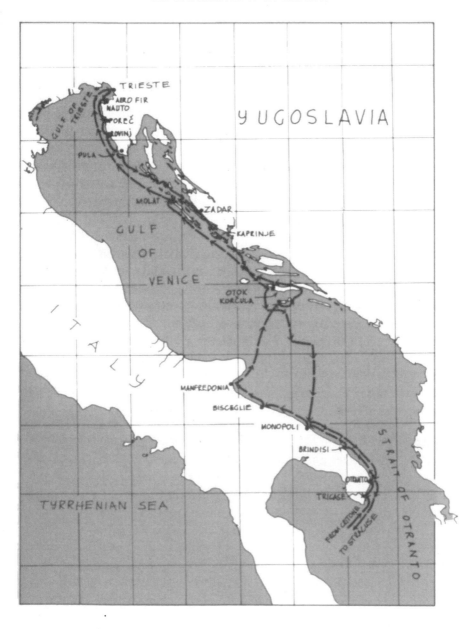

around the world to list any changes that affect navigation, lights, wrecks, newly discovered rocks, military maneuvers. Even if you buy relatively new charts from a general marine supplier, you will need a light list. They are issued yearly by the United States Defense Mapping Agency and the British Admiralty. Since each one covers a very large area (our Mediterranean light list also covered the Black Sea and Red Sea), its cost of six dollars is negligible. Every light, from the smallest fairway buoy to the biggest lighthouse, is listed along with its physical characteristics and a description of its supporting structure. Larry later depended on these descriptions of lighthouse structures to confirm his daytime positions while he sailed along the almost featureless east coast of Italy.

It is easy in retrospect to see all of the reasons Larry and I got into one of our rare deepseated disagreements on the voyage between Crotone and Tricase: fickle sailing winds; summer heat; concerns over the marital problems of some cruising friends, indecision over our own future (both long range and immediate), pressure to explore more during the shortening sailing season; concern over writing projects—but most of all the need to separate for a while and think about our unbelievably close relationship.

Unlike most shore-based couples who separate each day of the week for nine or ten hours to go to work, Larry and I had been within eight or ten feet of each other twenty-four hours a day for three years. Other than half-day shopping excursions now and then we had not been apart since England, when Larry had taken off for the Two Man Round Britain Race and I had sailed *Seraffyn* along the Cornish Coast. By the time we sighted the tiny port of Tricase we had agreed that I would take a holiday to explore Pompeii and Capri and Larry would sail *Seraffyn* north in the Adriatic.

Maneuvering into Tricase took some careful sailing. No chart shows this tiny fishing port—except for the Italian tourist council's cruising guide. Their sketch shows an entrance forty feet wide with a switch back turn into a 150-foot-wide, 400-foot-long mooring area protected by a sea wall. I am glad we beat into this tiny place under sail instead of powering in. Just 50 feet around the corner of the 25-foot-high sea wall was a maze of lines and moorings holding about a hundred small fishing boats. With an engine we would have fouled our propeller. We were moving at less than a knot, so we stopped by setting our ready-at-hand stern anchor from the walkway which topped a ledge on the inner face of the sea wall.

Seraffyn looked beautiful tied bow to among all the small diesel-powered work boats. I looked down from the only café on the steep cliff next to the harbor the next morning and watched as Larry prepared to maneuver out. We had agreed to meet three weeks later in Manfredonia—a post two hundred miles to the north, or to send a letter there in care of Poste Restante. I called "Good sailing" as Larry hauled back to his stern anchor, preset his jib sheet, then hauled the anchor on board. I was not sure he heard me as he worked hoisting his sails and setting his course to weave clear of the rocks at the entrance to Tricase. So I was not hurt when he did not wave until he had eased sheets to sail behind the point that hides this picturesque port from the sea. Then I hoisted my single seabag and started up the hill for the three-mile walk to town and a train station.

I was aware that either of us could decide not to be at Manfredonia in three weeks. But I was excited by the idea of being in Italy

Seraffyn at Tricase.

alone: free to think all my own thoughts, free to take care of only myself with no consideration for the needs and desires of a man, a boat, and the sea. The next weeks offered lots of time to consider my future. Did I really like voyaging or did I stay with Larry because it was easier than doing anything else? Was I willing to accept the constant careful planning and attention to details that made our life afloat safe? Could I accept the idea that in tight sailing situations Larry would be and act just like a captain? He was definitely the stronger, more experienced, more aggressive sailor of the two of us, and I knew that life with him would always involve sailing. Did I resent the restrictions of being part of a couple? (As Larry once said, "If you want to be independent then you have to do it alone. But if you want the strength, companionship, and security of being part of a couple, that's another thing.")

I had a wonderful holiday right from the first night on the train to Napoli. I met two young Australian girls who were on a world tour, and we spent the next ten days exploring Pompeii, Napoli, and Rome, seeing things with the fresh viewpoint of two art students. Then I spent four exquisite quiet days in Assissi, the enchanted village where St. Francis lived and studied. But after a two-day visit in Ancone with Mario and Maria from Lampedusa, I was feeling irresistibly pulled toward Manfredonia. My justification for heading to our rendezvous port four days early was that I was tired of traveling on trains and that I needed some lazy days sunbathing on the beach.

The train situation in Manfredonia was a mile from the harbor. Every small hotel and pension within luggage-carrying distance was full. One concierge finally suggested, "Leave your bags here and walk past the harbor. There is a real big hotel on the far side that must have one room vacant." Local telephones were out of order, so I set off. As I approached the harbor I could not believe my eyes: there was *Seraffyn*, with Larry in the water diving to scrub her bottom.

Our reunion was wet and wonderful. "I got here a few days ago hoping you would show up early," Larry told me. "These south winds are too good to miss. I sure hated single-handing. I felt so vulnerable all the time. What if I didn't make port by nightfall? Sure is easier to come alongside unfamiliar docks with two people!"

We both had come to the same conclusion during our time apart. Being together as a closely working couple was our first choice. For any two people living in the confines of a cruising boat, open and easy

The lateen rig
worked exceptionally well.

The two
sixty-year-old brothers.

communications are an absolute necessity—and a yearly separate holiday will add spice and tranquility to the relationship.

Larry had planned our reunion well. He had located a special fishermen's café, where we had thick, wine-flavored seafood soup and crusty bread. He had scrubbed *Seraffyn*'s bilges (a job I hate). His only bad news was that a fishboat had hit our boomkin and windvane—breaking the joint we had patched up after the collision in Ibiza. "This winter I'll make a complete new end for the boomkin," Larry assured me. "Meanwhile it's strong enough since the bronze wind vane bracket plate supports the backstay too."

Larry left me at 0300 the next morning. He had been fascinated by a lateen rigged twenty-four-foot open boat that entered the harbor about noon each day. In spite of a sometimes humorous language gap, the two sixty-year-old brothers who owned the eighty-year-old boat asked Larry to sail along with them one night while they fished for octopus. I had a good sleep in, then unpacked and shopped for some fresh stores while I waited for Larry to return.

At noon Larry was back full of admiration for what must be the last sailing work boat in Italy. "You would be amazed at how well that lateen sail goes to windward," Larry told me over lunch. "It's nothing but rough poles lashed together with bits of string. Not one spar is longer than the boat, so they can all be stored away easily. To add sail they just lash more canvas to the lower edge of the mainsail. The first reef is easy. The brothers just ease the lashings holding up the lateen spar and the whole sail plan comes down about six feet closer to the deck. It doesn't have so much leverage then. Sure is safe without a boom to hit you while you're working. Now I know how we could jury-rig *Seraffyn* if we broke our mast at sea. Our spinnaker pole and oar lashed together could be the lateen spar, our boom could be the mast, and one of our jibs could be lashed to that. We would be able to go to windward that way!"

Larry's enthusiasm was contagious until he started talking about breaking our mast. But it is always a possibility, so I could appreciate his interest in considering ways around the problem. Maybe this mental preparation is like carrying spare parts. If you have them on board, you never need them; if you go without, the original always seems to break down far from the nearest parts supplier.

Just before we set sail the next morning Larry took two nylon one-half-inch mooring lines from our "too good to throw away" locker, sewed new whippings on the ends, then rowed over to the octopus boat. The brothers were delighted with this gift, especially since their mooring lines were prickly old manila. Larry declined their return offer of an octopus. Somehow neither of us have come to like this so-called delicacy in spite of our Spanish and Italian friends' finest culinary attempts to change our minds.

Our general sailing plan was to work farther north along the Italian coast to circumnavigate the Adriatic with Trieste as the top of the circle and the Dalmation Islands of Yugoslavia as the far side. But strong northerly winds were blowing when we cleared the Manfredonia area. After twenty minutes of slamming into a twenty-five-knot wind, we easily changed our minds, eased sheets, and reached off toward Dalmatia and yet another arrest.

Once again, strong winds caused us to choose an anchorage that promised good protection but in the end presented us a problem. This time we encountered storm-force northerly winds during the night and lay hove to for six hours with the huge navigation light on one of the tiny westernmost islands of Yugoslavia serving as a comforting beacon three miles to windward. A huge VLCC (very large crude carrier) signaled to us as we lay comfortably, bow forty-five degrees from the wind, mainsail double reefed, and hauled close amidships with tiller tied to leeward. *Seraffyn* must have looked unbelievably small to them as their search light played over us in seas we were told later ran as high as twenty feet. So we took turns standing a cool watch in the cockpit since we had been given positive proof that this could be a shipping lane. By morning the wind had shifted to the northwest and eased to just a gale so we again reached off over a very nasty sea toward Korcula, which our British cruising guide raves about. But by noon the winds were definitely easing and we had learned how Mediterranean winds can turn off with almost no warning. So rather than risk spending a night becalmed in a choppy sea if we failed to reach the last twenty-five miles to Korcula, we changed course to sail five miles into what appeared to be a deserted but exceptionally well-protected bay on the island of Laskov. Our charts and pilots showed this island as almost unpopulated except for a tiny village on its northern side, five or six miles from our chosen anchorage.

That special sensation that comes when you sail from a gale-whipped, rolling, tumbling sea into the calm, still lee of a safe anchorage swept over us as the green clad entrance opened its arms in welcome. We had a delightful beat up the calm bay, tacking easily between the dangers marked on our chart. The afternoon sun was warm. The wind was much lighter in the lee of the high hills although an occasional strong gust heeled us until our leeward deck ran with water. We took an extra long tack at the head of the bay to decide exactly where we wanted to set our anchor. We were disappointed to see a small hotel had been built right in front of the nicest spot. So we headed for another shallow area in the bay about one-fourth mile away. A huge bang shook the air. A flare blazed in the air ahead of us. Neither Larry or I had any idea it was meant as a warning to us. So we sailed innocently on, talking about dropping the staysail in a minute or two and rounding into the wind to anchor. Then we saw two uniformed men run out from under the trees into the rocky beach and point their rifles right at us. Another flare burst just ahead of *Seraffyn*. Gun shots rang out, and we realized we had done something that someone in power did not like. Larry put the tiller hard to leeward. We tacked, sailed back in front of the little hotel, anchored, and took our sails down. This seemed to satisfy the armed soldiers as they put their rifles down as soon as we headed in the opposite direction. "Damn military takes over all the best anchorages," Larry groaned, "Portsmouth, Sada, the river at Bizerte, Clearcreek, here."

We decided against launching *Rinky Dink* since the wind was definitely moderating and we planned to sail onward in the morning. So we dug into the stack of new books I had brought back from my shopping spree in Rome.

I was just preparing dinner three hours later, Larry was checking the anchor and getting the oil lamps ready for the night when a large naval launch came into our bay. Guns were much in evidence as it pulled carefully alongside *Seraffyn*. Larry saw me climbing out of the cabin and said, "How do we do it?" just as a very portly gaudily uniformed man called in broken English, "You are under arrest."

Three inspectors questioned us this time and two climbed through the boat searching for weapons. We showed them our old 37 mm flare gun and again were glad that we do not carry any firearms while we cruise. After an hour the head official took our passports, ships papers, and Larry's international driver's license. "Why did you not go first to Split, Korcula, or Dubrovnic for a cruising permit?" he asked for the fifth time.

"There was a storm blowing," Larry explained again. I guess the official accepted this since he had had to plow through heavy seas to reach our bay. His uniform and the launch were speckled with drying salt spray. "Well, I am sorry for you," he answered, "Now you must sail to Korcula, where you will pay a two-hundred-dollar fine, then these papers will be returned to you. Until that time you are under arrest and we will be watching." Then he departed and landed next to the building that was now obviously a barracks, not a small hotel.

We slept soundly but both of us were up early, ready to set sail as soon as the first breeze came up. I was fuming over the whole affair and ready to abandon our papers and head to sea. But Larry reminded me, "This is a communist country, so let's tread real lightly. Those ships papers and passports are worth two hundred dollars worth of hassle to replace."

It was 0900 before a breeze filled in. On shore no one seemed to pay attention to us. In fact only two soldiers were visible as we tacked into the forbidden part of the bay to get weathering and clear the harbor. They ignored our presence. But we suddenly saw the reason for all the fuss. Just behind a tree-covered small point there was a series of large tunnels cut into the rocky shore. The bow of a submarine was just visible in the first one.

The pall of being under arrest, the threat of a two-hundred-dollar fine, and our unavoidable fear at being wrongdoers in a communist country dampened an otherwise pleasant day of sailing. We both tried to keep as busy as possible while we reached northward in light breezes on a calm sea. Helmer was steering, I was scrubbing the teak deck while Larry threw the canvas bucket over then hoisted it on board to wash the scrubbings away. On one toss he lost his grip. We both reacted as we had practiced for our man overboard drills. Larry easily picked up the wooden bottomed bucket as I steered just to windward of it. But when we settled back on our course we realized neither of us had thought to unclutch the wind vane. In these seven-knot breezes it had been easy to overcome its steering power. But in any heavier winds this omission could have cost precious time. So man overboard drill went on our list of boat chores.

It was after dark when we reached into the 1½-mile-wide Pelješac Kanal between Vela Luka and Luka Ploče. Four miles ahead on the northern shore of Vela Luka we could see the glow of Korčula. To starboard, the steep ridge of the granite mountains which form Luka Ploče rose to over five thousand feet within a half mile of the sea. Gentle warm breezes kept us skimming over the smooth waters. A huge full moon glowed against the towering cliffs. The aroma of pine from the tree-covered lower hills surrounded us. From the minute we followed the excellent navigation lights into that enchanted kanal until we tied up in Korcula, only one hundred feet from the base of one of the most beautiful walled cities I have ever seen, both of us were able to forget our arrest, our fine, and our fears.

They all came back the next morning. "What papers?" the port captain asked. "Arrest? What are you talking about?" the chief of police asked when we located his office. "I don't have your papers," the military adviser for the island told us after we had walked eighteen blocks and gotten lost three times looking for his office. "Try the port captain." We went back to square one and again carefully explained the whole affair to the English speaking port captain. "I'll give you a cruising permit," he offered. "Bring me your passports."

We went back to Seraffyn in defeat. Then a quiet gentleman came walking down the stone quay and asked us about Seraffyn. "I'm a retired naval officer," Lujo explained. "I've built a little schooner myself, its just across the canal." We invited Lujo on board and within ten minutes he took us in hand and solved our dilemma. Once again we went to the port captain's office. This time Lujo convinced him to search all of the "in" baskets on each of his subordinates' desks. The last one contained a note and all of our papers. The port captain read the note, shook his head, and tore it up. "Forget the fines, you didn't do any harm, but now let's make you a cruising permit!"

This document cost us nothing. It was never looked at by another official in all our time in Yugoslavia. But on page one were careful descriptions and maps of each closed military zone, including the area sorrounding Tito's summer island retreat and, of course, Laskov.

As soon as this was in our hands, Lujo looked at his watch and then called "Please sail over to my home for dinner tomorrow" as he ran to catch the ferry.

The two of us stood in front of the port captain's office clutching our precious papers, feeling slightly dazed by our good fortune and enjoying the smell of freedom for a few moments. Then we headed for the first money-changing shop we could find and later spent a small part of our unimposed fine at an excellent open-air restaurant on the seaward edge of the ancient city.

CHAPTER 18

~~~~~

The Other Side of Sailing

The Dalmatian Islands stretch along the Yugoslavian coast like a shredded ribbon thirty miles wide and two hundred miles long. The sides of the island chain closest to the mainland are green and indented with tiny harbors. The side facing Italy presents a bleak, steep-to, rock-faced appearance. Harbors on this seaward side are up to thirty miles apart.

Lujo pointed out some of those he had explored in his little schooner and recommended we stay outside the islands for our voyage north, then come inside for our return. "Even with our good navigation aids, you shouldn't sail at night on the inside. Too many rocks, and the Bora wind comes quickly." His advice made sense because the coast pilot had spoken in detail about this northeast autumn wind which whistled out of the Russian steppes and sometimes gusted up to eighty knots. Its full force rarely carried beyond the outer edge of the Dalmatian Islands. So going north against this possible head wind we would have easier sailing and room to heave to if necessary in the more open waters.

After Lujo and his brother Ivo, a mathematics professor from the University of Zagreb, made careful sketches of our windvane, we went ashore to meet the rest of their family. They had prepared a special treat: barbequed highly spiced meatballs. Momma, the eighty-one-year-old matriarch, still worked as an English-Polish translator. She unabashedly asked if we would bring her any good books we had finished reading on board. "Our government is probably the best there is if you have to live in a communist country. But they are still afraid of books!" she told us. That evening for the first of many times we heard the Yugoslavian litany, "While Tito lives, our own lives keep improving. But when he dies will it be the same?" Mom capped a peaceful, interesting family-type evening by playing quiet Beethoven sonatas on her battered old piano.

When we set sail bound for Trieste, Mom was on her front porch. She had found a huge white handkerchief and waved it until it was only a flashing speck five miles astern. It is strange how that tiny fading white dot brought tears to my eyes. There stood a woman who had lived through the middle of two world wars and a communist takeover yet still voraciously devoured novels in three languages and practiced piano for an hour each day. Her bewitching smile and twinkling gray eyes had made us feel like we had stepped into a magic circle of friendship.

We hurried north past the bleak out islands, sailing on nights when there was a fair wind, searching for an anchorage when the barometer started to fall or mares tales swept across the sky. One day when we were tied next to a tiny village quay, we varnished *Seraffyn's* mast because there was no breeze to fill our sails. So with the blessing of fair winds and warm late summer days we arrived in Trieste on September 15, two days before the first race of the 1976 World Half Ton Regatta.

The yacht club Adriaco is located on a pier in the middle of a small, extremely crowded harbor near the freight yards of Trieste. The floats surrounding the red brick building were almost filled with thirty-foot race boats from seventeen different countries. So we were not too surprised when the attendant on the dock waved us away, but we were a bit ticked off with his rude manner. The unexpected crowdedness of the overfilled harbor, the shriek of a steam engine shoving railroad cars along the dockside, the roar of cars on the main highway just behind the club, the shrieking factory whistles calling six o'clock quitting time, and the absolute lack of anchoring space came as a bit of a shock after three weeks in the quiet island anchorages of Dalmatia. "Come on, let's leave," Larry grumped. "Who wants to stay in such a dirty harbor anyway?"

"Oh, Larry, quit it," I snapped. "You wanted to see the races. Let's just tie alongside some fish boat for the night. Maybe the club will find a place for us if we talk to the right person." We slowly reached around the confined harbor and finally tied to a strange looking barge with vacuum cleaner like arms extending twenty feet into the air, a huge revolving brush on its front end, and large bins amidships. No one told us to go away. With dark, the roaring city sounds died away and we spent a comfortable night.

At eight A.M. laughing Italian voices woke us. "You must go away right now," the young man dressed in coveralls told us. "I have to collect the garbage!" Only then did we realize the barge we had tied to was a garbage scooper—the kind that cleans floating debris from harbor waters. I dressed quickly, grabbed my wallet, and headed along the shore for the yacht club while Larry rowed *Seraffyn* slowly around the harbor.

There was absolute chaos in the club manager's office: Reporters, race skippers looking for missing crew, waiters looking for change. But the manager still had a sense of humor. When I asked for a mooring space saying we were cruising members of the West Vancouver Yacht Club, he put his hand over his eyes and asked, "How big is she?" He slowly parted his fingers to look out his second-story window. *Seraffyn* slid jauntily into view, Larry slowly stroking with the single oar on the glassy morning water. The manager laughed with relief. "For her, of course we have space. Right here in front of my office where I can watch her."

I ran down to see the space he had indicated between two beautifully maintained fifty-foot wooden ketches. It was a bow on mooring less than twenty feet from the club's lobby. Then I ran out the docks to tell Larry.

Several eager hands took Larry's lines as he sculled into our assigned space. Within ten minutes we had met two Italian yacht designers, an Irish racer, and three local cruising sailors. We were informed that no foreign ocean crossing yachts had been in Trieste for at least three years. Only one other cruising boat was in harbor: *Kotara* the forty-five-foot ketch owned by Des and Annette Stock from New Zealand. They usually based their Dutch built ketch in Split, Yugoslavia, and now were in Trieste to support and assist their hometown New Zealand half-ton crew. All of the rest of the crowd that streamed by our bow was caused by the crews and entourages of the half-tonners plus all of the members of the Club Adriaco who had come to organize and assist with activities and events.

As soon as we could politely leave *Seraffyn*'s admirers, we walked over to the docks reserved for the half-ton competitors. Forty tubby, elaborately painted hulls bobbed and dipped as crews tried on new sails, adjusted rigging, or rushed around greasing and bolting on various bits of deck hardware. About halfway down the line a huge Canadian flag flew from the stern of one race boat. We hurried to see if by some remote chance it was anyone we knew. "Hey Larry," roared Vladimir Plasvic, a West Vancouver Yacht Club racer. "Heard you were somewhere in the Adriatic, thought you'd show up. I need you to crew." Larry hates being an observer so he looked at me, hesitated thirty seconds, then climbed on board saying, "Sure, Vlad, show me around the boat."

I stood on the dock laughing. Looks like I have a week to loaf, I thought. But no one loafs when a regatta gets rolling. I was recruited as chief shoreside cook and bottle washer. *Seraffyn* became the preparation kitchen for racing meals, message center, and coffee-break haven. Because of her proximity to the club's entrance, the aroma of each fresh perking pot of coffee seemed to add another Italian yachtsman to my morning coffee klatches. Soon they began bringing fruit and pastries each day. While Larry was out practicing, I made new friends, toured the town, and did a bit of varnishing. Then an hour before each race I boarded the lovely old ferry the yacht club had hired for press and officials. We feasted on magnificent four-course hot meals accompanied by wine and constant rounds of coffee or tea and lounged on padded deck chairs while Larry and 240 other men slaved to catch the best puffs of wind over tricky olympic courses and ate prepacked sandwiches.

Some top notch sailors competed. Paul Elvstrom from Denmark showed everyone the way around the olympic course with his near perfect tactics. Bill Carter and his raucous crew from San Francisco had chartered an Italian boat named *Selvaggia*, or *Savage Woman*, which suited them fine. But it was the irrepressible Irish, sailing a new boat by an almost unknown designer, who stole the show and all the Italian hearts. Harold Cudmore and his team from Cork had towed their Ron Holland designed *Silver Shamrock* across Europe behind an old Jaguar a month and a half earlier. By the time race week started, they had sailed as guests in all the Italian eliminations, plus ten local races, and gone over both the overnight race course and the long-distance race course. By the day before the first race their boat and food was ready, all the rigging checked, the hull scrubbed and polished, everything organized. So all during race week they could concentrate on racing during the days and playing during the evenings.

When the final uproarious awards party ended and the first half

One of my morning coffee klatches in front of the Club Adriaco. In the foreground is the only sad looking Italian we ever met.

The Italian owner willingly allowed these marker-pen translations.

tonner was loaded on a truck to be hauled toward its home port, Larry and I sat down at a small café for our first quiet hour alone together in close to a week. I heard his impressions of high pressure racing and we dissected the reasons the Canadians came out in the middle of a fleet of forty-two. "Not bad for a crew who arrived four days before the first race, who sailed on a chartered boat they'd never seen before," I said. They had been handicapped by having the Italian owner on board as sixth crewman. He was a good sailor, but since he spoke no English and not one of the crew spoke Italian, there were inevitable mixups, and only two of the people on board had ever sailed together before they arrived in Trieste.

The comparison between the Irish team's effort and our Canadian team's attempt taught me about the time, expense, and organization behind a successful world-class racing effort. Larry and I had worked on race committees in England and Mexico, so we were already aware of the work necessary for the success of a regatta like this one. Both the town of Trieste and the Club Adriaco had gone all out. And like all good hosts they breathed a sigh of relief when the last boat was safely loaded on its semi-truck and hauled away.

Then several of the warm local sailors who had been only fleeting hellos and casual drop in visitors, came over to *Seraffyn* to really get acquainted. The day before the last long-distance race ended, I had had time to go into the main post office. Two large packages were waiting. One contained our normal mail, but the other one held the first copy of our very own book plus some spare dust jackets. To say I was excited is a vast understatement. I could not wait to share this treasure! So I showed it to an Italian yacht designer, Carlos Sciarrelli, who stopped by for coffee an hour later. I wish Larry had been there to share the fun of hearing Carlos yell at anyone who passed, "Look at this, it's wonderful!" *Seraffyn* rocked with congratulating visitors. My coffee pot perked full time, and one visitor, a young naval architect from the local ship building yard, asked for a dust jacket, which he promised to return.

Now Carlos returned each day to invite us to a dinner or a concert or to introduce us to one of his special friends. This famous blustery intellectual had become a switch train operator in the yard in front of the Club Adriaco when he was eighteen. The daily sight of people going sailing, of lovely boats surrounding the handsome old club house, had enticed him to ask about sailing. Within a year he had designed and built himself a lovely eighteen-foot wooden sail boat. A club member liked it so much he asked Carlos to draw one similar but twenty feet long. Now, eighteen years later Carlos had drawn over 175 different boats, from twelve feet to over one hundred feet long. While we were in Trieste, Carlos had twenty beautiful custom designed boats under way in various parts of Europe. One evening at his seven-hundred-year-old home, Craiglietto, a boat builder who worked with Carlos almost exclusively, started an interesting conversation. What is the real cost of a custom built yacht? Carlos, who is almost a maniac about keeping graphs, charts, and figures, ran up to his designing loft and came back with the statistics he had kept for eighteen years. "Here are the figures for almost fifty of the boats I have designed. They were built in professional yards: some on contract prices, others on time and materials—all of them to the high standards set by Craiglietto. I have broken the costs down on a total displacement basis using a ton of two thousand pounds. It seems any type of custom boat—wood, steel, or fiberglass—can be priced by the ton. Right now in Italy the cost for materials on a simple boat with an engine and sails will be about $2000 a ton (1976) and the labor will be eight hundred hours a ton for a heavy displacement type hull—going up to about one thousand hours a ton for light displacement boats. So you can just find how much the yard charges for their labor, add the price for materials, and figure the cost for your boat within five percent." Carlos's figures started an argument that meandered through a dinner of baked lasagne, roast pork, three vegetables, three types of wine, then a dessert of white grapes cut in half, soaked overnight in dry white wine topped with brandy flavored cream and served with coffee. In the end no one could dispute Carlos's figures. We have checked them out with several top grade professional builders and designers in five different countries since then, and his figures do work within 5 percent. (Material costs in 1980 are running about $2800 a ton of displacement.) We've heard of many people who found boat builders willing to try producing a custom boat for less than these prices. But in the end they rarely turn out to be bargains. Either the builder skimps on materials or on his quality, or worse yet, he goes broke before he finishes your boat.

One way to save on the cost of a custom boat is to build part or all of it yourself. For amateur builders the time factor has to be increased by 25 to 50 percent per ton because of the learning curve involved. Material costs will probably increase by 30 percent since professional discounts are hard for the amateur to get. For people who start with a hull, deck, and house, the time factor can be decreased by one-third and the material costs increased by about one-sixth.

(A few years later we continued our discussion with Carlos by mail. He wrote, "When somebody comes to me for a boat that he wants to build himself, I, before all, clarify to him the number of working hours he has to face, the hours per month he has at his disposal, the logical number of years that will be needed. . . . My suggestion in most cases is, if you want to sail around the world, you must order a new boat or refit an old one if you are not rich.")

As we were leaving to walk back through the quiet streets of the old city, Carlos came part way with us. "Why don't you stay in Trieste

Seraffyn resplendent in her new Italian clothes. VENEZIANI LTD.

just ten days more?" he asked. "There is the last regatta of the season, and I will take my boat and challenge *Seraffyn.* " We told him about the end of the season growth on *Seraffyn*'s bottom plus our desire to see more of the Dalmation Islands before winter's Bora winds blasted through the Russian Steppes. The idea was inviting since we felt right at home in Trieste, but after two weeks it was time to move on. Carlos eyes took on the naughty twinkle we had come to recognize as trouble, "I have an idea that will make you stay," he said when he turned to leave.

Just as my coffee pot started perking the next morning, Carlos showed up with a box of cream-filled pastries and two friends. Fredrico de Minerbi was manager of Veneziani paint company's marine division. His fiery red-haired wife, Sabina, was advertising director. "We must print a brochure on how to paint a wooden yacht this winter," they explained. "We will pay for the expense of hauling your boat and give you all the paints you need if we can take photos while you work."

So two days later we were hauled clear of the water at the fine marina just fifteen miles north of Trieste in Manfalcone. With the full approval of the paint company we took this chance to strip seven years of accumulated bottom paint using the blow torch they provided. For seven days we scraped, sanded, and painted while a photographer sipped coffee and occasionally asked us to turn our paint can so his brand name showed. Two coats of red bottom paint, two coats of white topside enamel, a coat of royal blue on our whale stripe, and *Seraffyn* glowed proudly for her final photographs. We had even found time, and with the assistance of Fredrico, the materials to replace the boomkin stay chainplates which were bent from the two collisions earlier that summer. We also put five-sixteenth-inch thick, one-inch wide straps of bronze between each chainplate on our channels (the struts that hold the chainplates away from the hull so the shrouds clear our bulwarks). These straps took all the chafe from fenders and fender boards so eventually we saved a tremendous amount of maintenance work. We decided our next boat, if ever we built it, would have a bronze strap running on a raised rubbing strake for most of the length of the hull.

We had a special treat while we worked on *Seraffyn.* One of our old friends from Newport Beach now lived in the marina at Manfalcone on board his forty-five-foot charter yawl, *Vervaine.* Bob Riggs and his wife, Barbara, filled our evenings, helped us shop, and lent a hand sanding when the weather looked threatening. So our least favorite job of the winter was now crossed pleasantly and inexpensively off our work list, and when we arrived at the Club Adriacos closing day regatta *Seraffyn* was the second most admired boat in the fleet.

Carlo Sciarrelli scudded past us in a boat that drew everyone's attention from our glowing paint job. He had found eighty-five-year-old eighteen-foot *Bat* in a barn sixty miles from the water near the Austrian border a few years earlier. Her lovely varnished teak hull had required little restoring. Now she presented a stunning show as her ten-foot bowsprit and gaff rig spread almost six hundred feet of canvas above her open daysailor's cockpit.

The late autumn breeze failed before the first boat could reach the finish line. But the day was a delight of greetings and farewells as new friends traded tacks and our Italian crew, Carmelo Lucatelli and Gianfranco Gulli, worked to get *Seraffyn* at the weather mark right beside the one-quarter tonners. By the time everyone decided to call it quits and the committee boat came by to tow *Bat*, three other engineless cruisers, and us in for the after race dinner, it was turning cold. It was

The Bat.

207

October 18, and for the first time that year we put on our oven to warm *Seraffyn*'s cabin while we dressed to go out for dinner.

Just as we were stepping off the boat, the naval architect who had asked for the dust jacket from our book came down the dock. "Are you really leaving tomorrow?" Enrico Buschi asked. When we assured him we were, Enrico said, "I have made a small gift for you. If you do not like it you must tell me and I will not expect you to take it with you. Please wait for me in the club bar." Our curiosity was more than a little aroused as we waited for his return. When Enrico slowly opened the cardboard box to display an eighteen-by-twenty-two-inch oil painting of *Seraffyn* reefed down, beating across an angry sea, neither Larry nor I could stay dry-eyed. He had used an eighteenth-century style to dramatize our cover photo and create a painting that is still one of our most valued treasures. Because the painting still needed two weeks to dry thoroughly, Enrico had constructed a special extra strong box to protect it. When we set sail the next morning it was cold and sunny. Our lockers were full of fine Italian packaged products. Our guest book had seven new pages of signatures, addresses, and good wishes, and our port quarter berth was filled by Enrico's special gift. As we look back now, we realize only the threat of Trieste's cold winter kept us from finding a small apartment to rent so we could stay among these warm, fun-loving people for a while longer. We sometimes wonder how our lives would have differed if we had.

As we sailed toward Piran, the first Yugoslavian town on the Istria Peninsula, we were expecting some cold weather and possibly blustery Bora winds on our slow meander south for a warm Maltese winter. But we were not quite prepared for what we got.

CHAPTER 19

~~~~~~

Sirocco

We had experienced the repression and problems of communistic
regimes during our voyage around the Baltic in 1974. Russia
had been completely closed to us. Poland had been a depressing armed
camp where only an invitation from the Polish Sailing Association had
made an entry visa for *Seraffyn* finally materialize. So we were quite
surprised by the openness and relative prosperity of coastal Yugoslavia. Officials never once asked for our papers. We were free to sail
anywhere except the three closed military zones shown on our cruising permits. The villages and cities we visited were clean and prosper-
ous looking with excellent new schools and road crews busily repairing ancient roads now used more by automobiles and trucks than
donkeys or horsecarts. Then we learned of one of the main reforms
Tito had made to enrich his country's economy and raise morale under
his brand of communistic rule. After twenty years of the closed-door
policy common to most Soviet influenced countries, Tito had guaranteed people the right to obtain passports and visit abroad. He also
invited Yugoslavs who had been exiled during the revolution to come
home for a visit or to stay, and he guaranteed they would not be
detained at future departures. Only students who accepted government assistance for their college education were denied passports—
and only for five years after they had finished school so the country
could benefit from their experience.

As we sailed along the Dalmation Coast we met returned exiles
who had already become American, Canadian, or British citizens but
now felt free to spend summer or autumn holidays with their Yugoslav
families. Their small gifts plus the money they sent home from jobs

abroad helped enrich the local economy.

We met one fisherman from the San Diego, California, tuna fleet in a tiny Dalmation island village. He sent his parents thirty dollars a month, which enabled them to have some kind of meat five times a week. On this visit he had brought a small portable television, the first one to appear in a village of two hundred people.

Imported goods were noticeably absent from the shelves of the village stores we shopped in. Food was reasonably priced, but the selection of local produce was limited. All canned and packaged produce carried the same label from the state-owned co-op. The quality was average, but for items such as jam or fruit preserves, which were not considered staples, the prices were quite high. Our lockers were full from our stay in Italy, and we needed only fresh meat and vegetables. Laundromats were noticeably absent throughout Yugoslavia. On the one occasion when it was impossible to wash our own clothes on board because of constant rain, we asked every person we met, where we could wash and dry our clothes. Some clever person directed us to the local sanatarium, a rest home for people recovering from respiratory diseases caught in the mines of central Yugoslavia. The director very kindly invited us to use the laundry facilities and served us tea on the enclosed sun room while we waited.

The first days after we left Trieste were crisp and clear with light cold breezes that made us keep our sailing jackets well zipped. We day-hopped south, stopping each night at some of the most exquisite medieval towns I have ever seen. The sweet aroma of roasting chestnuts lured us to the street corner vendors who stood next to charcoal braisers—stirring the nuts and tossing advice to the inevitable chess players clustered close to the small fire on wrought-iron, roadside benches.

Handsome bronze statues of men who pointed batons or rode horses decorated the tiny cobbled squares, surrounded by carved stone steeples and granite office buildings. The autumn hills were ablaze with trees turning crimson and yellow as we sailed quietly by this rich peninsula which had often been the cause of border disputes between Italy, Yugoslavia, and Austria.

We had seven hundred miles to go to reach our planned winter re-fitting port, Malta. It was getting late in October and the first ten days of our southbound trip lulled us into stopping everywhere we could, sometimes only going eight miles to see some new anchorage.

We began dawdling more at each port. "The only strong winds anyone talks about for the Adriatic in October and November are the Boras. They're from the northeast so we can use them to run out of the Adriatic if it gets too cold," we rationalized.

We had only a short work list for the winter re-fit. Our publisher had shown interest in another book. But we would not have to be in Malta for that since we had started devoting two mornings each week to our project. Our cruising fund was still well reinforced from our delivery of the previous winter. So we did not have to rush and find work.

One hour out of Valuda, the last harbor on the Istrian Peninsula, we got our first taste of the up-to-then fabled Bora wind. The air was perfectly clear; the sea, extremely blue. The wind skimmed in like a flock of water birds, the first puff hesitant and kicking so whitecaps specked the sea to windward. Then the next puffs came with determination and settled in as if they owned the area. Within twenty minutes it was blowing over forty knots. The wind was right on our beam. We'd dropped our jib and reached along under the double reefed mainsail, Helmer steering while both of us climbed into wet-weather

Larry was eager to go out on our bowsprit to take this photo with our Nikonos underwater camera in 50- to 55-knot Bora winds.

gear. Then Larry tied a reef into our staysail, set it, and *Seraffyn* took off like a rambunctious racehorse. Spray broke across the foredeck almost constantly, and I went below to make sure the hatch dogs were good and tight before we cleared the lee of the land. Not a drop of water seeped through our decks or hatches. I climbed on deck with our Nikonos underwater camera and secured a drop board in place to make the companionway combing higher than the deck level. Then I snapped our canvas cover over the rest of the opening. This was glorious sailing. After all my worrying about the Bora wind, the actuality was only slightly uncomfortable and definitely exhilarating. Even in the more open water between the Istrian point and the first of the Dalmation Islands, *Seraffyn* surged confidently over the rolling whitecaps and through the flying spray at six knots. Larry climbed to the end of the bowsprit to shoot photos of our plunging, hissing bow wave.

When we anchored five hours later next to three commercial fishboats in Cibat and shed foul-weather gear, ski jackets, scarves, and boots for a rub down with fresh water, I was elated. I actually looked forward to the rest of the 650-mile trip.

For two more days we had wonderful sailing on moderate winds with nighttime stops in excellent anchorages. I am accustomed to absolute dry bilges in *Seraffyn*. For two or three weeks we had been taking on about a cup or two of water a day. I noticed this because we stored some extra bottles of Italian wine in the sump of the bilge and they came out wet. After the Bora wind, the leak increased to a gallon a day; Larry started tracing it immediately. The water was obviously coming from aft, under the cockpit, so he removed each sailbag until he could see our cockpit drains. Just above the seacock, water was oozing through the thick walls of the high-pressure hose we used to connect our self-draining cockpit to the through hull fittings a foot below our waterline. The repair took only fifteen minutes since we could shut off the "swing" seacock, remove the hose, cut four inches off, and re-fit it in place. These hoses had been made of rubber, wired with a steel coil, since that had been the only guaranteed, noncollapsible hose available when we built *Seraffyn*. After eight years, the rubber was deteriorating, especially on the tighter bends. So our work list had one more item on it. Fortunately we knew that a Maltese chandlery had the newer Neoprene and nylon reinforced noncollapsible hose for applications like this where there had to be a bend in the line and where metal angle fittings with their protruding hose clamps would have created a problem. Once again, I had the peace of mind that comes from knowing our boat was absolutely tight no matter how hard we pushed her. That small bit of peace came to mean a lot over the next month.

Our daily winds had started coming from the southeast now, a very odd direction for this time of year. For three days they were moderate. Then it hit, the dread sirocco. A huge high-pressure area formed over the Sahara Desert, a low formed over the Russian Steppes, and on twenty of the next thirty days we had gale force southerly winds with intermittent rain squalls and restless seas next to the islands and large square seas in open water. We located radio stations that had marine weather forecasts and faithfully set the alarm to listen to first an Italian broadcast (in Italian) issued from Brindisi, then the Yugoslav broadcast from Split in English, and finally an English one from Malta. They never once agreed. We would set sail when the Yugoslav radio forecast northerly breezes, and an hour later that damned sirocco had us tack on tack in a nasty beat. So we would ignore that radio report the next day and try the Italian or Maltese one with the same results. Finally we tried the best two out of three. Still no luck, every time we set sail we started out with fair winds and ran into a gale.

We wonder now why we were so damned determined to get to Malta for the winter. But each time the weather looked improved, we would set sail again hoping for better luck.

Thank God there were lots of island anchorages along the way. Calm nights snuggly secured away from the frustrating, howling winds and the pleasant personal encounters in almost every anchorage were all that saved us from growing to hate the Adriatic, the boat, and sailing.

It was blowing only force 6 from the southeast one morning. Our anchorage was between two uninhabited islands. We had been sitting there twenty-four hours already hoping for a wind shift. At 1000 Larry said, "Come on, Lin, we know how to beat. There's a neat looking harbor on an island just fifteen miles from here, let's reef down and try for it."

Unfortunately the island was separated from our anchorage by an assortment of small islands and just-exposed rocks that resembled a bomb field. There were absolutely no shallow spots to anchor between our present anchorage and that one harbor. In fact, one of the main problems in sailing along these coasts is the deep water that is right up to the shore—soundings of one hundred fathoms at fifty feet from the rocks were not uncommon. The channels between these islets and rocks were only about a half-mile wide, so as we beat tack on tack in the heavy wind our fifteen miles stretched until it was late afternoon, and we still had three miles of beating to go. By then the wind was gusting close to fifty knots. Again we had been putting in reef after reef until we were under double reefed main and reefed staysail. Then a gray heavy rain squall started to work its way north. We could see it gobbling one island after another. Now I really began to worry. We could only put in one more reef, the third in our mainsail. To leeward one-quarter mile were dozens of exposed rocks and a maze of unlit islands. We had one more rock to find and round before it was safe to begin the two mile beat between the two islands to where the tiny harbor lay. The only thing on our side was the fact that our chart showed a five-mile light on the end of the breakwater that formed one side of the harbor.

As the squall grew closer Larry, too, became more than a little concerned. "Lin, plot a course that is safe on a beam reach. One that will take us through the islands and outside into the Adriatic. Try to

We had to find that rock before we could go either way.

find the largest channel and keep the plot up to date," he said as he hand steered to gain weathering on each puff or wind shift.

I worked at our chart table, sweating in wet gear, two sweaters, and a jacket, my feet wedged right across the cabin, one hand ready to grab the bunk edge when we lunged over a particularly steep bit of chop. There was a safe passage through a two-mile-wide channel, which would mean only ten miles of reaching to clear into open water if we could only find that last four-foot-high rock.

I spent the next twenty minutes rushing from the chart to the foredeck trying to find that last rock we would need to clear for either course we chose. I took bearings off the points of the few islands that had not yet been swallowed by the fast approaching squall. I did not quite trust them as the spray and mist made island ends fuzzy and our motion made our handbearing compass swing and dip. Larry kept me up to date on the island-gobbling squall as it grew ever closer. *Seraffyn* beat surely into the five-foot swell the fierce wind set up in spite of the island only two miles to windward. Some hidden air current turned the thick, forbidding squall so it passed less than two hundred yards astern of us. We lost no visibility, the wind only increased momentarily to bury *Seraffyn*'s soaking lee deck just two or three inches more. Then we spotted the rock we had been waiting for. It lay like the glistening back of a sounding whale, guarding the entrance to Otok Kaprinje.

We beat surely up the one-half-mile-wide channel, riding much easier in the lee of the land—tack on tack, our 140 square feet of canvas pressing the bulwarks under water in the stronger gusts. Dusk was falling quickly, but we could see the stone pier with its unlit navigation lamp. Five or six people stood on its end in spite of the cold heavy wind. When we were only four or five tacks away from the paradisiacal village tucked behind the breakwater and a hook in the island, someone climbed the steps to the navigation light and lit a kerosene lamp that probably would not be visible three miles away. But now, with our goal just minutes away, this only made us laugh with relief.

An English-speaking villager took our bow line. "The whole village has been watching you. We couldn't figure out why you were going from one side of the bay to the other and tilting so much. But one of the old fishermen explained for us. We were going to send one of our fish boats out to help you but the wind is too strong for our small motors. Welcome to the Isle of Capri," he said.

"This isn't the real Isle of Capri," the lady next to him said, "but it's our Isle of Capri." As we spent the next two days recovering from our foolish, storybook sail, we forgot the difference in spelling and the difference in location—to this day we look on Otok Kapriji and its village of two hundred fishermen as our Isle of Capri.

We spent a quiet morning answering letters and finishing an article to send to Australia. Not one person disturbed us as we lay in front of the timeless village. By noon we had a dozen letters and small packages to mail. We walked a hundred yards along the stone sea wall, then climbed the stairs to the post office above the only store in town. The door was wide open. No one was inside. An old man was sitting on his front porch two doors down. When we reached the street again he called in Italian, "The postman is out fishing. I'll tell him you came by."

An hour later while I was cleaning up from lunch, the postman knocked on *Seraffyn*'s deck. "Bring your letters along," he said in English that we could easily understand. I was surprised when he put the same eleven-cent stamp on each item. Some were bound for Italy, some for New York, some weighed one half an ounce, others seven or eight ounces. When I tried to diplomatically ask him to weigh some of the larger envelopes, he laughed and said, "The officials on the mainland think we islanders are so dumb we can't read a scale. So they let us send everything for the same price. But we're not so dumb. We don't tell them we can read a scale." We later found our mail left two days later on the once-a-week ferry and arrived in New York and Australia within five days.

Each person who spoke English or Italian in the little village warned us, "Move your boat before the ferry comes in." We finally asked how large this ferry was and when we heard it was only eighty feet long, we almost ignored their advice. We were lying against a jog in the concrete pier at right angles to the main 150-foot-long empty ferry dock. That evening one of the villagers who had invited us to join his family for dinner came by to escort us to his home. He pointed to the pier beside *Seraffyn*. At least a dozen six-inch-deep notches scarred that solid concrete wall! Obviously they were the recent work of the same green vessel since flakes of paint still marked each one.

So we set our alarm for 0500. It was still dark when we got up and rigged a long stern line, then untied our mooring lines to let *Seraffyn* hang thirty feet away from the stone wall. A lovely force 3 southerly

The ladies of Kaprinje are very proud of their specially smoked and dried figs.

We were laying right next to a jog in the quay.

breeze held her in place while we sat on the sea wall watching half the village assemble to meet friends, families, and packages or leave for the day-long trip that allowed them three hours to shop in the market town of Zadar, since this same ferry would come through again late that evening on its way back to Split. By the time the rough old ship had disgourged its last crate of cargo, Larry and I had decided to sail onward for Split since the morning sun was warm, the breeze fresh and fair.

We hauled *Seraffyn* closer to the pier and began to take off her sail cover. The last person on the quay, the same lady who had greeted us when we sailed in out of the storm, called, "Where are you going?" "To Split," we both called back. She shook her head sadly as she walked away, then said, "Going to Split? I'm going home and going to bed."

Four hours later we began to wonder how she had guessed. We abandoned any hope of reaching Split, which now lay dead into the teeth of yet another gale. Instead we eased sheets, reefed to staysail and half a main, and headed for the tiny village of Primostan. Force 10 gusts of wind ranged down the hills and raked the bay with fingers of white as we scudded in. We carefully discussed our plans to drop the staysail, reach into the tiny bay behind a two hundred-foot-long stone sea wall, then gybe to come alongside the pier—which had a fifty-foot-long open space with good strong bollards for our mooring lines.

We had our lines and fenders oot out on deck and secured as we ran into the harbor. A dozen small work boats were moored with a maze of lines crisscrossing half the harbor to hold them well away from the rough stone walls. So we readjusted our plans to gybe a bit sooner than expected. I hauled the reefed mainsail flat amidships, straining my feet against the bulwarks, hands smarting in spite of the four-part purchase and an extra turn around the cleat. When Larry put the tiller to leeward another force 10 gust laid us decks awash with a jerk that almost made him loose his footing. We aborted that attempt at docking and worked out to more open water to discuss another plan. *Seraffyn* came about with only the double reefed mainsail set in spite of the roaring wind and short chop, but we kept the staysail ready to haul up just in case. On our second attempt we ran into the harbor under just double reefed mainsail, but this time I pulled it down before we gybed and Larry reached into the pier under bare poles. Three fishermen ran down the quay to take our lines and secure them.

By midnight the howling winds were well above hurricane force. (This was later confirmed by both newspapers and the anemometer at the harbormaster's office six blocks from our boat.) The waters inside the stone quay boiled like a caldron. Waves breaking against the twenty-foot-high sea wall covered *Seraffyn* with spray even though the fetch outside the sea wall was less than two miles. By morning we had every line we owned crisscrossing the quay next to *Seraffyn*. There were at least a dozen mooring lines plus our warping bower and as final protection, in case the three lines taking the heaviest strains broke, we had looped our anchor chain around the two-foot- diameter stone bollard. A beam anchor was set, with the help of the local fishermen, to hold *Seraffyn* safely away from the threatening stone wall. We wore our foul-weather gear and spent most of our morning tending chaffing gear and worrying as the three-foot-slop, spray, howling wind, and spitting rain created a scene which is bound to have been any sailor's vision of hell. A dozen local people worked to protect the small fishboats tied astern of us, they took turns pumping the open ones, replacing chaffed lines, and making sure deck cleats were holding. In spite of their best efforts, one of the twenty-foot diesel launches did sink in eight feet of water at the head of the bay. But just at noon three of the burly men ducked through the spray and pulled us toward a small café. With sign language and some Italian words they made it clear that they would watch *Seraffyn* while we warmed up over a hearty soup. By evening the harbor lay calm under heavy rain. It took us most of the next day to sort out our mooring lines and shorten those that had chaffed.

For some reason our run of sirocco weather seemed to make both Larry and I more determined to get south. We could have stopped for the winter in any of the charming villages of Yugoslavia. But none had the sort of shipyards, markets, movie theaters, and warm English atmosphere that we had encountered during our summer visit in Malta. Besides, we looked forward to being in a place where English was the major language, just to have a respite from the constant strain of difficult communications that is part of foreign cruising. We also knew the more efficient English mail and communications system would allow us and our publisher to catch up with each other, and in the back of our minds was the comforting knowledge that we could always get boat repair work to fill our coffers if our current writing scheme failed.

Writing was beginning to be an excellent, almost magical, way for us to finance our cruising life. We could do it wherever and whenever we liked. On rainy days, we could hide inside the boat, coffee pot perking, and while away the time over our pads and typewriter. On calm sailing evenings we could discuss and outline new writing projects. When we were kept in port by either a lack or an overabundance of wind, we could stroll around and fill the hours taking photos for some future article.

But there are some frustrating logistical problems when you write from a floating home like ours. Mail mix-ups and delays sometimes meant we had to wait four or five months to learn if an article had been accepted. The package of mail we lost in Tunisia contained three checks that would have provided almost a month's worth of crusing funds each. It took nine months to reach us finally in Malta. Checks for our work had to be cleared through the mails which sometimes meant we had to do without for a month while we waited for the ponderous wheels of the international banking world to grind our dollar checks into the proper channels to produce Italian lira or Maltese pounds. Our publisher and magazine editors endured similar frustrations when they could not even find us to check on changes they wanted to make to our copy. So more than one printing schedule was missed while we enjoyed ourselves meandering about the sea.

The winter in Malta did eventually sort out many of these snags, including getting our royalty checks changed into travelers checks. So maybe the terrible sailing along the way had been worthwhile.

But as we struggled south against the now prevailing south winds, we began to wonder. Up until this time we had noticed special days of sailing in the fickle Mediterranean. Now we counted the easy sailing in hours and underlined any fair winds in our log. Even a reach in gale force winds became a reason to celebrate. It took us 360 hours of sailing during forty days to make good 740 miles. We hove to nine different times from 5 hours to over 48 hours. We returned to port three times when sailing conditions deteriorated while we were still within sight of the breakwaters. Our worst squall, a northerly or Temporali as the Italians call them, screamed over the toe of Italy after the barometer dropped ten milibars in less than two hours. Its force 10 winds lasted 35 hours.

By Sunday the twenty-first of November we were lying in Syracuse Harbor only eighty miles from Malta. With our goal now so close we had decided to wait until every weather report we could get forecast fair winds and no gales. The second morning, just like magic, Italian, Maltese, Greek, and French shortwave radio meteorological reports called for westerly winds averaging from force 3 to force 5 over the whole Mediterranean Basin. This was too good to pass up! Even though there was absolutely no wind where we lay in the old harbor, Larry set our oar in place and we rowed out to clear water to wait.

Sure enough, by noon we were reaching on an ever-growing breeze, a beautiful westerly. A rain squall passed over us but was soon gone leaving only a force 3 breeze. At 2000 just when it was my turn to take the watch, the navigation light on the breakwater at Porto Palo came clear. This is a well-protected fishing harbor on Sicily's southeast tip. The distance from there to Malta is fifty-five miles. Since it was my watch, Larry left the choice up to me, "If you want a night in port, call me when we can tack and clear into Porto Palo. But if you want to keep right on for Malta, that's fine with me."

For almost thirty minutes I agonized over the decision. The wind was just forward of the beam and almost warm. I only had on a sweatshirt and jeans. The sea was calm and glowing with phosphorescence. I went below and tapped the barometer. It did a little jig and landed in the same spot again. I scanned the skies, the stars sparkled brightly. I spun the radio dial hoping to find a weather report, no luck. Then I went on deck, watched *Seraffyn*'s wake as she scudded along under full lapper and main, "God, I'm getting chicken," I thought to myself. Then I deliberately went below and wrote in the log "On to Malta."

Within an hour Porto Palo was only a memory. I had been able to ease sheets to a real absolute beam reach, and we were making five knots bound right for Marsesmett Harbor. At 0300 we were hove to in a westerly gale with ever-increasing seas. By 0700 Larry started making some calculations. "If it blows like this for two days, we'll be driven seventy miles east of Malta because of the currents, and that doesn't include our drift. I'm going to set the reefed staysail and see if I can steer toward Malta. You stay in the bunk. I promise I'll heave to again if things look unsafe," Larry told me.

I listened while he dropped the double reefed main and lashed it down. Then scrambling sounds from the foredeck told of his struggle to reef and hoist the staysail. As soon as we were actually underway the incredibly rough motion made me seasick. It is hard to describe the motion of a five-ton boat reaching over twenty-five-foot current and wind-caused seas at four knots while forty-five- and fifty-knot gusts of wind shove against a sixty square feet of sail at the top of the waves with half that amount in the troughs. To begin with, *Seraffyn* is absolutely tight, so my bunk was dry and warm. But stray pots rattled, and a can in the locker thunked under my bunk on each lurch and roll. No matter how I wedged myself in I was rolled back and forth by the motion. My head felt close to bursting, my ears felt chaffed and raw from the pillow, tears lay ready to flow. Every few minutes I would scoot myself around in the bunk to open the canvas companionway cover and peer out into the cockpit. Each time Larry would spot me and say something cheery from his roped-in position next to the tiller. Each time I would resolve not to ask him to heave to until he suggested it. After an hour and a half he called, "I've got Malta, maybe eight or nine miles ahead now. Hang in there Bubbles, I'm going to set the triple reefed main and try to get some weathering just in case."

Helmer steered while Larry worked with a jib sheet tied securely around his waist. The motion got worse, but only spray broke against our decks—even though I could feel *Seraffyn* being shoved bodily to leeward in the breaking foam of the jumbled seas. I felt her seem to stall when Larry headed bow into occasional breaking rollers. But mostly I felt terrible, just praying for an end to the throbbing in my head and the blinding feeling behind my eyes. An hour later Larry asked me to try finding him something, anything, to eat. For the first time in my life, slicing a piece of bread was beyond my ability. I barely managed to hand him a hardboiled egg and half an apple from the basket next to the sink. When I opened the companionway expecting to hear the full shriek of the wind, the sun was glaring bright on our soaking decks. Larry took his token lunch and looked at me; shock changed his face. I guess I was the proverbial seasick green. Though I wasn't heaving, I was close to passing out. "Get back in the bunk," Larry commanded. "Try to hold on just an hour more, we're high enough to lay Valletta Harbor. If the entrance is too rough we can sheer off for Marsaxlokk on the south of the island."

Less than thirty minutes later there was such a distinct change in our motion that I rushed on deck worried and ready to help. Malta lay less than two miles ahead, and the seas had been disturbed by the shoals and points so that they now ran almost on our stern. Larry eased sheets for a ten-degree course change, and the breakers began to lay down. Within minutes we reached past the roaring surf on either side of the entrance to Marsesmett Harbor. My headache cleared almost instantly and the pain was replaced by a feeling of insatiable hunger. The wind dropped by almost half, baffled by the buildings and hills. I worked quickly making a potato salad and omelet to serve as soon as we were at anchor. Larry unreefed the whole mainsail and worked into our favorite mooring area between Manuelo Island and Sliema.

When that anchor went down it was exactly eight years and one hour from the moment *Seraffyn* had been launched. I am sure that the five hours of sailing from Syracuse to Malta had been the hardest she had been through in her whole life.

A familiar voice called across the water, "Come and have a shower, where you in from?" We spotted Graham and Marie Newly on their sixty-five-foot power yacht, tied among the winter fleet. Within fifteen minutes we rowed over to take them up on the offer. "Looks like you had a good wind for your sail," Graham said as he welcomed us on board. "Good wind?" Larry and I both crowed. "It's blowing at least force 9 out there!"

"Is it?" Graham asked, looking out his wheelhouse wind at the tiny whitecaps that ran through the harbor pushed by occasional twenty-five-knot gusts. Larry and I just looked at each other then we looked out to where *Seraffyn*'s salt encrusted cabin sides reflected the afternoon sun. Who cared if no one knew we had just sailed through a storm? We knew and our confidence in our little ship was stronger than ever as we went below for the promised drinks and a hot bath.

CHAPTER 20

~~~~~

Malta

The day after we sailed into Malta, I dug out forty packages of tortellini, linguini, and spaghetti noodles we had bought in Trieste. Then we took the familiar bus along the harbor drive into the old, downtown part of Sliema. It was fun to be back in a place we knew. This had happened only twice in eight years of cruising and each time we had enjoyed the feeling of familiarity, of knowing the ropes just enough so that street names, offices, and stores meant something to us.

Sally welcomed us like long lost friends even before she saw our load of noodles. "I've found you a wonderful place," she shouted over her shoulder as she scurried to the kitchen for a bottle of wine and some glasses. An hour later she led us down a narrow cobbled alley and stopped in front of a wrought-iron grilled door in a row of identical four-story stone houses.

Within an hour we had paid a fifty-dollar deposit for the first months rent on the top floor apartment above a Maltese second cousin of an uncle of Sally's. Our winter home had a magnificent iron-grated street door, which opened directly onto thirty-seven stairs leading up to a two-bedroom furnished apartment. A secret interior door led from our front room up onto the flat, parapeted roof. The next day we loaded our clothes, writing supplies, and favorite souvenirs into a taxi for the one-and-a-half mile move to our new nest.

Within a week we were glad we had moved off the boat and into a home where we could feel the pulse of this foreign city. Our landlady spent a morning taking me to meet her favorite business friends—the green grocer in his basement shop just six doors down the street, the wine vendor with his horse-drawn cart, and the butcher, who only worked on Wednesdays and Fridays. She helped us locate a piano to rent and movers willing to haul the six- or seven-hundred-pound instrument up thirty-seven stairs; she found a typist to hire and showed us the best places for hot tasty workman's lunches at thirty-five cents a plate.

So on Tuesdays we left our empty wine bottles at the bottom of our steps and thirty-five cents underneath each bottle that we wanted refilled with a rough but definitely drinkable table wine. On Thursdays we left our flower basket on the steps with fifty cents beneath it, and when the flower lady knocked, we opened our bedroom window to call down our preference: daisies, mums, narcissus, and, in early spring, iris, and daffodils. On Fridays the noisy horse-drawn cart with its one hundred-gallon oil tank came rumbling down our narrow street, the oil man's echoing call of p-a-r-a-F-I-N pulled us from our writing and we ran to check our heater tank then rushed down all thirty-seven steps to buy another gallon of fine kerosene for twelve cents.

The tailor just around the corner started fitting custom-made jeans to our definitely non-Maltese shapes for less money than brand-name pants. When we asked him about the superb new sewing machine sitting unused at the back of his shop he said, "That is one my son bought when he thought of becoming a sailmaker. But we earn so much more making jeans for English companies. So it sits." Larry asked if we could rent the machine to build ourselves a new genoa. The tailor and his wife refused to take our money but immediately moved the machine into their unused back room. So we ordered the cut and shaped panels for a 365-square-foot, five-ounce genoa from Paul Lees, our sailmaking friend in England, and started a project that intrigued our neigbors and the tailor.

The only open space large enough to spread out the whole unfinished sail while we planned and cut the patches, reef points, and tabling was on our rooftop. So we would plan and prepare our sewing for the day while one rooftop neighbor showed us his racing pigeons or another called across the street to display the perfect rose he had grown in soil he had carried onto his rooftop by the basketload from a friend's farm outside the city. Then we would bundle up the sail, take our scissors, thread, and tape, stumble down four flights of steps, around the corner, and through the tailor's shop. We would spread the sail as well as possible in the six-foot by seven-foot back room and carefully sew on patches and reef points while the tailor's wife told us about her widely dispersed family and all their hopes and dreams. After two weeks of working each afternoon we had built a reefing genoa. We also learned to repeat the silly ditty that used to infuriate me when my mother said it, "As you sew so shall you rip." We had had to patch a hole we accidentally cut in the brand new sail when we were trimming thread ends. But when we carried that sail out of the tailor's shop, boarded the local bus, and paid an extra fare of seven cents for the space it took, we were like expectant parents. We rowed out to where *Seraffyn* lay on her mooring. Then we set that seemingly huge genoa. It fit better than we had hoped. We were delighted about the three hundred dollars we had saved by finishing it ourselves, and we had learned much more than could be counted in monetary terms.

Larry is a fanatic about smooth-setting sails, so we marked the few adjustments we planned to make, took the sail back to the tailor's shop, and did the final stitches. Both the tailor and his wife seemed thrilled

Sewing patches onto our new genoa.

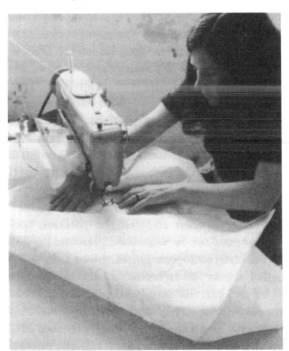

with the bottle of Scotch whiskey and bouquet of roses we brought as a thank you. Each time we saw them on the street they insisted, "Come use our machine any time." So occasionally we did and on Christmas Eve we joined their family for a drink of wine and some special cakes.

As a special treat, partially to save my sanity and Larry's supply of patience, we decided to hire someone to type the final drafts of several articles we were writing. Julia Stansby, a Maltese-born English girl, willingly did our work and decided we should get to know her adopted homeland better. So she and Chosie, who was her boyfriend and a Maltese professor of English from the local secondary school, included us in their weekend picnics. On Thursday afternoons we would all get together early and ride through the outskirts of Sliema in Chosie's rickety sports car. After twenty minutes on a narrow winding road that passed through four small villages, we rode into a small valley three miles from Malta's northern tip. There in the center of the carefully cultivated farm lands, Edward Cassar-Torreggiani had a small stable. On days when Edward was not busy with his contractoring work in Valletta, the tiny country's capital, he would join us as we rode his beautiful Arabian horses along the fields and out onto the smooth beach. Then we would all gallop along the sandy shore, our horses kicking up the salty water. We would walk our sweating mounts back to the stable in the fading light and stop at a huge sandstone trough to water them. The brother and sister who cared for the stables were both in their early seventies. They would be waiting barefoot on the cold cobbles of the courtyard to help us groom the horses before putting them in their stone stalls.

In spite of living only fifteen miles from Malta's main city, the old couple had never been to Valletta and never once had a chance to learn English. The only time they wore shoes was on Sundays when they walked four miles to the church in the small town overlooking this quiet valley. Each time we came we brought a six-pack of Seven-Up for the old couple and before we climbed into Chosie's car for the ride home, we would stop in their one-room house that was lit by an oil lamp and listen to stories of local farm problems while Chosie or Edward translated.

We could not quite believe that people on an island as small as Malta had not once left their home village in seventy years. But Paul Ripard, who owned the local ship chandlery, confirmed this when he invited us for an afternoon flight on his small airplane. "Time means nothing to the older people here," he told us as we skimmed through the crystal air just high enough to see how small this fifteen-mile-by-twenty-five-mile country was. Then we circled low over Valletta, and Paul pointed out a huge stone dome being built on top of the main Catholic church. "One man and his helper have been working on that dome for nineteen years now, cutting each piece of sandstone with handsaws, shaping it with files. He plans to finish it within six years so he can retire at the mandatory age of seventy," Paul told us. We later went to see this incredible 140-foot-by-100-foot oval dome. It was a study in patience with each fifty-pound block set perfectly together. No plans had been drawn, no transits set. The old dome builder had been taught his trade by his father—the last in a one thousand-year line of craftsmen—and the dome was perfectly oval and gracefully arching toward its final spire.

For almost two months *Seraffyn* was too torn apart to take out sailing. We had removed her maple sink counter because it had started to rot at the corners. Now Larry spent his afternoons laminating a new

Valletta and its Oval dome from Paul Ripard's plane.

one out of ash. He used ash to build a new spinnaker-whisker pole and a new end for our boomkin. We found some teak and built rails on top of our bowsprit with limber holes for gaskets to make it easier to lash the sails down. Then Larry replaced a piece of the cabin top trim that had been damaged years before. Meanwhile, I put four coats of varnish on all the worn spots inside the boat plus extra coats on our hatches and cabinsides. Our decision to move into an apartment made all of this work a lot easier. We no longer had to clean the boat up each night before we tried to use the galley. Rainy days no longer interrupted our progress because we could take work home and spread it out in our flat. When we saw how much surge there was in the harbor during the frequent northeasterly gales that winter we were doubly glad we were not living on board. Because of the shape of this very large harbor and because of its stone and concrete straight-sided sea walls, any swell that came through the entrance ran around in circles, curled around the harbor edges, and magnified until all of the hundreds of yachts moored stern to began to surge up and down, back and forth in seven-foot circles. Lines and tempers frayed during these five-day sieges. Topsides were dinged, and taffrails were damaged. Even on seventy-foot powerboats the motion sometimes became bad enough to scatter dishes that had been set on the table.

Seraffyn rode very well out at anchor. But a strange ruling by a bureaucrat newly elected to the government of Malta forced us to take up her mooring and tie her Mediterranean-style six weeks after we arrived. So on stormy days we took the bus down twice a day to check her lines. We had taken our chain to be galvanized and tested, so we set our stern anchor on a nylon rode. We just happened to be on board three days later when her one half-inch stern line parted, and we noticed the change in motion just in time to stop the bowsprit from hitting the sea wall. Fortunately we had a trip line on the stern anchor. When we recovered it we found the line had been chaffed through by some rusty object on the bottom. So this time we reset the anchor with thirty-six feet of chain so there would be no line near the bottom. As soon as our chain came back from being galvanized we set it out instead of the line. This incident made us later advise people, "If you plan to winter in Malta, take your boat out of the water and find an apartment, or stay on board at all times until some newer government lets you anchor off."

Many of the sailors who brought their boats to Malta for the winter either had them hauled out and stored at the shipyard or hired local people to watch their lines and fenders while they flew to their homes for the Christmas holidays. But almost half of the yachtsmen in Malta stayed on board that winter, including an international collection of some of the most interesting sailors we have come to know. Humphrey and Mary Barton, an English couple, were spending their seventh winter here. *Rose Rambler,* their thirty-five-foot Giles-designed wooden cruising sloop was vastly different from *Seraffyn.* We spent many boisterous evenings comparing these differences over rum and lime juice in the Barton's warm cabin. Humphrey had crossed the Atlantic twenty-one times on boats under forty feet. He had written a lovely book about one of these voyages—the story of *Vertue 35,* a twenty-five-footer he had sailed to New York—and founded the well-respected Ocean Cruising Club for voyaging sailors. Humphrey had expounded the idea of always taking all-female crews: for comfort, a well-run ship, and amiable company. His wife, Mary, was one of these crews. He proposed to her after an Atlantic crossing and they were married at a real cruising man's wedding ceremony in Antigua. Now she is a veteran of several Atlantic crossings and thousands of miles of Mediterranean cruising. On Humphrey's birthday a dozen cruising friends planned a surprise party at Sally's restaurant. It worked wonderfully and the hit of the evening came after Humphrey again told Larry he should give up bowsprits, sculling oars, and beamy boats in exchange for an all-inboard rig, a 50 percent ballast ratio, and a diesel engine. As their discussion reached its usual dead end, Humphrey, who had just turned seventy-seven years old, waited for a moment's silence. Then he stated in a firm voice, "Larry Pardey, all that's wrong with you is you are old-fashioned."

Jack Jensen and Nancy Spencer were wintering here on their Cruising Cal 46, *Satori.* They were from *Seraffyn*'s birth place of Newport Beach. Jack had started the company that built all of the Cal boats. He loved racing and resented the poor light-wind performance of his present boat. He and Larry got into some interesting evening discussions about designing a two-tonner with a removable cruising interior that would enable Jack to cruise from regatta to regatta, remove the excess weight, and enjoy being involved in world class racing.

Our home port of Victoria was represented by Ray and Dot Compton, who had bought a forty-five-foot steel boat, *Blue Onion,* in Holland. Their plan was to earn the money to buy their perfect small cruiser

Humphrey and Mary Barton. Humphrey was the founder and admiral of the Ocean Cruising Club. He died during a 1980 cruise around the Aegean at the age of eighty-one.

Ian Staniland.

An afternoon sail with Julia Stansby, her two sons, and Chosie.

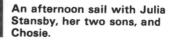

by sailing this boat home from Europe to sell it for the much higher prices steel boats were bringing in Canada. The only snag is that they were enjoying cruising so much they still had not reached Canada two years later to sell the boat. But Ray had found he could just support their habit by doing welding and engine repars with the equipment he carried on board. Larry helped him build a wooden dodger frame on *Blue Onion*'s cabin top in exchange for a new, custom-welded, stainless steel oven grate and some welding on our anchor chain.

Winter seemed to fly by. We had more than enough to keep us busy. Our writing did earn us enough for our limited cruising needs. There was lots of wood work available if and when we needed it. Social evenings, weekend parties, movies, and plays made life seem very full. As soon as *Seraffyn* was reassembled we were able to take our new friends sailing around the harbor or, on warmer days, south to the wonderfully old-fashioned fishing village of Marsaxlokk. We took a few long weekends and visited the well-protected harbor on Malta's northern island of Gozo, a place where time really did stand still.

It was during these weekend jaunts that we got to know Tom Forrestal and Ian Staniland, two very unique people who gave us a real insight into the question of children and cruising. Susan and Richard Blagbourn had cut short their cruise through the Greek Islands because a baby was on the way. They arrived in Malta early in autumn, and by the time we arrived, three-week-old Christopher Blagbourn was the center of attention. Richard had found a job as live-aboard caretaker on a seventy-foot powerboat. So his thirty-two-foot *Taganita* was hauled and stored at Manuelo Island shipyard. After many hours of debate and indecision the Blagbourns had decided that cruising with a five- or six-month-old infant was not their cup of tea. So *Taganita* was up for sale, and Richard had arranged an intersting position with his old architectural firm in Canada. I wondered what my reaction would be in the same situation. Life with a new child requires a lot of readjustments. Life on a new cruising boat also requires a big readjustment.

Then we got to know Ian, a wiry twenty-six-year-old with dark eyes and a suave appearance. His parents were among the first of the charter boat owners who migrated between the eastern Med and the West Indies year after year. Ian had been born in a Maltese hospital and moved on board the fifty-seven-foot wishbone schooner *Carrina* when he was one week old. Two months later, right on schedule for the winter charter season in Antigua, the Stanilands set off across the Atlantic. Ian had grown up on board beautiful *Carrina*—except for six winters spent in a private school in England. He had worked as first mate and at the age of nineteen took over as captain. Now he was buying *Carrina* from his parents so they could retire on board a thirty-eight-foot motor sailor. We learned that Ian had never worn a safety harness or a life jacket. Once he could crawl, his parents allowed him free run of the decks with their eight-inch-high bulwarks. They taught him to swim and were amazed at his innate sense of survival. After almost falling overboard once at the age of five months, Ian never again tried to go under the lifelines. Now Ian was lithe as a cat, and only once did we hear a near complaint from this successful charter skipper. One evening after a huge luxurious dinner prepared by his professional cook, Zillah, we sipped a fine bottle of sherry in the warmth of *Carrina*'s burgundy velvet and mahogany paneled main salon. Ian sighed, "I wonder what it would be like to store the boat away in a covered shed then work in a London office for a year? You know, a whole year when I could go without worrying about anchors dragging, sails rotting, or varnish deteriorating."

Forty-five-year-old Tom Forrestal had a completely different story on the idea of children and cruising. He had a successful contracting business in New York. But his doctor told him he had only two or three years to live due to a prematurely aging heart. He never told his wife or family about his health problem. Instead he said to his perky wife, Jo, and their nine daughters, "Some day I'd like to buy a bigger boat and go cruising." The memory of happy summers spent sailing along the coast of New York made this sound like a good idea and within a few weeks they had talked *him* into doing it right now. Tom ordered a Morgan 51 and spent four months and close to fifty thousand dollars modifying it. Then the family set off from New York with six of the daughters on board. A year and a half later we met Tom, Jo, and some of his girls—who range from eleven to twenty-four years old. The older girls had jobs or were in school so they could only join the boat for two or three months each year. Tom taught Jo and the five younger girls how to handle and maintain the boat themselves. One learned basic diesel mechanics, one studied about radios and electronics, and Jo varnished and painted like a professional.

Eight months after we left Malta that winter, we sailed into a small Greek harbor and saw *Liberty* and several of her crew anchored just off shore. "Where's Tom?" we called. "Come over and we'll tell you," Jo called. As soon as we had set our anchor we dove over and swam to *Liberty,* where we learned Tom had died suddenly the morning before we sailed into port. Only when Jo called her brother-in-law did she learn that Tom had expected this all along. We spent the next three days discussing Jo's biggest dilemma, Should she and the girls continue their planned cruise? I hope our encouragement was one of the reasons she and the six girls cruised two years more, including crossing the Atlantic. We often heard of the instant party whenever this ship full of handsome women tied up in some harbor full of cruising sailors.

We have often considered having children of our own, and the confident, healthy young people we saw on these boats plus several dozens we met throughout the Med convinced us that if we had children we would prefer they grow up on a cruising boat. We would be able to control their education ourselves, and the ever-changing cus-

Tom Forrestal and five of his nine daughters.

toms and new ideas would help them cope in today's confused world. As for concern about missing the company of children their own age, we never met an unhappy child who had gone cruising before the age of fourteen. Their parents might sometimes have felt confined, since it is even harder to find a babysitter around cruising boats than it is on shore. Having a child along does mean cruising will require extra money and maybe a four-foot addition to the boat. Almost every parent found they needed a second dinghy to allow them and their children more freedom in port.

After much careful thought I have decided I would wait until a child was one year old before taking him or her cruising. Diapers, special food, and the worry of early childhood diseases would make life afloat uncomfortable before then. I would also hesitate before asking a child over fourteen to leave a normal shore life for a brand new life afloat. Unless the young person already loves sailing and dreams of cruising just like his parents do, this upheaval right when their own social life is forming creates a sullen and unhappy atmosphere that does not belong in the confines of a small cruising boat. After discussing this with many cruising families we have found the cruising success rate with children between the ages of one and thirteen is surprisingly high. It is almost never the children who want to stop. But for first-time cruises with children between the age of fourteen and eighteen, the success rate drops tremendously.

On the thirty-first of March 1977, we moved out of our flat and back onto gleaming, clean *Seraffyn*. I love the cozy warmth of our little boat. After the huge space we had lived in all winter, she seemed like a perfectly fitted cocoon. We planned to set sail as soon as possible for the Greek Islands. Since there were no restrictions against laying at anchor in Marsesmett Harbor for short periods, we untied the bow lines and pulled *Seraffyn* back to her stern anchor and then sailed to our favorite anchorage. Soon after, an approaching storm set up a surge in the harbor.

Ian and several of the charter skippers who planned to leave for Greece at the first sign of clear weather, had organized a farewell dinner and evening at the casino. I shall never forget the weather that evening. Rain squalls swept through the anchorage with forty- or fifty-knot gusts of wind. We carried our dress clothes in plastic bags as we rowed ashore wearing foul-weather gear. We changed on board *Carrina*. The restaurant we went to was in a cellar and it had a roaring fire going in the fireplace to keep us comfortable. After dinner we all ran from our taxis to the casino, which was built along the cliff edge, and I wished I had worn a wool sweater instead of my sleeveless dress. Heavy breakers pounded at the rocks one hundred feet below the parking lot, and someone in our crowd laughed and said, "Nice night not to be at sea." Then the sound of rolling dice, croupiers calls, and the chatter of elegantly dressed people shut the sea from our minds. Larry and I had a great time watching our twenty-dollar limit slowly dwindle away on the turn of a card while the casino served us complimentary drinks. Three hours later we donned our foul-weather gear and rowed back to *Seraffyn* through the steady rain laughing about the jokes and sea stories we had all shared.

The next morning was sunny, still, and warm. Ian called over, "A big ketch sank last night. Right at the harbor entrance. Two crew got ashore okay."

We climbed into *Rinky Dink* and rowed about three-quarters of a mile to where two varnished masts poked through the surge and swell just sixty feet from the steep-to rocks. As we maneuvered next to those gently swaying spars with their tapping halyards, I got a queasy feeling in my stomach. The outlines of the fifty-five-foot wooden hull were just visible thirty feet below. "So close but yet so far," was Larry's sad comment as we rowed less than three hundred feet and came back into the protected waters of the harbor.

Paul Ripard told us the whole sad story later that day. The owner of the ketch, an Italian sailor from Naples, called to find the costs for hauling his boat in Malta for a spring re-fit. Since the price was about half that of Italian prices, he asked Paul to recommend a Maltese sailor to help sail the boat three hundred miles from its home port. All went well until they ran into a northwesterly gale their third day out. The owner was tired and probably a bit scared as they approached Valletta late at night with squalls and force 9 winds. "Let's take down the sails now and motor in," he told the crewman. "The harbor is easy to sail into with this wind," the very experienced Maltese sailor told him. "It's a beam reach. There's plenty of room inside where we can take the sails down."

The owner started the diesel and insisted on taking all of the sail down as they approached the harbor entrance. He cast loose the jib sheet as the crewman eased the halyard. The sheet went overboard and fouled the spinning propeller. The engine ground to a stop. The jib

The top of the ketch's spars moved with the surge.

was halfway down and flogging. The owner yelled to his only crewman, "Go see what is wrong with the engine!" The boat hit the rocks before they found the problem. The first surge bashed a hole in her side, the second surge lifted her away from the rocks. Both men jumped clear as she went down. Then they swam almost a quarter mile until they found a place where they could climb up on the rocks; they survived—battered, cold, and scared but uninjured.

Paul told us the Italian insurance company had just called and told him, "The ketch is only insured for winter lay up in Italy until the fifteenth of April. If only the owner had called before he set off we could have put a rider on his policy. As it is, there is absolutely no coverage."

This tragic loss of a magnificently built teak and mahogany fifteen-year-old ketch was the culmination of a maze of "if onlys." If only the owner had heeded his crewman's advice; if only he had left the jib set until they got inside the harbor; if only he had held onto the end of the jib sheet; if only he had decided to hoist sail and head back to sea when the engine failed; if only he had checked with his insurance man before he set sail.

Now the Maltese government declared the wreck a menace to navigation and gave the owner three days to remove it. Weather forecasters throughout the Med predicted strong easterly gales within the next four days. Robin—a professional skin diver who was staying with a Canadian couple, Jeff and Heather Hillyard, on their Dutch botter yacht—suggested he and Larry try and figure a way to salvage the boat in repairable condition. Kelly Wilson—an American sailor who alternately worked four weeks on the oil rigs in the Red Sea and cruised four weeks on his thirty-foot race boat—joined Robin and Larry and provided his twelve-foot inflatable dive boat. Robin provided the tanks. Larry provided his Nikonos underwater camera, and they dove on the wreck to take photos that would show the Italian owner their ideas. They found the keel of the ketch wedged between two huge boulders. That is why she still stood upright. "She was a real beauty," Larry told me that afternoon. "Now there's no cabin left, the stem is broken, and there is an eight-foot hole in her port side."

The Italian owner had already left Malta. He was unreachable. So the next day the government authorized the local salvage company to lift the wreckage and recover their costs by selling whatever equipment they could. Two days later we watched as the ruins of the

Larry inspecting the sunken ketch.

fifty-five-foot ketch were dragged off the bottom on wire slings. They cut the hull almost in half, so only her fittings and engine were worth salvaging.

On the fourth day the predicted easterly gales set in and blew for five days. We spent the time like all of the other crews and skippers who were ready to be on their way to the Greek Islands. We shopped, puttered with the rigging, slept in, but mostly we all ended up together on one boat or another, or in the local café or bar. And sooner or later that ill-fated ketch would sneak into the conversation. Someone would start out, "If only. . . ." Inwardly each of us would shudder as we wondered about the decisions we might make on some future storm-tossed night when luckier sailors would be sitting in a nice warm bar waiting to say, "If only. . . ."

CHAPTER 21

The Turning Point

I t is strange that two sheets of paper influenced the whole direction of our lives. The plans Lyle Hess had sent us early in the summer had been the catalyst for literally hundreds of hours of discussion. First we talked about maybe building a new boat some day. Then evening discussions started changing from "If we build a new boat . . ." to "When we build the new boat. . . ." By the time we arrived to spend the winter in Malta our midnight chats started out, "We don't need another boat, *Seraffyn* does everything we want."

I noticed we spent a lot of time looking at wooden boats in the shipyard or mooring areas, comparing construction methods, and noting nice woodworking details and fittings. As we re-fitted *Seraffyn* I would say, "On the next boat, let's find space for a dirty-clothes hamper." Larry would ask, "What about using fir for the new boat's boom? It doesn't bruise as easily as this spruce does."

We finally sat down and made a list of pros and cons headed, "Should we sail directly back to California and build a new Boat?" The pro list grew slowest: we want more space so we can have a solid-fuel heater and be warm when we visit Norway and Scotland; we want to try using some of the new tricks Larry learned from other boat builders; if we figured a way to earn the boat-building funds as we went, we could sell *Seraffyn* to provide a nest egg for our distant future; the building would be done at home, and we had not been home for eight years, except for occasional one-week visits.

The con list was easy: cruising was too much fun to quit; we were right at the gateway to the most exciting part of the Med; why be fool enough to give up three years of cruising just for a heater; if the visit home was the problem, why not just store *Seraffyn* and fly home for a year; to sail to California would be at least 14,500 miles, since we do not like ocean passages that much, why not just continue gunkholing for five or six years more—Greece, Turkey, Israel, they all lay ahead.

Our cruising friends came down strongly against giving up a summer in the Greek Islands. "Come on, let's plan a rendezvous in Corfu next winter," one said. "How about meeting in Istanbul come August," another one said in conclusion to any discussion we started.

But as we set sail from Malta we made our decision. "Logical or not, I'm really interested in getting involved in a big project," Larry told me. "You know, watching something grow and develop under my own hands." All through our eight years of sailing we had had problems to solve on *Seraffyn,* things to learn, systems to simplify. Now she was like a finely tuned instrument. Everything worked perfectly. There were no changes left to make, only simple maintenance and occasional adjustments lay ahead. One of our favorite parts of cruising had been learning about our boat and her ability. Now we knew her like a book. It was time to change and keep our minds growing. In spite of my own reluctance to changing a very enjoyable way of life, I remembered what Robert S. Lewis, the principal of my Sun Valley, California, High School told me when I was eighteen: "Add something completely new to your life every three years, something that will force you to think about and explore new ideas. Then you'll always have things to look forward to and be excited about."

Our decision immediately opened unlimited areas to think about: what kind of construction should we use, where shall we build, and —first and foremost—which way should we sail to California. We knew we wanted to build our boat somewhere in California for several reasons: it is easy to earn money repairing boats there; building materials are readily available because of the huge marine industry; the weather is easy on boat builders; and, our old friends and family all live on the West Coast.

We spent hours over the *Ocean Passages for the World.* East about from Malta, through the Red Sea, across the Indian Ocean to Singapore, then north to Japan, across to Victoria, and finally south to California would be 14500 miles—with one 2200-mile passage and one 4500-mile one. There would be places to stop to break the remaining 7800 miles into chunks of 1200 miles or less. West about meant 14,400 miles: Gibraltar, across the Atlantic, north hard on the wind to Hawaii, then across to the United States West Coast—three passages of at least 2500 miles each. Larry solved the problem in the time-honored cruising man's way. "To go east we have to be at Suez by the fifteenth of August. To go west we have to be at Gibraltar by the first of October. It's only April now. Let's make the decision on your birthday, the first of August. That gives us at least three months to enjoy the Greek Islands and that's one place I'm not going to miss."

Seraffyn's bowsprit lifted to the first ocean swell, and we eased her reefed lapper and full mainsail just a bit to lay a course of forty-five degrees—with Valletta Harbor on our stern, and four hundred miles of open sea on our bow. Weather reports from three different countries were favorable. The boat was in perfect condition, our lockers brimmed with fresh and canned supplies. The bilges were full of duty-free liquor. As soon as we were three miles away from Malta, Larry set the wind vane and broke open the first bottle of my favorite: Bristol Cream Sherry. Though it was early in the afternoon, he proposed a toast, "To Malta and to our future. May all our decisions be as interesting to make as the ones we've thought about this winter."

Two days later we had covered almost half of the four hundred miles between Malta and the Ionian Islands. Gray clouds covered the sky, the wind backed, and by noon heavy rain kept us inside *Seraffyn* while Helmer steered a steady course. The wind increased until Larry reluctantly climbed into foul-weather gear to take down the reefed jib and set the staysail. "Hey, look at this," he called after the jib was down and bagged. I climbed out of the cozy quarter berth and cautiously slid open the hatch. "What?" I yelled. My shout caused a flurry of blue within three feet of my head. A tiny land bird had arrived and taken refuge in the relative dryness and calm of our upside-down dinghy. (The pram fits like a cap over the hatches and keeps most of the rain out—so I, too, was inside the six-foot-eight-inch upside-down dinghy.) But that bird was too tired to care and soon settled back on the underside of the wooden thwart.

Another blue bird landed on our spray-washed foredeck while I stood there. The strongly gusting wind caught under his tail and blew him halfway down the side deck. Both Larry and I laughed at this clownlike new arrival. But when he also fluttered into the protecting dinghy and settled on the thwart next to our first bird, Larry decided, "Looks like we're in for a blow. Can't lay our course so let's heave to now." He secured everything on deck, lashed the tiller to leeward, hauled the double reefed mainsail in flat, then came dripping below after one last glance at our little blue companions. "Nearest land is over one hundred miles away, they must have been blown off by pretty heavy winds," Larry said. We felt those winds in an hour. They shrieked through the rigging and threw spray across our heaving foredeck. Rain hit the cabinsides like a tattoo of hail. Larry heard shrill sounds from our two bird visitors, climbed from his bunk, and slid the hatch open just enough so he could stick his head through. Over a dozen more birds had landed on *Seraffyn*. Unfortunately, two of them were brown and obviously unwelcome under the dinghy. The two outcasts tried to find shelter against the cabin in our very open cockpit.

Larry waited just until he could use the excuse of lighting the oil navigation lamps and then said, "How about padding some buckets with old rags? I'll put the birds in and bring them below. They'll die out there."

I must admit I was feeling a bit under the weather from the surging, lifting motion caused by the ever-growing seas. Lethargy, the need to plan each move so there was a safe hand hold and place to land, plus the cold that waited just outside my sleeping bag, made me unenthusiastic. But Larry's almost pleading eyes convinced me. When he climbed into his wet gear and struggled out the companionway, I got out of the bunk, found the rags and buckets, then stood waiting to receive each soaked, trembling ball of feathers. Fourteen tiny brown bodies lined one bucket. Eight slightly larger blue ones filled another. Then I lit each of the running lights Larry handed in.

When Larry climbed down into our tiny salon and stripped off his soaking foul-weather gear, he found some crackers and crumbled them into each bucket. Then he placed the bird buckets securely under the cockpit. I managed to make an exquisite dinner of peanut butter and jam sandwiches swilled down with red wine. Then I climbed gratefully back into my bunk only to get out once every other hour to check the limited horizon. There was never a sound from our castaways.

When the alarm went off at 0700 to arouse one of us for our hourly deck check I only half opened my eyes and hoped Larry would get up first. The wind was down a bit, seas were still rough. But bright sunlight made the world seem far nicer.

Larry scrambled out of his bag and opened the companionway cover. Sunlight streamed in, and all twenty-two birds came to life at the same time. The cabin became a blur of wizzing brown and blue wings. Birds flew onto the chart table, landed on the stove, fluttered into the forepeak, collided with Larry, sat on my head—and each left his calling card to prove he had been there. It took Larry almost ten minutes to shoo the last chirping, evasive bird out onto the slowly drying deck. Meanwhile I could not climb out of the bunk without landing on the white bird droppings which covered the settee next to me, so I just lay there convulsed with laughter, tears running down my cheeks. I braced against the lee cloth while Larry grumbled and searched out the droppings to mop them up. Then he set a pot of coffee to perk and its warm aroma filled our nine-foot-by-eight-foot cabin and lured me from the bunk.

At 1100 Larry took a sun shot and fixed our position. With the current, we had been set just far enough north to ease our sheets and reach toward the islands. The last of our bird friends had taken flight and headed downwind with our best wishes. So we set sail. At first Larry hand steered while the triple reefed mainsail and reefed staysail pulled us across the wind jumbled seas. By evening Helmer was steering as we carried full sail and the storm-caused lumps began to smooth out.

For the next two days the fickle Mediterranean behaved and gave us perfect sailing. At dawn on our sixth day out of Malta, islands broke the horizon. We rushed toward them at almost six knots: Corfu to the north, Levkas, Cephelonia, and Ithaca to the south—the Greek Islands, Ulysses' home and the ultimate goal of almost every wandering sailor.

In spite of over a hundred other ports and landfalls to look back upon, this one seemed the most exciting of all. For as we stood on deck, watching the islands growing firmer and larger, I think both of us knew this would be a major turning point in our lives. Like Ulysses, we would leave the warmth and protection of Ithaca and sail into an unknown future.

Lin.

JANIS PRATER

Larry.

~~~~~~

Pardeys' Expanded Wind Speed Chart

All sailors try to put a number on the strength of the wind. "It was blowing twenty-five, gusting thirty . . ." the North American will tell his friends at the yacht club bar. A Frenchman will raise his glass and sigh, "We had a great breeze, eight meters per second, then. . . ." The British will meet at the pub and talk of another race cancelled because, "It was blowing force nine; force nine sea, too."

Even with a good anemometer, each of these numbers is only a guesstimation unless it is a reading taken from a shore station within one unobstructed mile of your position. Unless your boat is standing level and absolutely still with its anemometer mounted at exactly thirty-three feet above sea level, your reading will be affected by the waves, the speed of your boat through the water, its angle of heel, and its motion. Guesses without an anemometer are even more apt to be in error. If you are beating, the wind seems ten knots heavier than when you are running. If you are seasick or tired, it is twenty knots heavier.

Through the years we have come to rely on the British method of gauging winds. Because it is far less specific, it is much more accurate. It should be rembered that the force of the wind increases as the square of its velocity.

The following chart is one derived from the Beaufort scale, along with our own comments. When we refer in our books to having had winds of over force 8, these have been confirmed by radio or newspaper reports. Winds of lesser speeds are from our own estimates based on sea conditions and what sail area we could carry.

The size of your boat and its displacement will affect your actions in different wind speeds. A fifty-footer of medium displacement might be kept sailing safely in winds a force higher than what *Seraffyn* would be able to handle. But on the other end of the scale, the owners of the fifty-footer might not enjoy the sailing at force 2 or 3 as much as we do.

One interesting thing we learned about wind speed during our voyaging in the Mediterranean was that wind strength is affected by humidity. Moisture-laden wind is heavier and will heel a boat more than will dry winds. The famous, very dry Santana wind, which blows off the California desert in fall and winter, creates great sailing even when it gusts force 9. A moist and cold mistral wind blowing off the coast of France might see every boat hove to, or considering a storm anchor.

During the past twelve years of sailing, which represents somewhere between 40,000 and 50,000 miles on *Seraffyn* and at least another 19,000 on deliveries, we have found winds of force 5 or less more than 65 percent of the time. We have spent less than five hundred hours in winds over force 7, which represents only 2 percent of the time we have spent at sea.

These notes refer to the chart on the following four pages.

*We use *Seraffyn*'s staysail as the first reef or first sail increase when we're cruising. Instead of changing from our lapper (number 2 genoa) to our large genoa, we would first set the staysail. Only when that proved insufficient would we get out the larger sail— one of the things we like best about the cutter rig.

**Our general rule is one drop board for each reef in the mainsail—because our companionway sill is below deck level. One drop board brings it high enough so that water running along the side decks or slurping in the cockpit can't find its way below. If we had cockpit combings we would arrange our first drop board so its top would be above the combing level.

***We have found it pays to keep a balanced sail plan whenever we are running in winds over force 6, i.e., as much sail on one side of the mast as on the other. If you run with just a headsail, the boat will roll badly. This balanced sail plan is also safer. If you have to, you will be able to get on the wind more quickly. This can be vital if someone falls overboard or you have to change course to avoid some object in the water or an approaching ship.

****Most of these tactics depend on a combination of wind and sea conditions more than on wind strength alone. For the first few hours after a storm blows in, the seas will be calmer than the description given for the Beaufort scale. After a storm the seas will often stay rougher than expected so you may have to lay hove to even though the wind is down a force or two. Currents, tides, and the proximity of shoals or land will also affect the sea conditions.

PARDEYS' EXPANDED WIND SPEED CHART

Pardeys' personal scale	Beaufort scale	Speed in knots measured at 33 feet	Meters per second	Maritime description	Sea height in open water after several hours	Deep sea criteria
TOO LITTLE WIND	0	LESS THAN 1	.5	CALM		Sea mirror-smooth.
	1	1–3	.5–1.5	LIGHT AIR	1/4 FOOT	Small wavelets like scales, no crests.
ENOUGH WIND	2	4–6	2–3	LIGHT ꓵꓵꓣꓣꓓꓣ	1/2	Small wavelets still short but more pronounced. Crests ꓵꓵ, ꓵꓵꓵꓵꓵ ꓵꓵꓓ ꓵꓵ ꓵꓵ break.
	3	7–10	3.5–5	GENTLE BREEZE	2	Large wavelets. Crests begin to brea Foam is glassy.
	4	11–16	5.5–8	MODERATE BREEZE	3 1/2	Small waves becoming longer. More frequent white horses.
	5	17–21	9–10.5	FRESH BREEZE	6	Large waves begin t form; white crests more extensive.

Seraffyn's crew reactions	Sail **we would carry**
Get out a good book; go swimming; take out the mending or bosun's work. Serve cocktails.	Take down all sail; secure the halyards so they don't slap. Set the sun awning.
For beating, this can be the most special wind there is. Helmer starts to steer on all points as soon as the boat is moving at least one knot, unless the sea is sloppy. Downwind, this is boring.	Beating: Large genoa, full main Reaching: Nylon drifter only Running: Drifter and small genoa wing and wing
Now this is sailing. The boat barely heels on a beat, gurgles on a run. Helmer is in complete control. All hatches open, cushions on deck for sunbathing.	Beating: Full genoa, staysail and main Reaching: Everything we've got Running: Drifter and small genoa wing and wing Spinnaker if we are ambitious during the daylight hours
Fastest, most comfortable beating conditions. Moving close to hull speed on a reach. Downwind, the decks are steady. If it were like this all the time, everyone would be sailing.	Beating: Lapper, staysail and main Reaching: Large genoa or lapper, staysail and main Running: Same as for force 2 (we never carried the spinnaker at night) *
On a beat there is a small risk of spray across the foredeck. So the cushions go below. Cocktail glasses are exchanged for mugs as the boat heels until its deck just touches the water. Running and reaching start to be exhilarating.	Beating: Lapper and main Reaching: Lapper, main and staysail Running: Lapper and main, wing and wing, or spinnaker for fun
Beating isn't as much fun. Spinnaker is a handful if there are only two of us on board. Helmer needs a bit of damping with shock chord to prevent over correcting on a reach. All hatches are closed and dogged. Companionway is left open **	Beating: Reefed lapper, maybe one reef in main Reaching: Reefed lapper, full main Running: Lapper and main wing and wing.

Pardeys' personal scale	Beaufort scale	Speed in knots measured at 33 feet	Meters per second	Maritime description	Sea height in open water after several hours	Deep sea criteria
TOO MUCH WIND	6	22–27	11–13	STRONG BREEZE	9 1/2	Sea heaps up; white foam blown in streaks
	7	28–33	14–16	NEAR GALE	13 1/2	Moderately high waves of greater length; crests begin to form spindrift. Foam blown in well-marked streaks.
	8	34–40	17.5–20	GALE	18	High waves; dense streaks of foam. Crests begin to roll over.
HEAVE TO	9	41–47	21–24	STRONG GALE	23	Very high waves with long overhanging crests. Surface of the sea becomes white with great patches of foam. Visibility affected.
STORM TACTICS	10	48–55	25–28	STORM	29	Exceptionally high waves. Sea completely covered with foam.
	11	56–63	29–32	VIOLENT STORM	37	The air is filled with spray and visibility is seriously affected.
PRAY	12	64+	33+	HURRICANE	EXTREME	

Seraffyn's crew reactions	Sail we should carry
Seal off the foredeck ventilator and put the chainlocker sock on to prevent water from getting below. Get a good book and wedge yourself in place.	Beat: Staysail, one reef in main Reaching: Reefed lapper, one reef in main Running: Reefed lapper, full main
One-pot meals are served in a bowl with extra napkins. If it's a long voyage and the wind is dead on our nose we might heave to and wait for a wind shift. Reaching Helmer needs a tight shock cord to prevent over correcting.	Beating: Two reefs in main, staysail Reaching: Staysail and one reef in main Running: Staysail and one reef in main, wing and wing •••
Prefer to heave to if it is a beat. Reach carefully, watching the seas. If currents are against the wind and crests start to break, heave to.	Beating: Double reefed main and reefed staysail Reaching: Staysail only Running: Staysail and double reefed main, wing and wing Hove to: Double reefed mainsail ••••
Generally hove to. But in smooth seas we have beat into winds like this. We've found reaching is usually unsafe in force 9 seas. Running is okay when seas are regular.	If we are near a lee shore, we try to beat with three reefs in the mainsail, two in staysail, work to gain sea room. Hove to: double reefed main, but near lee shore set storm anchor to cut drift. (Fortunately to this date we have always had sufficent sea room to just heave to, so we have never had to beat in force 9 seas with force 9 winds.)
Make sure we are hove to so that we are drifting dead downwind and not fore-reaching (moving forward) at all. Set topping lift up to take strain off leach of the riding sail. Put in another drop board.	Hove to with triple reefed main. We have beat in winds of this speed, but it was in the lee of the land with only three to five miles of fetch, so seas had not built up to the breaking point.
When rain or spray hits your bare skin, it stings. Dig out the nuts, raisins, bread, and candy bars. Most storms of this intensity are short lived (12 hours or less) except in the north Atlantic or roaring 40s.	Triple reefed mainsail, sea anchor out to assure boat is held about 50 degrees to the wind and continues to drift *dead* downwind. All deck gear removed. This is when it especially pays to plan your storage so nothing clutters your deck or needs special lashing. All drop boards in. Start watch on sea anchor chaffing gear.
We've only been in two -12 hour hurricanes. Don't care to try to gain the experience to comment fully on them. So far our tactics have been the same as for force 11 with hourly checks to prevent chaff on the sea anchor rode.	Probably remove all sail, ride to sea anchor alone.

About the Authors

"After voyaging tens of thousands of engineless miles under sail, penning more useful marine books than Hiscock and Moitessier combined, and receiving more awards for their pursuits than Tom Hanks has for his, Lin and Larry Pardey are entitled to their well-earned nautical opinions." — Herb McCormack, editor-at-large, *Cruising World*

Lin and Larry Pardey have been called "the enablers". Their books and videos have encouraged sailors of all ages to stop dreaming and start doing. The knowledge they share has been earned during the four-plus decades they have been voyaging together, years during which they completed both east-about and west-about circumnavigations on board their own self-built, engine-free cutters, *Seraffyn* and *Taleisin*. During their most recent east-to-west voyage, they sailed below four of the great Southern Capes, including Cape Horn. An avid racing sailor from the age of 17, Larry worked as first mate on the 140-ton, 85-foot schooner *Double Eagle*, voyaging on her to Hawaii and along the coast of Mexico before meeting Lin. Larry, along with Leslie Dyball, won first on handicap in the exceptionally stormy 1974 Round Britain two-handed race. Lin and Larry have delivered more than two dozen boats across oceans and raced on their own and on other people's boats. To date, Lin has sailed almost 185,000 miles and Larry has accumulated over 200,000 miles at sea.

In 1996, Larry received the International Oceanic Award from the Royal Institute of Navigation, presented by the Princess Royal, Princess Anne for meritorious voyaging using traditional navigation methods. During the same year, Lin received the Ocean Cruising Award for being the person who has "done the most to foster and encourage ocean cruising in small craft and the practice of seamanship and navigation in all branches." In 2000, both were inducted into the Cruising World Hall of Fame. In 2009 the Cruising Club of America awarded Lin and Larry their prestigious Far Horizon Award.

Lin and Larry's articles have appeared in: *Cruising World, Sail, Good Old Boat, Wooden Boat, Practical Sailor, Yachting World, Yachting Monthly, Classic Boat* (UK), *Cruising Helmsman* (Australia), *Boating New Zealand, South African Yachting, Nautica Brazil,* and *Yacht* (Germany).

Their books and video programs have been published in the United States, England, and New Zealand; and translated into German, Russian, Italian and Japanese.

Lin and Larry recently sailed through the Line Islands then south to New Zealand to celebrate Larry's 70th birthday. Between cruises to explore the coast of Northern New Zealand, Lin finished writing her eleventh book, a memoir called *Bull Canyon: A Boatbuilder, A Writer, and Other Wildlife.*

If you enjoyed this book, you can continue the adventure -

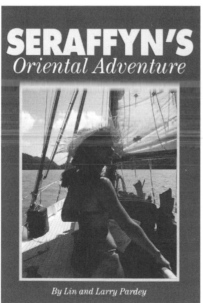

These books along with Lin and Larry's newsletter and cruising tips
can be found at **www.landlpardey.com**

"If this DVD doesn't inspire you to get out cruising, nothing will." – *Cruising World*

"Just like their books, **Cruising Has No Limits** mixes good story-telling with practical advice." – *Boating New Zealand*

Join Lin and Larry on board *Seraffyn's* bigger sister, *Taleisin* as they share three great adventures – a song-filled summer on Ireland's rugged western shores, a child-enhanced meander through the tropical Brazilian islands south of Rio de Janeiro, and an amazing seven month 4x4 journey through southern Africa.

This program plus the Pardeys' instructional DVD's

Get Ready to Cross Oceans
Get Ready to Cruise
Storm Tactics

Available at
**www.landlpardey.com,
amazon.com**

or as downloads at
www.thesailingchannel.tv.

Also available as rentals
www.youtube.com

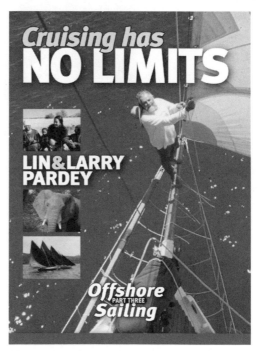

The adventure continues with *Bull Canyon: A Boatbuilder, A writer, and Other Wildlife*

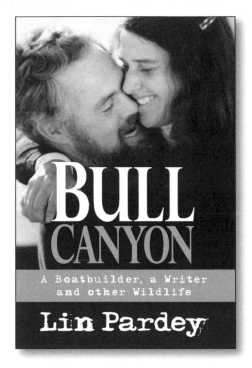

"Significant, highly romantic, and admirable. With many homespun snapshots included, readers may feel as if they're following the fantastic adventures of an old friend." *Publishers Weekly*

"Challenge isn't a bad thing, as Lin Pardey and her husband Larry live off the adventure of it. *Bull Canyon: A Boatbuilder, A Writer, and Other Wildlife* is a combination book of true adventure and memoir as they find their home in an abandoned stone cottage with little in the way of luxury, but which gives them what they wanted, a place to build a boat and live a simpler and more rustic life. But no place is a one hundred percent paradise. *Bull Canyon* is a riveting memoir of the path less taken..."
– *Midwest Book Review*

" This lilting memoir will complete those who read the *Seraffyn* books and send the rest of its readers to them in search of that dream and adventure!"
– Deb Fowler, *Feathered Quill*

All Pardey books are also available as ebooks from Amazon Kindle or itunes bookstore.